# The Whigs' America

# The Whigs' America

## *Middle-Class Political Thought in the Age of Jackson and Clay*

Joseph W. Pearson

UNIVERSITY PRESS OF KENTUCKY

Scholarly publisher for the Commonwealth,
serving Bellarmine University, Berea College, Centre
College of Kentucky, Eastern Kentucky University,
The Filson Historical Society, Georgetown College,
Kentucky Historical Society, Kentucky State University,
Morehead State University, Murray State University,
Northern Kentucky University, Transylvania University,
University of Kentucky, University of Louisville,
and Western Kentucky University.


*Editorial and Sales Offices:* The University Press of Kentucky
663 South Limestone Street, Lexington, Kentucky 40508-4008
www.kentuckypress.com

Maps by Dick Gilbreath.

Library of Congress Cataloging-in-Publication Data

Names: Pearson, Joseph W., 1979– author. | University Press of Kentucky.
Title: The Whigs' America : middle-class political thought in the age of Jackson and Clay / Joseph W. Pearson.
Description: Lexington : The University Press of Kentucky, 2020. | Includes bibliographical references and index.
Identifiers: LCCN 2020022875 | ISBN 9780813179728 (Hardcover : acid-free paper) | ISBN 9780813179742 (PDF) | ISBN 9780813179759 (ePub)
Subjects: LCSH: Whig Party (U.S.)—History. | Whig Party (U.S.)—History—19th century.
Classification: LCC JK2331 .P43 2020 | DDC 324.2732/3—dc23

This book is printed on acid-free paper meeting
the requirements of the American National Standard
for Permanence in Paper for Printed Library Materials.

Manufactured in the United States of America.

Member of the Association
of University Presses

*To Erica*

# Contents

# Introduction

This book is about politics, exploring the general outlook of a group of Americans called *Whigs*. Between 1834 and 1856, the Whigs were one of the two great political parties in the United States, battling their opponents, the Jacksonian Democrats, for office, prestige, power, and ideas. Boasting famous members such as Henry Clay, Daniel Webster, and William Henry Seward, they supported tariffs, banks, internal improvements, moral reform, and public education.

Yet, in a deeper sense, this work is about more than politics. At bottom, it is about people and explains how nearly half of nineteenth-century Americans saw their world during the thirty years before the Civil War. In democratic nations, politics is about more than policies, reflecting also the underlying attitudes and worldview of society. T. S. Eliot described this sort of analysis as a search for what he called *the prepolitical.* "And my defence of the importance of the pre-political is simply this," he explained in 1955, "that it is the stratum down to which any sound political thinking must push its roots and from which it must derive its nourishment."[1] Thus, this book is a political history that is interested in the deeply felt, shared cultural soil beneath Whig politics. *The Whigs' America* explores how Whiggish Americans understood human nature, society, and the role of the state and explains how they reflected on the past and anticipated the future. It is about how Whigs revealed their understandings of the world, not only on the stump and in the legislative halls, but also in their churches, schools, and lyceums, in their newspapers and journals of opinion, and sometimes even in their letters and diaries. I believe that the use of public power was only a part of a larger view of the world. Indeed, this book shows how Whigs talked among themselves and how they described their goals and the ends they thought most appropriate to achieve them. Finally, it is about how Whigs persuaded each other about the righteousness of their cause and the dangerous implications of the ideas of those who opposed them.

Understanding the Whigs matters because they were the first political party speaking for, to, and about America's rising middle class. *The Whigs' America* argues that American Whigs shared an observable middle-class worldview. This perspective informed their politics because it grew out who Whigs were. They were people who were more excited about the future than afraid of it. They believed that human nature tended to be violent, stupid, and self-serving when left alone. Consequently, they often refused to leave people alone. They promoted voluntary associations such as temperance societies, lyceums, and literary clubs because they wanted to bring people together and encourage self-improvement. Whigs were not grumpy misanthropes who dismissed mankind as hopeless; they argued instead that individual restraint was crucial to a good society.

Terms matter. Throughout this book, I use *middle class, bourgeois,* and *bourgeoisie* to describe Whiggish Americans. The precise meaning and application of the term *middle class* has challenged scholars such as Peter Gay, Lawrence R. Samuel, and Deirdre McCloskey for decades. I do not attempt to parse out social categories on the basis of income or wealth per se; instead, I try to describe the frame of mind that found this view of the world appealing. Often aspirational or imagined, a middle-class worldview deeply influenced the way in which many antebellum Americans sought to live their lives. As I see it, then, Whigs were middle-class because they valued prudence, temperance, and thrift, seeing these ideas as virtues to guide their lives and their politics. Further, they were comfortable with the impersonal, market-oriented world growing around them and eager to use public and private institutions such as schools, legislatures, and banks to promote their values and protect their interests. In the antebellum United States, as in most subsequent eras, being middle class is more about mind-set than material means, and shared ethics matters more than similar incomes. Middle-class people are often cautious and prudent, putting their trust in public institutions and their faith in the government entities, large and small, that they create. And America in the decades after the War of 1812 witnessed the rise of bourgeois political, social, and cultural dominance.[2]

Were all antebellum Americans of middling means Whigs? Probably not, at least not if the term *middle class* is understood in a strict economic sense. Andrew Jackson, the beau ideal of the Democratic cause, lived much of his adult life enjoying ease and comfort bought by slave-grown wealth, military fame, and political power. Yet, despite his tremendous success, he never quite felt like he had arrived and always worried that unseen, illegitimate powers beyond his ken were working to destroy him. He and those who supported him trusted few, valuing loyalty and liberty most of all. Old Hickory won almost every contest that mattered yet never felt secure. Thus, when we look at the middle class as a shared worldview and not simply a collection of people whose incomes are, relative to those of their neighbors, neither exorbitant nor meager, the sort of folks who lived their lives along bourgeois lines and found meaning in middle-class terms were much more likely to be drawn to the Whigs than to the Democrats. Could a Democratic American be prudent, thrifty, and temperate? Sure. But he was unlikely to judge his favored politics, politicians, or policy in those terms because he valued other things more. It was not so much that a farmer in Ohio or a laborer in New York was a Democrat and a merchant in Louisville or a banker in Philadelphia was a Whig in any deterministic way. No. Instead, a farmer with modest means who saw his world more in aspirational terms of what it might be was more bourgeois in his political outlook than the affluent banker who pined for supposedly simpler times in a mythical past of his own imagining. The key idea is not that Whigs met economic criteria (i.e., enjoying material affluence that was neither meager nor extravagant) that Jacksonians did not, or vice versa, but that Whigs thought about themselves, their world, and the future in far more middle-class terms and, crucially, felt little need to apologize for that point of view.[3]

Most Americans lived, worked, and worshipped in the thirty years before the Civil War in small, rural places, it is true, but Whigs saw their world in terms of what it might become. They wanted to build a modern nation, linked together by improved infrastructure, economic opportunity, and sober habits. They embraced an evangelical Protestant morality, nurtured a vision of success built on merit, and feared the day when public appetites slipped the collar of prudence and modesty. As with most middle-class people, they greatly cherished order. They also had a broad sense of community and believed that the state should promote individual and broader group efforts to work together. Indeed, their bourgeois worries about human weakness and the need for improvement also led them to embrace conviviality, comity, and compromise. Henry Clay once remarked: "Let him who elevates himself above humanity, above its weaknesses, its infirmities, its wants, its necessities, say, if he pleases, I never will compromise, but let no one who is not above the frailties of our common nature disdain compromise." And most Whigs would have agreed. In a general way, their entire political program can be understood as a vast, hopeful effort to knit isolated Americans together. They were deeply optimistic about America's possibilities, so long as individual Americans developed self-control.[4]

Henry Adams distilled much of the antebellum era's political strife when he observed: "Of all the parties that have existed in the United States, the famous Whig party was the most feeble in ideas and most blundering in its management; the Jacksonian Democracy was corrupt in its methods."[5] Often snakebit with bad luck and bad timing, the Whigs never achieved the electoral success of their opponents, the Jacksonian Democrats. Yet Adams was wrong to argue that they shared no underlying philosophy. Whiggery was rich with ideas because Whigs saw their world through middle-class eyes firmly fixed on the future. Resolutely focused on progress, they wanted to build a modern nation, one linked together by improved transportation, economic opportunity, and sober habits.[6] Comfortable in most respects with the dynamic world around them, they often tried to speed change up.

Like all people, however, antebellum Whigs had blind spots. Their middle-class reverence for order meant that they often tolerated oppression and inequality for the sake of compromise, civility, and stability. Whigs' embrace of evangelical Protestant Christianity and their belief in a rigorous, active, virtuous citizenry made for a potent xenophobia toward Catholic immigrants, who were, they thought, too hopelessly enthralled to their clergy to be good Americans. Their faith in institutions meant that Whigs overlooked the ways in which those institutions can harm the broad mass of common people. Their reflexive dismissal of the local ties and personal connections that mattered so much to Democrats in favor of the broadly collaborative but rootless world of commercial exchange could, if not attentively balanced with family and friends, rob life of meaning and purpose. Often their schemes failed, and common men and women lost. For every Erie Canal success that states like New York enjoyed there were also botched public works like the failed 1830s Illinois railroad effort that left the Prairie State mired in deep debt for nearly a decade. Most Whigs, in the aggregate, also saw slavery as a necessary evil that they had to tolerate to keep the country together. Here again, their middle-class willingness to compromise in order to preserve social order meant that they looked past their moral unease. To be fair, like most Americans of the era, they saw black people as inferior to whites. Southern Whigs were also supportive of slavery in ways that northern Whigs were not because their political fortunes and daily lives were deeply entwined in the "peculiar institution." But, North or South, Whigs were *far* more likely to favor emancipation (usually gradual and compensated), condemn racial violence and the expansion of slavery, and admit an ethical disquiet with black chattel slavery than were their Democratic opponents.[7]

The aspirational, striving nature of the Whigs' political thought repelled their Democratic opponents. Democrats did not trust their plans or believe their assessment of human depravity and the need constantly to collaborate. Instead, they saw only coercion and control in Whigs' efforts to push public cooperation forward through social organizations and the state. This sort of oppression they feared most of all. Jacksonians were nostalgic for a past that they felt slipping away and afraid of a future that they could not predict or control. They understood liberty in stark, intimate terms, and they worried constantly about its loss because their faith in government was small. Most would agree with Thomas Jefferson that "the natural progress of things is for liberty to yield, and government to gain ground." Jacksonian Democrats worried deeply about the loss of personal autonomy and local independence due to the slippery scheming of distant financiers and their political lackeys. It was not all hyperbole. A fair bit of evidence justified Democrats' concern with concentrated wealth, their distaste for shadowy financial dealings that always seemed to leave a few rich and many ruined, and their disgust with politicians who strengthened the ties of money to power. Political arguments often came down to perspective. Where Democrats focused on the failures, trying to limit the damage, Whigs focused on the successes, trying to expand the benefits. Democrats saw government as the last, best shield protecting a vulnerable people from the excesses of concentrated power. Whigs saw it as the first, best economic engine, especially state legislatures attentive to the people, helping generate opportunities for middle-class happiness for all who were disciplined enough to achieve it. Suspicion ran through the heart of Democrats' political thought, and it was why Whig arguments never persuaded them. In Jacksonian eyes, Whigs were at best naive and at worst sinister politicians who wanted the people to pay for their own ruin through foolish taxes that funded boondoggles, cozy legislative arrangements with banks and moneyed interests that favored only the haves, and usurious tariffs that strangled competition and inflated prices.

Accordingly, Democrats embraced a caustic, confrontational political style that was geared toward breaking down perceived artificial privileges and concentrated on limiting the reach, power, and scope of all levels of government. At bottom, Jacksonians felt increasingly lost in a world in which too much seemed to be changing too fast.[8]

Yet in antebellum America change—both vast and varied—seemed society's only constant, and it was vast and varied indeed. One hundred and fifty years of clinging to the Atlantic coastline from the settlement of Jamestown in 1607 through the close of the Revolutionary era in the late eighteenth century ended in fits and starts as a colonial world of isolated cabins, farms, and villages begrudgingly gave way to an integrated world of cities, credit, and commerce and a flood of settlement west over the Appalachian Mountains. From 1800 to 1830, the population of the United States doubled from five to ten million. Fueled by natural increase and immigration, moreover, it would continue swelling to over thirty million by 1860, a staggering surge of over 500 percent.

During the same sixty years, the nation's borders rapidly expanded from timid outposts on the Atlantic Seaboard, sprawling south to the Gulf of Mexico and west to the Pacific Ocean. Yet dynamic change went far beyond demography or geography. Beyond question, then, the mammoth territorial growth that helped define the era (see map 0.1) also drove home contradictory feelings of hope and doubt in the minds of many. The ways in which people talked, traveled, bought and sold goods and services, worked with each other, and even understood time itself were different. The antebellum United States was a dynamic, often bewildering place, with a vibrant, almost scandalously young population. Life seemed faster, harsher, and more impersonal because in many ways it was. In the teeth of these transformations, Americans contested their depth, breadth, pace, and meaning. Their country was becoming modern under their feet, evoking both a middle-class response and an agrarian reaction. Thus, Whigs and Democrats carried on a bitter ideological war for America's soul in elections, pamphlets, sermons, literature, and even art and music. Fiery debates over banks, tariffs, internal improvements, slavery, and territorial expansion reflected deeper divisions over life as it was and life as it ought to be.[9]

As Whiggish people saw things, then, individual self-control, social collaboration, and state support for infrastructure and uplift were essential. In their view, traditional hierarchy, communal bonds, and even the social

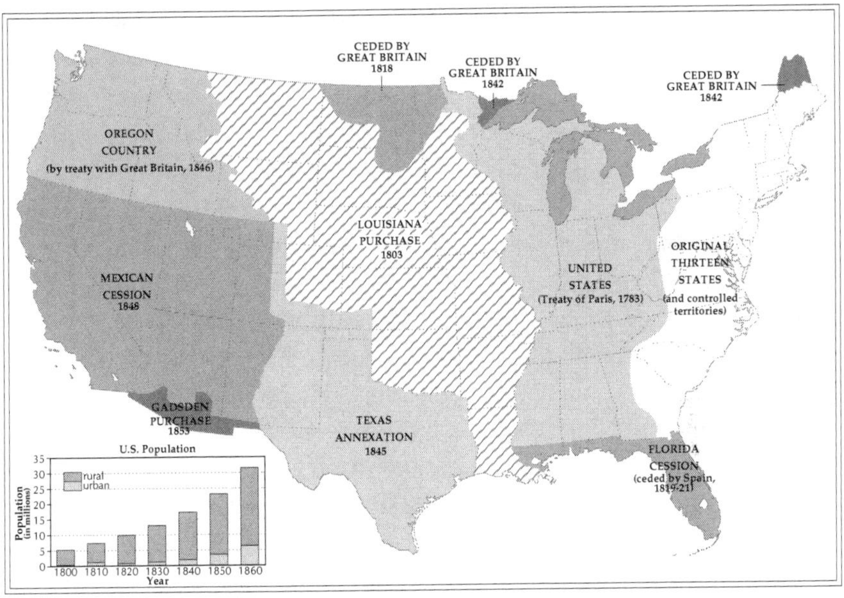


Map 0.1. Territorial expansion during the antebellum era.

fabric itself were splintering as a consequence of what scholars have often termed *transportation, communication,* and *market revolutions.* Whigs' worries about social changes mirrored those of their Democratic neighbors. But their answers differed. Individuals were freed in troubling ways from both the limits and the responsibilities of the old colonial world. Probably most Americans worried about this problem, but people came to different conclusions about the best remedy. Jacksonians longed for a smaller, more personal world and strove to maintain independence from all forms of coercion, both real and imagined. Whigs were often impatient with this nostalgia, working instead to build a more integrated social order through collaborative effort and association. Hope ran through the heart of the Whigs' political thought, and it was why Democratic fears rarely concerned them. The challenge of the times lay in whose vision of the future and whose understanding of the past would shape American society going forward. In the short term, Andrew Jackson and his Democrats tended to win the presidency, both houses of Congress, and a goodly portion of elections for the statehouses and governors' mansions throughout the era. Their appeal to the sum of all fears—justified in some respects, such as the exploitative potential of corporations and banks—struck a chord with a populace buffeted by constant change. Jacksonians' worldview clung to an agrarian past that was dying hard. The middle-class perspective from which the Whigs drew their strength saw the coming world more clearly and were better prepared for it, even if that vision did not always equal electoral success.

I contend that all politics flows from a collective mind. Consequently, this book explores those *general* ideas and attitudes about life that American Whigs would have breathed in with the air. It is about the casual assumptions that they often took for granted, the conclusions that they considered obvious, and a partisan perspective that most would deny was partisan at all. Like most Americans, they simply considered their views plain common sense, rejecting any notion that other perspectives might be legitimate too. The fact that Democrats felt the same way and that both groups argued over vital aspects of social life goes a long way toward explaining why political debates were often so nasty. Politics drew Whiggish people together around a common vision as they attempted to use the state in its service and, in the process, revealed their understanding of their world and persuaded others of their ideas' virtues. Thus, the worldview that Whigs shared was built from the past that they sought to escape, the present that they worked to improve, and the future that they hoped to build.

I do not divide Whigs into separate camps, such as evangelicals, entrepreneurs, or modernizers, as other scholars have done, though I concede that a great deal of latitude existed in terms of which aspects of Whiggery appealed most strongly to different people in different places at different times. It is also true that not all Whigs shared the same intensity of belief. Yet this worldview resonated with a vast array of future-looking people in large cities and small villages, in factories and on farms, and in the varied statehouses across the country as well as in the halls of Congress. The world that the Whigs promised to build attracted those Americans seeking achievement, community, and meaning through collaborative effort and self-control. In some ways, it came down to different ideas about time itself. Whiggish people tended to see themselves traveling through time into a future that was open to almost boundless possibilities, one where progress, ideas, and resolve made history. Time was, they believed, what they made it, for ill or not, and success came to those who could bend the future to their will. On the other hand, Democratic people often saw time as a series of reactions to the expected and the unexpected, privileging providence, destiny, and fate. Time happened to them, regardless of clever plans or shrewd schemes, and only the sturdy, the stalwart, and the strong endured.[10]

A broad study of general patterns will obviously have exceptions. Sectional concerns such as tariffs, territorial expansion, and slavery were powerful riptides that created local concessions to broader forms. Indeed, black chattel slavery lurked as a broiling acid beneath the body politic, slowly, implacably dissolving the social, cultural, and political bonds that held America together. A catastrophe of blood, tears, and dust loomed. However, at bottom, Democrats were not Whigs because their respective worldviews differed. Whigs and Democrats did not agree on what America's past meant, what challenges mattered most in its present, or what the future should look like. Where Whigs saw opportunities for prosperity, Democrats saw exploitation and possible ruin. While Democrats worried that change was occurring too fast, Whigs wanted to speed things up. Where Whigs aspired to build a connected, modern world that would, they believed, be better than the one in which they lived, Democrats looked to defend the best of what they felt was slipping away, doubting all the while that *future* meant *better.*

Although many Whigs probably would not articulate these notions with the concision striven for here, most would recognize this summary as an accurate effort to explore and explain the way in which they saw their world. Whiggery appealed to those Americans seeking achievement, community, and meaning through collaborative effort and self-control in a world growing more and more impersonal. It drew together people who worried that failing to cooperate or promote personal discipline would lead to widespread barbarism and a general degrading of social life. Thus, *The Whigs' America* is about the essential ways in which Whiggish Americans understood their world, the reasons and strategies they used to change it, the gaps, inconsistencies, and blind spots in their political vision, and the ordered, happy future that they believed their dreams would create.

# 1

# The Individual

> True national freedom, in the American view, rests upon moral groundwork, upon the virtue of self-possession and self-control in individual citizens.
>
> Philip Schaff

In democratic nations such as the antebellum United States, political parties brought together groups of individuals with shared ideas, anxieties, and aspirations, ostensibly to win elections. But that is a thin reading of their importance because the ideology woven into the fabric of campaign rhetoric, polemic, and song echoed the beating heart of what mattered most to antebellum people. Whiggery was the political culture of America's rising middle class, the partisan expression of a bourgeois worldview. Jacksonians lionized yeoman agriculture and its attendant agrarian worldview above all. Whigs saw room for virtue in other places, perspectives, and occupations, describing the middle class as *plain, honest, hardworking, virtuous,* and *successful.* The key idea is not that Whigs met certain material criteria that Jacksonians did not but that they thought about themselves and their world in far more middle-class terms and celebrated that point of view.[1]

Then, as now, political culture was built first on individuals. Daniel Webster explained this idea in 1833, noting: "The actual character of the government can never be better than the general moral and intellectual character of the community."[2] And, since communities are made up of individuals, a deep reading of Whig political culture must begin with Whig thinking on the promise and possibilities of individual Americans. Whigs' attitudes toward human nature, the proper understanding of liberty and equality, and the role of families in shaping individuals were crucial to their view of the world.

## Human Nature

"But men are men, the best sometimes forget," Shakespeare wryly observed in *Othello* (2.3.256), culling nearly a millennia and a half of popular wisdom and intellectual inspection on the darker aspects of human character. And, for their part, most Whigs agreed, maintaining a healthy skepticism about human nature. The world that Whigs sought to build was a partisan middle-class response to their particular understanding of individual character. Their reading of biblical Christianity taught them that human nature was at best flawed and that the depths of its darkness did not vary noticeably across classes, races, or genders. But they also believed that the possibilities for improvement—for the kinds of people individual Americans might become—were as vast as the continent stretching out before them. Though they shared with Jacksonians an appreciation for Christian notions of human weaknesses, they thought more was possible from more kinds of people. Indeed, in many ways they demanded it. But what were they reacting to? What sort of upheaval was occurring that demanded a middle-class response?[3]

In the years between 1820 and 1850, Americans endured a staggering succession of changes that, taken together, freed individuals from centuries of similar living conditions, roughly thrusting everyone into a modern world, whether they wanted to go there or not. In these three decades, the population and the sovereignty of the United States were extended from the Atlantic to the Pacific. The Atlantic world that for two centuries Americans had traveled in, traded in, and died on, clutching the coast in colonial farms, villages, and towns, was now linked by trains, roads, canals, and railroads to the vast North American continent stretching westward beyond the Mississippi River. An agrarian lifestyle with roots in the medieval past was rocked by a passion for building cities on windswept prairies seemingly overnight. Old bonds of patriarchy, paternalism, and hierarchy gave way to the draw of cheap land in the West, cheap labor in the cities, merchant opportunities almost everywhere, and a thriving, risky general spirit of go-ahead that coursed through the heart of the antebellum years. Not everyone was happy about these shifts in society. Many Americans felt satisfied with their country the way that it was. They craved space, certainly, but they did not want to surrender their autonomy, independence, or station to the modernist ethos of their neighbors. Andrew Jackson spoke for them, and, if theirs was a political outlook that protected slavery, ignored social violence, and dismissed the future's possibilities for the present's comforts, they also rightly saw the abusive potential in the new social and economic arrangements gaining traction among the rising mercantile interests. Individuals were cast adrift in cities, left to trust as best they were able the bosses and managers that replaced the old apprentice-journeyman-master artisan system, based so firmly on family and reciprocity, with one of cash exchange, alienation, and expediency. Crafts were now jobs, craftsmen hired laborers, and nothing but supply and demand linked labor and capital. These changes could be soulless, soul-crushing, and cruel to individuals most of all, at least as Democrats saw things, and they vowed to fight against them.

Others saw that the old ways were dying no matter what anyone did. They argued that sulking about a fading world did little to create meaning, prosperity, or happiness in the new one in which all must live. Henry Clay spoke for them, and, if theirs was a political outlook that took too rosy a view of commercial exchange, had too little of an appreciation for the human cost of their policy failures, and was perhaps too ready to throw present comforts into the hazard to win future glories, they also correctly understood that America was destined to be an urban world and that success would follow those who were comfortable with change. All of life's meaning was not wrought by hand, they argued, and a life earning money, managing people, or developing technical systems of communication, transportation, and industry had merit too. A world of comfort for all who would earn it was at last possible, and they would defend those possibilities forever. Individuals were indeed adrift, Whigs conceded, and, absent guiding principles and strong institutions, their descent into savage barbarism would be swift. Humanity's fallen nature was fertile soil for vice. And everywhere they looked coarseness, ignorance, and brutality were rising.

Whigs believed that Americans' disturbing penchant for violence, drunkenness, and ignorance justified their skepticism about human nature. In 1839, for instance, perhaps the most famous Whig, Henry Clay, argued that American society was rife "with all the violent prejudices, embittered passions, and implacable animosities which ever degraded or deformed human nature." Clay's language is telling, and the words he chose in describing human nature were common to most Whiggish Americans. Across the country Whigs shared a common reading of social ills that often described humanity as violent, embittered, degraded, and deformed. From the Illinois prairies, to the rolling river country of West Tennessee, to the piedmont of Kentucky, to the rocky farms of New England, American society and Americans themselves, Whigs believed, suffered from a lack of order.[4]

For their part, Jacksonians often rejected Clay's reading of American individual character. In 1837, the staunchly Jacksonian periodical the *United States Magazine, and Democratic Review* declared: "We have an abiding confidence in the virtue, intelligence, and full capacity for self-government of the great mass of our people—our industrious, honest, manly, intelligent millions of freemen." For Jackson's supporters, white men were stolid, dependable, virtuous, and hardworking, if only left alone. For them, *common* was no insult and *striving* no boast. Whigs shared their optimism, at least in terms of what was possible, but believed that Americans, unimproved or unrestrained, were dangerous to themselves and to one another.[5]

Whigs did not have to look far to see evidence of human depravity. In the decade after Jackson's election alone, the news was littered with tales of American brutality. In 1834, just outside Charlestown, Massachusetts, for example, an angry drunken mob assaulted a boarding school for girls run by Catholic nuns, putting the chapel, the bishop's lodge, the stables, and the nuns' living quarters to the torch. Truly barbarous, at least in the eyes of many stunned eyewitnesses, was the razing of the cemetery and the disinterment of Catholic dead. And similar scenes occurred throughout the era with disturbing regularity. A year after the Ursuline convent burned another mob in Vicksburg, Mississippi, strung up five gamblers without benefit of trial or jury. "The wife of one of the sufferers, half distracted at the cruel treatment and murder of her husband," one shocked account of the gamblers' deaths held, "trembling for her own safety, in tears begged permission to inter her husband's body—it was refused!" In 1835, Protestants and Catholics brawled on the streets of Cincinnati, gouging eyes, ripping out hair, and stabbing one another.[6]

As figure 1.1 demonstrates, this scene was repeated again in Philadelphia in 1844. Even more gruesome, in 1836 a free black man in St. Louis, Frank McIntosh, was burned alive after killing a white sheriff during a brawl. Finally, in the fall of 1839, New York governor William H. Seward was forced to send in the state militia to quell violent protests in and around Albany stemming from unjust lease and rent practices.[7]

It follows, then, that the possible future descent of the amoral and unlettered into barbarism that haunted the Whig imagination was based on

Fig. 1.1. H. Bucholzer, *Riot in Philadelphia, June [i.e., July] 7th* (New York: James Baillie, July 23, [1844?]). Lithograph. Prints and Photographs Division, Library of Congress, Washington, DC. "Tensions built up in 1844 when the Roman Catholic bishop persuaded school officials to use both the King James and Latin Vulgate bibles. Protestant mobs burned two Catholic churches on May 7, 1844. On July 7, 1844 rioting broke out again, necessitating intervention on the part of the state militia." https://www.loc.gov/item/2003654121.

more than middle-class worry. In 1837, for example, another mob formed in Vicksburg, Mississippi, publicly mutilating and murdering a fifty-year-old white man for offering free passes to slaves. "In the broad light of day," the *Vicksburg Sentinel*'s editor grimly noted in 1837, "this aged wretch was stripped and flogged, we believe within hearing of the lamentations and the shrieks of his afflicted wife and children." The mob cut off his nose and ears, flayed his skin until the ribs were exposed, and continued beating him until their bloodlust ebbed. Before retiring to drink and song, they left him swinging in a magnolia tree, a creaking corpse rotting in the fall breeze. "In the name of heaven to what is this country coming?" the outraged local editor implored. "When is the spirit of turbulence, outrage, and barbarism to have an end? Upon what principle do these enemies to the peace and happiness of society arrogate themselves to the right of dispensing with the laws of the land at pleasure?" At bottom, he tapped into the greater Whig concern that there *was* no principle beneath this violence save a fevered thirst for one man's blood.[8]

Mob violence offers a rather obvious example of Whiggish fears of barbarism. Indeed, most discerning Jacksonians objected to the excesses of lynch mobs too. The difference between these two lines of thought, however, lay in their reading of social disorder's depth and breadth and its underlying causes. For Jacksonians, a bit of bedlam was an unfortunate but necessary price to pay for healthy republican liberty. After all, as New York Democrats stressed in 1847: "It was here upon this Continent that the sentiment was first promulgated, 'that all men are born free and equal,' . . . [and that] the blood of those who uttered that God-like truth, was freely poured out on many battle fields." The people could be rowdy, true, even occasionally violent and cruel, as the preceding examples demonstrate, but those instances were exceptions that must be endured to secure the larger freedom and independence of all.[9]

For Whigs, on the other hand, mob law was but an outward symptom of a more serious social ill. "It is easy to see how idle must be all pretense of principle," Louisville's Whig *Daily Journal* brooded in 1845, "when a body of politicians proclaim the tactics of slaughter and of rapine; give notice that whoever can kill an opponent shall strip his body, carry away his watch, and tear off his epaulets; and call to their ranks everything that is sanguinary in point of feeling and rapacious in purpose." What was barbarism, they wondered, but the inevitable result of a lack of middle-class civilization and, more important, cultivation? In their view, Andrew Jackson's America sorely needed both. In 1847, for instance, Horace Bushnell compared antebellum America to Israel in the era of the Judges. "It is a time of decline towards barbarism," he noted. "Public security is gone. The people have run wild. Forms are more sacred than duties." Worse, the people often mistook vices for virtues: "The villain and the saint coalesce, without difficulty, in one and the same character; and superstition, which delights in absurdities, hides the imposture from him who suffers it."[10]

The problem was bigger than violence and ran deeper than disorder. Intemperance, irreligion, ignorance, stupidity, and sheer laziness were spreading as fast as the country's borders. "This world was never made for people to dwell on in idleness," wrote one Whiggish woman who put her faith in individual hard work, "and yet more than three-fourths of the human family fail in contributing to the support and welfare of the race."[11]

Whiggery was built on the middle-class premise that men and women must continually seek improvement and avoid indolence at all costs. "Upon this subject, the habits of our whole species fall into three great classes," the Illinois Whig Abraham Lincoln argued in 1847, "useful labour, useless labour and idleness. Of these the first only is meritorious; and to it all the products of labour rightfully belong; but the two latter, while they exist, are heavy pensioners upon the first, robbing it of a large portion of it's [*sic*] just rights. The only remedy for this is to, as far as possible, drive useless labour and idleness out of existence."[12]

But how? How could Americans correct inherent tendencies toward violence, sloth, and drink while improving their character to secure a better future? Whigs believed that the process began with a realistic understanding of human nature. Their understanding of human nature flowed first from Christian Holy Writ and the idea of original sin. But what does that mean? "Original sin is a condition," one useful reference explains, "not something that people do: It is the normal spiritual and psychological condition of human beings." Adam and Eve chose to disobey God in the Garden of Eden, and their transgression forever stained their descendants. During the decades before the Civil War, this concept was powerful and grew out of deep intellectual, social, and religious roots.[13]

Popular culture opens useful windows into prevalent ideas of a given era. Thus, the New York printers Nathaniel Currier and James Merritt Ives offered prints, pictures, and lithographs that mined popular sporting and literary motifs, everyday life, and religious themes. In their 1835 print *The Tree of Death—The Sinner,* they stressed that the fruits of humanity's wickedness led all men and women through a cascading life full of folly, misery, and despair (see fig. 1.2).

Absent the saving power of God's grace, most believed that a cold grave and a hot afterlife awaited all. Antebellum Americans disagreed on many of the theological details, of course, but the consequences of religious choices concerned almost everyone, and the weight of original sin was often heavy. "The Bible told us that human nature was depraved," the *American Whig Review* reminded readers in 1845, "that the thoughts and imaginations of men were evil continually, that they loved darkness more than light, and that the heart was deceitful above all things and desperately wicked."[14] If left to their own devices, Whigs believed, men and women would sink back to depravity, even barbarism. And the violence, ignorance,

Fig. 1.2. Currier & Ives, *The Tree of Death—the Sinner* (New York: Currier & Ives, ca. 1835–1855). Lithograph. Prints and Photographs Division, Library of Congress, Washington, DC. "Devil watering tree of sins and skeleton about to chop it down." https://www.loc.gov/item/93512425.

and stupidity reported in newspapers across the country on an almost daily basis seemed to corroborate their fears. Thus, Whiggish reformers refused to leave people alone.

Yet Whigs also maintained that individuals diligently working—within families, voluntary associations, and churches and even governments—could overcome their own shortcomings and reach for a better tomorrow. In 1842, Henry Clay stressed that strict economy and frugality in both public and private affairs would solve most economic ills and benefit the whole people.[15] To be sure, the fear of social declension and the promise of communal development were crucial ideological cogs in the urge for improvement itself, more broadly understood. If individuals curtailed their baser instincts, Whigs believed, much was possible. "We believe in man's capacity for self-government," stressed Daniel Webster. "We desire to see the freest and widest dissemination of knowledge and of truth."[16] Whigs like Clay and Webster rejected the idea of static individualism and embraced the notion that men were not simply good enough on their own because they believed that everyone must always work toward improvement or inevitably fall back into savagery. "If you leave a thing alone you leave it to a torrent of change," Whigs might echo one dour modern apologetic. "If you leave a white post alone it will soon be a black post. If you particularly want it to be white you must be always painting it again." It was the proper method of keeping white posts white and vice-ridden men virtuous that made all the difference.[17]

Along with the Bible, Whigs turned to the founding generation for wisdom and guidance. The framers' views of human nature seemed to confirm Whiggish assumptions. "But what is government itself," James Madison famously explained, "but the greatest of all reflections on human nature? If men were angels, no government would be necessary." Men were not angels in 1788, most Whigs agreed, and the frequency of mob violence, public intemperance, blanket stupidity, and cold-blooded murder suggested that their character had not noticeably improved in the subsequent half century. Beyond doubt, and certainly beyond Madison, George Washington loomed largest in the imagined landscape of antebellum American political thought, and, during the fifty years before the Civil War, his words resonated in an often deeply felt way. "A small knowledge of human nature will convince us, that, with far the greatest part of mankind, interest is the governing principle," he pointed out in 1778. "Few men are capable of making a continual sacrifice of all views of private interest, or advantage, to the common good."[18] For Washington as well as for Clay, *unrestrained* ambition and *narrow* interest, or seeking one's own prosperity without sufficient regard for broader social responsibility, were among the greatest weaknesses of human character. But Whigs argued that, if those ambitions and interests were harnessed and directed toward the common good, greatness was possible.[19]

Association and collaborative effort to achieve the common good was the bourgeois antidote toward selfishness, and Whigs believed that those positive proclivities were most prominent in women. In light of the "groveling passions of mankind," Boston Whigs argued in 1841, "the best and purest feelings of our human nature are excited by woman." If human nature carried a lodestone of sin, it was lighter and less pronounced in women. In this view, women's virtues hinted at the possibilities for the general improvement of humanity. A society that could produce talented educators, authors, and publishers such as Elizabeth Ann Seton, Frances Sargent Osgood, and Sarah Josepha Hale offered great hope for the future. "The prevailing manners of an age depend, more than we are aware of, or are willing to allow, on the conduct of the women," one Whig periodical noted in 1840. "Those who would allow the influence which female graces have in contributing to polish the manners of men, would do well to reflect how great an influence female morals must also have on their conduct." Most Whigs believed that women offered an antidote to selfishness because they emphasized cooperation more than individualism. Of course, women struggled with original sin as well. Uncultivated by education or not properly restrained by religion, a woman's nature could be every bit as savage as that of a man. Yet most Whigs believed that women offered the best glimpse of the moral heights to which humanity might aspire, and this faith helped carve out a niche for women in Whig political culture that was rarely rivaled among the Jacksonians.[20]

In addition to room for women within their political culture, Whigs maintained hope for blacks as well. Certainly, the vast majority of white Americans believed that blacks were inferior to whites, and Whigs by and large agreed. Yet they held out the possibility for blacks' moral and intellectual advancement. More crucially, black men were *men,* properly understood, and not merely sentient brute animals, fit only for manual labor. "Is the black man morally accountable to God, or is he not?" Daniel

Webster wondered. "Has he a right to murder? Has he even a right to steal?" In this view, it was hypocrisy or delusion for any state or so-called statesmen to argue that blacks were little more than talking cattle, on the one hand, and then punish them for crimes, on the other. "If he has neither the right to murder nor to steal, it is on account of his intelligence and moral responsibility which teach him its sinfulness." If complete political and social equality seemed a radical impossibility for all but the most rock-ribbed of Whig reformers, the moral ground before the cross of Christ was surprisingly level. Webster spoke for many Whigs when he said: "I regard slavery in itself as a great moral, social, and political evil." Although Webster was no abolitionist, both abolitionism and emerging early feminism drew their intellectual sustenance from *Whiggish* soil.[21]

To be fair, the picture shifts the further south one looks. If pressed on the subject, most southern Whigs tried to follow Henry Clay down a path of moderation. "I am, Mr. President, no friend of slavery," Clay explained in the US Senate in 1839. "The searcher of all hearts knows that every pulsation of mine beats high and strong in the cause of civil liberty. Wherever it is safe and practicable, I desire to see every portion of the human family in the enjoyment of it." High-minded in a vague way, he qualified his vision when specifics were involved. "But I prefer the liberty of my own country to that of other people; and the liberty of my own race to that of any other race. The liberty of the descendants of Africa in the United States is incompatible with the liberty and safety of the European descendants." Whigs like Clay expressed regret with the presence of slavery in their midst, hope that future generations might find a way to deal with it, and an irritation with partisan extremism that debated nothing else. Clay himself probably believed his call for moderation, but his moral position was undermined by the scores of slaves that he owned in Lexington, Kentucky. Indeed, southern Whiggery was strongest among the restless planter and nascent merchant classes because both embraced the bourgeois possibilities that black chattel slavery opened and shared northern Whigs' commitment to reform, restraint, and cooperation. Dixie's Whigs embraced the vision of their northern counterparts, but they chose different paths to achieve it. Throughout the antebellum years, few investment opportunities were as consistently lucrative as the trade in human flesh. In a grim, remorseless way, southern Whiggery revealed the dark side of the middle-class path to the future. Comfort carried cost, and sometimes those costs were paid, not by individual sacrifice, pluck, and thrift, but by other people. So long as slavery was ignored on the national political stage, partisan unity endured, and southern Whigs supported the same policy proposals as their northern neighbors. Thus, although most Whigs in the South and Middle West, were proslavery or at least antiblack, they made room for education, infrastructure, and moral reform in their party until the sectional crisis of the 1850s made deferring the slavery question impossible. And, across these same years, it is almost ludicrous to try to imagine room in the party of Jackson, Polk, or Buchanan for abolitionists such as Frederick Douglass, William Lloyd Garrison, and Arthur Tappan or early feminists such as Susan B. Anthony, Elizabeth Cady Stanton, and Lucretia Mott, Whiggish bourgeoisie all.[22]

Although Whigs championed equality before God and the law and held out hope for improvement across races, classes, and genders, they did not believe that all men and women were born equally intelligent, hardworking, responsible, or deserving of status and acclaim. According to the *American Whig Review,* the military demonstrated this principle well, elevating to power men who were "educated, intelligent, moral, modest and brave." Whigs smarted under criticism from Jacksonians that their policies and principles were geared toward protecting the affluence of the few at the expense of the many. As they saw things, material disparity was the expected result of unequal ability, merit, and effort. "And when the victory [of want over wealth is won], how is the state to be governed? Is every man to do what is right in his own eye?" one Whig editor dismissed social-leveling thinking in 1841. "This, indeed, would be a paradise, yet is it not a 'paradise of fools'? Let the horrors of revolutionary France answer this question." Whigs sought to turn the debate to one of improvement for each individual relative to his aptitude and industry because they believed that levelers were shortsighted.[23]

Whigs' reading of human nature began with skepticism and original sin, but their hopes for individual improvement were vast. In America, relished Baltimore Whigs in 1832, "private enterprise and personal industry are encouraged."[24] The antebellum United States was a young nation with a young population, and any faithful reading of its history makes it difficult to overstate most Americans' sheer optimism and ambition. Andrew Jackson was born in 1767 in a dingy colonial frontier cabin in the South Carolina wilderness, a forgotten subject of the British Crown. The earliest memories of his greatest rival, Henry Clay, born a decade later in the Virginia backcountry, were of the uncertain American struggle for independence. The two men came of age in a dynamic country stumbling, tripping, and finally running west. The steamboat, railroad, telegraph, sewing machine, and mechanical reaper, to name but a few wonders of the era, noisily elbowed one another out of the way as technology raced territorial expansion to astound, amaze, and baffle Americans living through these years. This was a world of astonishing growth. And human nature might be flawed and crass when unimproved, but Whigs saw in the newness of America a grand historical opportunity. "Gentlemen, we are at the point of a century from the birth of Washington," the famed Massachusetts orator and politician Daniel Webster boldly declared in an 1832 speech celebrating the first president's birthday, "and what a century it has been! During its course, the human mind has seemed to proceed with a sort of geometric velocity, accomplishing, for human intelligence and human freedom, more than had been done in fives or tens of centuries preceding."[25] The petty superstitions, incessant wars, and oppressive class distinctions that continued to mar Europe had not yet taken root in America, many Whig polemicists rather generously observed. Thus, the promise existed for previously unfathomable achievements, beginning first with moral character. "This generation would be forward indeed to ask for other signs than it enjoys," William Seward assured New Yorkers in 1839, "that our race is ordained to reach, on this continent, a higher standard of social perfection than it has ever yet attained; and that hence will proceed the spirit which shall renovate the world."[26]

In fact, Whigs' support for the vast network of benevolent reform, including most notably the American Temperance Society, the American Anti-Slavery Society, the American Bible Society, and the broader common school movement, flowed from their bedrock faith in the improvability of individual men and women and, through them, American society itself. Whigs often waxed rhapsodic on this point. "That the world is bad enough we well know," one New England Whig conceded in 1836, "and yet wholesale and uncompromising censures of mankind we cannot relish or approve. There are redeeming qualities in the worst of men, and we do not well to condemn without limit." It is both telling and ironic that Whigs' fears of humanity's present condition invigorated their faith in its future potential. And most Whigs felt that their ideas offered the most pragmatic opportunity to secure social and individual improvement. Although their political creed was certainly based on a distrust of executive power, with all the dangers it portended, Whigs held out greater hope for legislative action, voluntary association, and individual activity. "The Whig cause is *practical* in all its tendencies and aspirations," Frederic S. Hill's Boston-based *New England Galaxy and United States Literary Advertiser* explained in 1836. "It has no sympathy with doctrines that recognize the equality of human rights, but stumble at propositions calculated to produce equality in social condition."[27] But the crucial difference between Whig and Jacksonian reform thinking was the recognition of unequal talents and the earnest desire to see Americans rise by striving and education and not by measures that only punished the successful. Democrats would dispute that they were interested in punishing success, arguing instead that they just wanted to be left alone and that the government should protect the little guys as well as the bigwigs. Democrats' defense of white, male equality was grounded in their need for political solidarity against enemies whom they feared combined money and power to oppress them. They thought that most people were basically good, if only left alone and that, even if human character had its warts, it was beyond the legitimate scope of government action to do anything about it. Whigs disagreed, believing instead that human nature was fundamentally flawed and that no two men or women were ever born perfectly equal in intelligence, industry, or piety, yet they also nurtured an abounding optimism that men and women could rise with diligent effort. As they understood human character, then, Whigs held that individuals should work for personal improvement daily. While Democrats lionized a rugged individualism where Americans rose or fell on the strength of their own will and virtue, Whigs qualified their understanding of free will by pointing to social, economic, and political context.[28]

Regardless, Whigs valued order in their personal lives because they saw two general paths before them. America offered the world's best chance to reform the minds and morals of men and women as they rose in material affluence, intellectual sophistication, and ethical refinement. But barbarism was the likely result for all who shunned benevolent progress. Whigs stressed hard work and social engagement, first within one's own family, and then as a productive member of society. They demanded a great deal of people. Individuals must discipline their passions and control their base desires. Whigs dismissed Democratic concerns with coercion as irrational and silly because of their middle-class trust in public institutions, a trust that was sometimes naive and misplaced. Even so, self-restraint and enlightened virtue were for them the surest badges of the truly moral man. Indeed, they believed that all men and women held a sacred obligation both to their forebears and to their posterity to develop character through disciplined instruction in the family, school, and church. For Whigs, finally, any talk of rights must be balanced with a deep appreciation for responsibilities. The Whigs' vision of America called on engaged, improving citizens, staving off apathy and ignorance to pursue the common good.

## Liberty and Equality

Whigs' worldview first reflected their belief in individuals' frail but improvable character. However, a deeper reading of their understanding of liberty is important because antebellum Americans debated the proper definition, application, and scope of it. Nearly everyone conceded that white Americans enjoyed liberty as their birthright from the Revolutionary generation, but what was liberty, many wondered, rightly understood? Near the end of his public career, for example, Abraham Lincoln pointed out: "The world has never had a good definition of the word liberty, and the American people, just now, are much in want of one." Noah Webster's famous dictionary offered no fewer than ten different definitions in 1830, demonstrating the term's importance to the American public—and also its slipperiness.[29]

For most literate Americans, then, liberty was first understood as "freedom from restraint, in a general sense, and applicable to the body, or to the will or mind." Yet Webster further qualified and clarified the word's meaning. First, he distinguished between natural and civil liberty. Natural liberty was well-nigh impossible in civil society, in his view, because "it is a state of exemption from the control of others, and from positive laws and the institutions of social life." On the face of it, "exemption from the control of others" sounds like a crude ideological shorthand summarizing antebellum Americans' emerging individualism. But Noah Webster was the elder cousin of the rising Whig Daniel Webster, and for both men such a simple understanding of liberty was not just wrong but dangerous.

Thus, the Websters spoke for most Whiggish Americans in their argument that individuals must put their civic faith in institutions and reverence for the law; pell-mell exemptions from either courted disaster. "Civil liberty," they would have argued along with Webster's *Dictionary,* "is the liberty of men in a state of society, or natural liberty, so far only abridged and restrained, as is necessary and expedient for the safety and interest of the society, state or nation." Because Whigs believed that, without restraint, liberty invariably became license, a refined notion of civil liberty was important to their understanding of the individual. Indeed, the bourgeoisie valued liberty as long as it was checked by order and self-control. And a society weakened by a lack of restraint teetered toward barbarism, which was precisely what middle-class Whigs feared most for the antebellum United States.[30]

But how could misunderstood and misused liberty threaten American society? Whigs looked first to individual character and the ballot box. Universal white male suffrage was by and large an accomplished fact by the time Andrew Jackson left the White House in 1837, but its consequences mattered more to Whigs than did its achievement. "We must live by universal suffrage, or perish," New York Whigs allowed. "If we can imbue with knowledge and virtue the mass, we shall live; but if irreligion and profligacy predominate, sure as the march of time, we fail."[31] Republican government relied heavily on the virtue of its citizens to select wise rulers who would chart a safe, prosperous course for the ship of state because democracy reflected the electorate's character. Given the assumed soundness of Whiggish policies and principles, Jacksonians' electoral successes baffled Whigs. If the people voted for Democrats, Virginia Whigs believed, "they will be shewing themselves to be wanting in virtue, at the same time, that they are unfit to be free." Such a result seemed to demonstrate the American people's susceptibility to galling demagoguery and base flattery. Did superior policies and principles deny Henry Clay the presidency? Whigs asked, pondering his narrow, crushing loss in 1844. "No, it was the vile work of a *faction,*" the *American Whig Review* explained, "which knew no motive and sought no end beyond its own triumph." The term *faction* was a calculated charge meant to conjure in the public mind images of cabals, courtiers, hucksters, and hacks. Factions played to fears, not hopes, and eroded common ground.[32]

Demagogues misused liberty to pervert political life through the wanton corruption of individual voters with lies, bribes, and high talk. "We are in the midst of a crisis," Elizabethon's *Tennessee Whig* observed in 1839, "when the great principles of civil and religious liberty, are all at stake."

Most Whigs would agree with their East Tennessee brethren, seeing their world as a place where "unprincipled demagogues and pilfering subordinates, of a corrupt and base-begotten administration—a band of depraved and profligate scoundrels, backed by the Devil himself, the first great enemy of 'all righteousness,'" were all "seeking the destruction of [the] republic." Indeed, Whigs felt that discerning men and women understood or ought to understand that Old Scratch and the political backbiters who aped his methods goaded the dissolute, intemperate, and stupid to ruin with seductive appeals to passion and pride.[33]

It is not shocking, then, that Whigs also grew wary at any mention of rights without duties because in their eyes that sort of rhetoric simply masked the pursuit of individual interest. "Christianity proclaims liberty," one Whiggish polemicist acknowledged, "but it is not a lawless liberty. It must not be a selfish liberty. It has relations to others, and must regard them. It has opportunities of usefulness, and must improve them. It needs restraints, and must not scorn them." Middle-class Whigs believed that individuals needed liberty to enjoy true freedom, and they stressed responsibility and order far more than did their erstwhile Jacksonian brethren. Indeed, most echoed Edmund Burke's explanation in the 1790 *Reflections on the Revolution in France:* "I flatter myself that I love a manly, moral, regulated liberty as well as any gentleman of that society." Yet, for Burke and America's Whigs after him, it was a love of liberty that was couched in the often messy context of real life. "Am I to congratulate a highwayman and murderer who has broke prison upon the recovery of his natural rights?" Burke offered Whigs consolation in another aspect as well. "While the Reformer is certain to be applauded if successful, because his object is definite and clear to everyone," the *American Whig Review* reminded Whigs in 1852, smarting after Winfield Scott got crushed by Franklin Pierce, "the Conservative, whose influence is felt rather than seen, must content himself with but a small measure of that public approbation which he feels to be his due." In the face electoral defeats, Whigs urged each other to stay the course and look to the future for vindication.[34]

Daniel Webster challenged Americans to be worthy of liberty. "To be free, the people must be intelligently free," he explained during a public dinner in 1833. "To be substantially independent they must be able to secure themselves against want, by sobriety and industry; to be safe depositories of political power, they must be able to comprehend and understand the general interests of the community, and must themselves have a stake in the welfare of that community."[35] Thus, Whigs believed that true liberty meant cultivation, restraint, cooperation, and order. "From the beginning of time, three things have been sacred among man," the *American Whig Review* pointed out in 1845, "their Liberty, their Religion, and their Honor. For the first, they appointed laws; for the second, creeds; and for the third, manners."[36] Manners mattered. Yet almost every newspaper, periodical, and broadside carried worsening tales of public disorder and the growing failure of individuals to control themselves.[37]

For their part, Jacksonians often understood individual liberty on a sliding scale of chains and fetters. The more coercion and control an individual faced, the less free he or she became. Democrats often worried that Whig proposals such as expanded banks and credit were ominous attempts to rob the people of their independence and liberty, to say nothing of their money. "The people of this great state fondly imagine that they govern themselves; but they do not!" William Leggett seethed in 1834. "They are led about by the unseen but strong bands of chartered companies." As Leggett and other Jacksonians like him saw things, banking directors, stockholders, and their agents, aided and abetted by scheming Whigs, played a shell game with public policy to bribe the people and control them with their own money. "These evil influences are scattered throughout our community, in every quarter of the state," he explained. "They give tone to our meetings; they name our candidates for our legislature; they secure their election; they control them when elected." While perhaps overblown, Democratic fears were not completely unfounded. Then, as now, banks and moneyed interests were not above using their capital resources to sway policy decisions. Yet Jacksonian concerns were larger than banks and credit and deeper than electoral corruption.[38]

To the narrowed gaze of observant Democrats, Whigs' understanding of liberty was not simply wrong but the stalking horse for a new American plutocracy. Because Jacksonians thought of liberty in stark, personal terms, they were unmoved by Whig appeals for restraint and virtue. Democrats embraced a more personal understanding of liberty, while Whigs tended to see it in more communal terms. Of course, it is inaccurate to suggest that Democrats did not value order. They did, but they largely rejected Whiggish definitions as calculated sophistry, a web of rhetorical deceit meant to manipulate. And, in a sense, they were right. The modern world Whigs sought for themselves and their posterity required virtue, thrift, and personal restraint. Individuals must control themselves, they argued, or society must do it for them. Democrats also suspected that the control that Whigs sought did not end with self-restraint.[39]

For antebellum Americans, the line between prosperity and ruin was not at all clear. And one of the starkest contrasts between Whigs and Jacksonians was the side on which they believed they were destined to fall. Though nearly everyone experienced doubt regarding their prospects, Democrats tended to feel that anxiety far more keenly. Consequently, Jacksonians' thinking on liberty often reflected worries about individual failure and oppression. The language that they used spoke of masters, slaves, freedom, and servility, and, in nearly every instance, they feared that they would end up as losers. "Money is powerful," the Mississippi Democrat John W. Gildart warned in 1836, "and exerts a secret and invisible influence over the actions of man. Indeed, we may look upon it as the ruler, the master, [and] the disposer of his temporal duties." But, in Democratic eyes, it was not simply money or the institutional protection of wealth that threatened liberty but the bourgeois reforming impulse within Whig political thought itself. In 1836, William Leggett explained Jacksonian misgivings about reform, cautioning: "We might say, indeed, of religious reformers too, that they have threatened, rather than persuaded; that they have sought to drive men, rather than allure." Reformers might couch their aims in lofty words but at bottom they sought to unjustly restrain a free people. "It is not enfranchising the few, but enslaving the many." For most Jacksonian Democrats, American liberty at its most essential was, as a result, freedom from outside control, coercion, and servility.[40]

Whigs championed white male equality before God and the law, but they doubted that all men and women were equally intelligent, hardworking, responsible, or deserving of status or acclaim. In their eyes, Democrats practiced bad politics because they often elevated men "to offices of trust and emolument without any merit or pretense to merit."[41] Material disparity was the expected result of unequal ability, merit, and effort. Whigs smarted under criticism from Jacksonians that their policies and principles were geared toward protecting the affluence of the few at the expense of the many. They believed that history showed that mankind had never been equal and thought it foolish to deny this fact. John Pendleton Kennedy, for example, argued that individual success was "dependent upon the merit and good character of the person."[42] Yet Whigs argued that—given their varying degree of talent and ability—all individuals could rise on the strength of their own exertion and persistence to achieve success. Democrats were not simply moaning misanthropes in the face of Whiggish Pollyanna paeans, it is true, and many of their worries about the corrosive potential of corporations were borne out in some degree in subsequent generations. But the antebellum political worldviews often talked past one another, Whig confidence in a prudent, prosperous future making little sense to wary Jacksonians, skeptical of vague promises of a better tomorrow seemingly, to their eyes at least, at the expense of a comfortable, independent today.[43]

Conceptualizing equality also became a sticking point as Whigs and Democrats often talked past one another on this point as well. No one disputed that white men enjoyed an equality of natural rights or an equal standing before God and the courts, but partisan rhetoric grew heated when the question turned to material disparity. "Nothing but the most wild imagination," Boston Whigs charged in 1839, "has ever tempted men to believe that a state of society could be made to exist, in which all men should possess an equal amount of property."[44] Perfect equality was impossible, all seemed to agree, yet Whigs were more comfortable with inequality than were Democrats in part because of their understanding of individualism itself. If, as Democrats believed, the American people were basically good, if only left alone, then lingering inequity signified structural flaws in social and material institutions. "If the inequalities of artificial condition bore any relation to those of nature; if they were determined by the comparative degrees of men's wisdom and strength," William Leggett argued in 1836, "or of their providence and frugality there would be no cause to complain. But the direct contrary is, to a very great extent, the truth." Whigs doubted that a state of nature was any more equal than human society and in the main found Leggett's argument superfluous. All men might indeed be equal in a state of nature, yet that equality was born of barbarism and its enjoyments were short-lived.[45]

Thus, Whigs grew impatient with what they viewed as baseless Jacksonian fears and found their opponents' understanding of liberty incoherent. Just as they believed that human nature was flawed but capable of improvement, so too they understood liberty as not so much freedom *from* coercion as freedom *for* association and uplift. Calvin Colton, Henry Clay's biographer and a Whig pamphleteer, argued that embracing self-sacrifice and cooperation as prerequisites for liberty "is a feeling, which dignifies man, ennobles his nature, and allies him to a higher order of beings."[46]

Democratic rhetoric pleading freedom from compulsion therefore seemed to Whigs like a bad-faith appeal for the socially dangerous freedom from restraint. "But when we look more carefully into the phenomena of the civilized world around us," Virginia Whigs observed in 1851, "do we find that any obligation is habitually regarded as sacred in private practice; or is any duty habitually enforced by the strong coercion of public sentiment, or the stronger influence of the conscientious observance of the right? There is none. The ideas of obligation and duty have given place to considerations of gain and expediency." For middle-class Americans, habits, obligations, and duties were more than mere words. Consequently, Whigs worried that, absent the social and cultural ties of American institutions (i.e., schools, voluntary associations, churches, civic clubs, etc.), Jacksonians' faith in so-called rugged, go-it-alone individuals was a foolish wager destined to fail. It is unfair to suggest, as many Whig polemicists often did, that Democrats did not value sobriety, responsibilities, or social institutions. Instead, it is more accurate to note that Whigs wove those values into their energetic reading of the proper scope of the public sphere in ways that Jacksonians thought were rude, costly, and even dangerous.[47]

Jacksonians struggled mightily to trust people beyond their immediate, everyday interactions with them, and, when they cast their eyes toward the future, they shuddered at an impersonal, urban world where independence and liberty were a fairy tale told by an older generation to remind the young of America's paradise lost. Not surprisingly, Whigs saw things much differently. Americans' liberties tempered by Protestant religion and restraint, they believed, were and would remain the envy of the world.

Temperance reform efforts illustrated this point well. What threatened men's capacity for ordered liberty and self-government more than the corrupting influence of alcohol? Reformers argued that whiskey, rum, and strong foreign beer promoted barbarism and licentiousness. Horace Mann even went so far as to suggest: "Society is infinitely too tolerant of the roué,—the wretch whose life-long pleasure it has been to debase himself and to debauch others."[48] Most Whigs agreed that, once otherwise free individuals took that first tantalizing sip, they set themselves on an inevitable road to ruin. The New York printer and lithographer Nathaniel Currier and his partner, James Merritt Ives, illustrated this argument well with their 1846 lithograph *The Drunkard's Progress* (see fig. 1.3).

Along with similar engravings from other artists such as the Kellogg brothers, *The Drunkard's Progress* presented the cycle of failure and

Fig. 1.3. N. E. B. & E. C. Kellogg, *The Drunkard's Progress* (New York: Kelloggs & Thayer; Hartford, CT: E. B. & E. C. Kellogg; Buffalo: D. Needham, ca. 1846). Prints and Photographs Division, Library of Congress, Washington, DC. "Print shows an archway of the nine steps of a drunkard's progress, beginning with a man in fancy dress having 'a glass with a friend' and then his gradual decline in society with poverty & disease, criminal activity, becoming a bum, and his eventual 'death by suicide'; two men, one on horseback and another with sacks, are in foreground." https://www.loc.gov/item/2002706811.

disappointment that began with the ill-fated "Morning Dram," which led to "the Grog Shop." From those innocuous drams grew a taste for drink and, worse, a taste for vice. Wavering in unsteady gait as his family starves, "the Confirmed Drunkard" suffers from his "home falling apart" and watches his "family evicted" and his "home up for auction." Booze ruined his life and the lives of his wife and children, now destitute. In the end, the drunkard takes his own life in the grips of suicidal ennui and his family is thrown out in the street. If the argument stopped here, probably the majority of Democratic Americans would agree. Drunkenness could leave intemperate people indigent. Whigs took the social consequences a step further. If enough fathers were drunks, then a critical mass of families would become beggars, dependent on society for support, and incapable of development or growth. For their part, Democrats usually acknowledged that alcohol could destroy a man's life, they just believed that it that was nobody's business beyond the drunkard, his kin, and his friends. The Democratic view of liberty gave wide berth to individual determinism, even if those choices were questionable in a broad sense.[49]

The idea that something could be done about drunkenness in society was rather new. In 1826, for instance, when Lyman Beecher and Justin Edwards founded the American Temperance Society, most Americans believed that alcoholism was a simple, unfortunate by-product of life and, at best, hoped to mitigate its effects on alcoholics' families. Indeed, one of the starkest ways in which the new wave of middle-class reformers differed from its forebears was the rejection of the notion that drunkenness was incurable and drunkards incorrigible. "Turn now, to the temperance revolution," Abraham Lincoln warmly asked a group of reformers on Washington's Birthday in 1842. "In *it* we shall find a stronger bondage broken; a viler slavery manumitted; a greater tyrant deposed. In *it,* more of want supplied, more disease healed, more sorrow assuaged. By *it* no orphans starving, no widows weeping." Pragmatic and discerning almost to a fault, Lincoln's prairie-born Whiggery rarely got so carried away, but he warmed to the temperance message, sounding the call for reform like a camp meeting preacher at Cane Ridge, Fairfax, or Rochester. "Happy day," he prophesied, "when, all appetites controlled, all passions subdued, all matters subjected, *mind,* all conquering *mind,* shall live and move the monarch of the world. Glorious consummation! Hail, fall of Fury! Reign of Reason, all hail!" Though Lincoln eventually came all the way around and set his will against its existence entirely, throughout the antebellum years temperance served as a moral cause that helped salve the bourgeois conscience regarding slavery, bridging sectional differences with middle-class morality while pointing the reformers' gaze past the coffles and pens to the alehouses and saloons.[50]

No doubt, Whiggish people believed that drunkenness was a social cancer. For Whigs such as Lincoln, alcohol represented a sinister threat to personal liberty because of strong drink's erosion of individual morality, responsibility, and self-control. For instance, one Whiggish merchant in New York warned potential job seekers that any clerk he hired "must be a man of good moral character, and not interested in any place where intoxicating drink is usually retailed."[51] Although a teetotaler, Lincoln coupled his hope for an American future free from the effects of draught and drink with compassion for the drunkard. "In my judgment, such of us as have never fallen victims, have been spared more from the absence of appetite, than from any mental or moral superiority over those who have," he cautioned temperance reformers. "Indeed, I believe, if we take habitual drunkards as a class, their heads and their hearts will bear an advantageous comparison with those of any other class." It was probably a nod to both moral breadth and shrewd tactics that pushed Whigs like Lincoln toward a more considerate stance. Few people seriously consider changing their habits while being harangued as hopeless reprobates.[52]

Hard-line teetotalism flowed from reformers' frustration with the slow progress of moral suasion, but, for more pragmatic Whigs such as Henry Clay and Abraham Lincoln, inflexibility was counterproductive. Conversions based on cajoling, overwrought moralizing, or downright abuse tended only to increase the rolls of backsliders or push the wayward to other vices. One gruff New York Whig reminded browbeaters: "The teetotal pledge prevents no man from chewing opium like a Turk."[53] Reform flowed more naturally from Whiggish thinking, and reformers were more at home in Whig ranks because bourgeois thought stressed process over destination. And, in addition, Whigs believed that "the trial of men's virtue never comes but when they are called on to maintain their principles at some sacrifice."[54] At its heart, the Whig world required a genuine, lasting reform of individual proclivities and inclinations. Indeed, reform was a process without end, inculcating the people with a desire for ongoing personal scrutiny and improvement. Only then would individuals have the moral strength to use their liberties wisely and preserve them. Only then would men begin to trust one another and extend the social capital so necessary for an integrated, modern middle-class society.[55]

Beyond the dangers of drink and the possibilities for individual reforms, Whigs also worried about the excesses of liberty at the ballot box. George Caleb Bingham's famous 1852 painting *The County Election* illustrates this well (see fig. 1.4). The sheer diversity of the American polity is the most striking feature of this work. Bingham shows serious voters engaged in heated debates alongside a nearly unconscious drunk whose friends are *carrying* him to the polls. One fellow seems about to fall over after a fight. The candidate stands high on the steps talking to prospective voters, of course, but he does not dominate the scene. Instead, it is *the*

Fig. 1.4. George Caleb Bingham (American, 1811–1879), *The County Election* (1851–1852), oil on canvas (35 7/16 × 48 3/4 inches). Saint Louis Art Museum, Museum Purchase 124:1944.

*people,* sometimes riotous, inebriated, and distracted, that matter most. Indeed, Bingham includes a banner that boldly proclaims: "The Will of the People the Supreme Law." *The County Election* demonstrates Whigs' rock-ribbed belief in American democracy, broadly understood, but it also expresses reservations about democracy's excesses in the age of Jackson.

Echoing their more caustic reforming brethren, most Whigs thought it foolhardy to trust voters plied with drink to choose leaders wisely. That Bingham refuses to flinch from portraying drunkards marring the franchise that supposedly confirmed their liberties does not mean that he, and other Whigs like him, was terribly hostile to popular democracy. Instead, he offers an honest, even idealized vision of Election Day in America. American democracy was not always pretty. Indeed, electoral results, corruption at the polls, the profligate use of spoils, and the lack of education and discernment troubled a wide array of concerned people throughout the era. Yet they put their trust in the ultimate judgment and wisdom of the American people. To middle-class eyes, Whiggery was not a stalking horse for a new moneyed aristocracy, nor was it claptrap, empty of substance or sincerity. If Whigs urged improvement, restraint, and uplift, it was because they believed in a glorious American destiny. That destiny need not manifest itself in territorial conquest but should instead look to the comfort, intelligence, and sophistication of posterity.

## The Family

Whiggish men and women understood human nature as vice ridden but also held out the possibility that diligent individuals could improve with effort and restraint. Like all Americans, moreover, Whigs idealized liberty and equality, though they qualified each by emphasizing order and merit. They first learned values such as self-control, hard work, temperance, and thrift as children in families. Thus, middle-class Whiggish families gave birth to, molded, and nurtured individuals along social and cultural lines consistent with Whig thought. Consequently, a more thorough reading of Whig views on the family, broadly understood, is crucial to understanding the individual's role in the America Whigs wanted to build.

At first glance, this notion seems obvious, even trite. Jacksonian Democrats were the products of families too, and the importance of family life is common to the human condition. Accordingly, it is doubtful that a Jacksonian would dispute the New York Whig Daniel Barnard's argument that "the Family must be held sacred." However, the *kind* of individuals families were supposed to create varied considerably among Whigs and Democrats. For Whig political culture, then, the family instilled moral character, essential for maintaining virtue in an individualistic society, character that would manifest itself through industry, frugality, and temperance. Jacksonians would probably agree that all families should promote these and other values, but most importantly they stressed that their families were the first link in a social chain of loyalty, trust, and intimacy. And for Democrats that chain was not very long. As they saw things, families shielded their members from the worst vagaries of an impersonal world; protection was their ultimate aim. Whigs would agree that defense was where the family's role began, but for them it did not end there. Families socialized their members for participation in the middle-class world. Through the examples provided by mothers and fathers, Whig families demonstrated the importance of social harmony, deference to hierarchy, the crucial qualities of respectability and self-control, and the need to collaborate with others to achieve broader prosperity.[56]

Despite America's overwhelming agrarian character, Whigs tended to champion the urban, middle-class ideal. This is not surprising, given their shared bourgeois imagination. Whigs tended to think of domestic life as society writ small, and their understanding of the role of mothers reflected this thinking. Sarah Josepha Hale, for instance, the formidable editor of the widely popular *Godey's Lady's Book and Ladies' American Magazine* argued: "She [the mother] is a soul on fire with the hallowed flame of affection, and filled with that overflowing abundance of virtue, high principle and purity."[57] For Whigs, then, motherhood was infused with a near holy sense of decency. Although Democrats might also say as much, the kinds of people they wanted mothers to create differed. Building on ideas of feminine respectability, Whigs stressed mothers' roles in shaping their children's character. In 1840, Daniel Webster lauded motherhood in cultivating virtue, explaining: "It is by the promulgation of sound morals in the community, and more especially by the training and instruction of the young, that woman performs her part towards the preservation of a free government."[58] In Whig social thought, then, the work of women instilling good habits in their children such as honesty, sobriety, compassion, and tenderness was vital because they were preparing them for an impersonal, middle-class world that demanded cooperation with neighbors, colleagues, and friends. Aside from these general understandings, however, what it meant to be both a woman and a mother was neither fixed nor constant. One useful way of thinking about the unsettling social and cultural changes that antebellum women endured is in terms of the differences between sentimental or romantic womanhood and more bourgeois femininity. For their part, Whig women embraced a more middle-class understanding of woman, wife, and mother and were often proud of it. They taught their children Whiggish understandings of individualism, tempering its worst effects by stressing cooperation, and did their best to live out its example in the wider public world.[59]

Mothers were crucial in shaping Whig individuals because, for the Western middle class, women embodied the three Christian virtues of faith, hope, and love. In Whig thinking, these virtues were crucial to living a moral, successful life. Whig mothers, moreover, offered a pious example for their husbands and children to emulate. "That man is what his mother made him," the Whig editor of the *Christian Advocate and Journal* explained. "Often, children without praying parents grow up not only without religion, but are decidedly vicious, and sometimes close their lives in prison or on the gallows." And mothers occupied the praying heart of the family, properly ordered and understood. Their piety undergirded their purity, lending moral weight to their broader cultural perception as exemplars of virtue. One formerly whiskey-soaked sailor in New York agreed, claiming to have turned back to God on the memory of his mother's moral instruction. Explaining his repentance and salvation to Whig reformers in New York, he recalled with remarkable awe the way his mother read the Bible to the family each night before bed. "The truth was, his mother had taught him to read it in the days of his childhood. She had taught him to reverence the Bible, and the Sabbath, and the name of God," a report noted. The memories of drunks are famously unreliable, yet the emphasis on motherly devotion is telling because of the way in which both reformers and reformed framed their efforts as living up to a mother's moral example. No doubt, many antebellum women shared in a common culture of religious devotion, yet Whig women interpreted and applied Christian moral strictures with decidedly bourgeois principles.[60]

Women were supposed to use their moral influence to inculcate a reverence for education, paving the way for both the uplift and the social participation that most Whigs believed so important. "To the woman," wrote a Whig woman in 1843, "it belongs to elevate the intellectual character of her household, to kindle the fire of mental activity in childhood, and to keep these steadily burning with advancing years." For most Whigs, this idea was more than a polite suggestion or a vague aspirational longing. As we have seen, society trusted women to educate children in and inspire men to piety and purity because of their perceived moral superiority. "She is not only the mother of our children," *Godey's Lady's Book* explained in 1831, "but she is emphatically the framer of infant minds. Tis her prerogative to watch over the first dawning of intellect, and shape the character of the future man." The Whigs' America demanded that mothers help mold individuals with piety, prudence, and self-restraint, then send them out into the modern world.[61]

Mothers further reinforced Whig values by strengthening family hierarchies with maternal love and respect. To be sure, submission and domesticity were essential virtues of bourgeois or true womanhood, but, as Whigs saw it, these ideas were not meant to repress or degrade women. "Husband and wife are not one, but two," stressed the *American Whig Review* in 1845. "They are but contracting parties." A proper understanding of deference, then, meant mutual association, and family roles smoothed individuals' way in a world that required cooperation. In the context of families, a proper regard for hierarchy extended back from the state and society, drawing support from the home. "For this purpose, it is needful that certain relations be sustained, which involve the duties of subordination," Catherine Beecher argued in her famous *Treatise on Domestic Economy.* "There must be the magistrate and the subject, one of whom is the superior, and the other the inferior. There must be the relations of husband and wife, parent and child, teacher and pupil, employer and employed, each involving the relative duties of subordination." In this way, everyone at one time or another was subordinate to someone else. Because Whigs argued that subordination was a vital part of social harmony, they did not fear hierarchies or see in them servitude and the loss of independence, as did Jacksonians.[62]

The engraving *The Happy Family* (see fig. 1.5) drives home these points. In the bourgeois Whig view, women were not imprisoned in their homes, chained to a life of miserable drudgery cooking, cleaning, and mending. Instead, they were the first guardians of society's future (i.e., children), and on their shoulders rested the important charge of instilling crucial values that would shape character, for ill or not.

"To render the family state what it should be," one New York Whig argued, "pains must be taken to make it the scene not only of subordination and good order, but of improvement in interesting, useful knowledge, and rational, innocent enjoyment." Thus, understanding one's role or place in society did not preclude uplift, in Whigs' view, because association, often including unequal reciprocal relationships, was the surest path to success. Democrats often dismissed such thinking as degrading and argued that Whigs' plan would lead to isolated, lonely ruin. A short story that appeared in the premier Jacksonian magazine the *United States Magazine, and Democratic Review* in 1845 illustrates their worries well. The author details the family follies wrought by the Whiggish path: "In this way the mother is left alone. Her son is at college. He leaves there for a wider career, but not to return to his home. . . . Wearied with life without purpose or occupation, that mother becomes a prey first to ennui, and then, perchance, to

Fig. 1.5. John Sartain (engraver) and Eliza Leslie, *The Happy Family* ([Philadelphia], January 1843). Mezzotint by Sartain expressly for *Miss Leslie's Magazine.* Prints and Photographs Division, Library of Congress, Washington, DC. "Print shows a family gathered in a parlor for tea; seated at a table are the father, holding a book and with a young daughter leaning on his knee, and the mother, pouring tea, also present are another daughter standing on the left, holding flowers, a nurse or maid holding an infant, and a small dog sitting on a cushion next to the table." https://www.loc.gov/item/2015650253.

superstition. . . . From step to step she will sink into the toils of the designing, until her prospect of happiness for life is destroyed; or her mind is over taken with inanity, and adjusted to the idle and profitless duties which are left her to perform."[63] The middle-class world that the Whigs worked so blithely to build undermined, in Democratic eyes, the personal bonds of family, robbed daily life of meaning, and prepared Americans to accept degrading servility. Whigs usually shrugged off such concerns as banal, arguing instead that arrangements such as employers and employees or superiors and subordinates were inevitable and that advancement and prosperity came to those who could negotiate them successfully. In many ways, moreover, Whiggish women shrewdly used their platforms and the public perception of their higher virtue to pursue potent political initiatives such as education and temperance reform and public care for the mentally ill. The Whig Party offered a public place for women that was largely unavailable among the Democrats. Whig families nurtured the worldview that made this sort of political participation attractive.[64]

By the 1830s, moreover, what it meant to be a man and a father was also disputed and elusive. Indeed, the ways in which Whigs thought about fatherhood reflected their partisan aspirations and anxieties. One way to understand these changes is to think of antebellum American masculinity in terms of two broad archetypes: the heroic artisan and the self-made man. A heroic artisan was independent, strong willed, and honest. He was agrarian and nostalgic, if not always in employment or living situation, then in temperament and outlook. He loathed feeling trapped and longed for the imagined freedom of a yeoman past that he sought to preserve from the mechanistic onrush of modernity. "How completely we are hemmed in on every side," William Leggett bitterly echoed this idea in 1834, "how we are cabined, cribb'd, confined by exclusive privileges!" Conversely, the self-made man was defined by a life on the go. Competitive and self-assured, he was a man of *busy*ness, of personal and public connections, and usually one who believed that the future was not constrained by the past and that future success was not mitigated by past ruin. Owing to their disparate ideological outlooks and the sorts of men both wanted to become, Democrats such as Leggett often lauded the supposedly go-it-alone individual or heroic artisan, while Whigs championed bourgeois notions of self-made men.[65]

Yet by *self-made* Whigs did not mean isolated efforts toward personal gain in constant battle against a cruel, unfeeling world. Instead, for them, individualism was a "reflective and peaceable sentiment," and to be self-made meant simply that individual destiny was tied to individual character, industry, and ability.[66] Self-made men grabbed life by the horns and worked hard to win the future. In 1838, the Massachusetts Whig Theodore Russell explained that a self-made man was "made for action, and the bustling scenes of moving life, and not the poetry or romance of existence."[67] Of course, it is both a mistake and a distortion to read these archetypes or the men they described as either all good or all bad. Indeed, Jacksonian and Whig men, at least in a material sense, drifted between both types over the course of their lives as circumstances and context dictated. However, in the world they imagined—in the ideal both strove toward and against a bit—more fixed distinctions emerged.

For their part, Whigs tended to lionize the self-made man, at least as the notion was qualified and understood in middle-class Whiggish terms. Indeed, Henry Clay first used the term *self-made man* in 1832 in a defense of protective tariffs as a public means to help the industrious rise. "In Kentucky, almost every manufactory known to me," Clay pointed out, "is in the hands of enterprising, self-made men, who have whatever wealth they possess by patient and diligent labor." Self-made men mattered to the Whiggish ideal of family because they bridged the gap from private to public. Fathers taught their children how to connect without getting exploited, how to strive so that they might thrive. As Whigs saw it, self-mastery, thrift, and temperance were the backbones of American masculinity, properly understood, yet the self-made man was shaped by both family and society. Middle-class Whig men were supposed to demonstrate discipline and demand temperance and courage. These were lessons handed down over time, and, like most Whigs, Daniel Webster believed that this sort of patrimony linked generations together. The opportunity to make something of oneself was essential to liberty itself and fundamental to all freeborn Americans. "Our fathers have earned and bought [liberty] for us," said Webster in 1826, quoting John Adams, "at the expense of their ease, their estates, their pleasure, and their blood."[68] An 1840 lithograph that burnishes William Henry Harrison's rustic appeal demonstrates Whiggish thinking in this regard well (see fig. 1.6).

An extravagant yarn that gleefully blended fact and fiction, Harrison's 1840 Log Cabin Campaign, so named because of the campaign fable that he began his life in a crude log cabin along the Virginia frontier, was a set

Fig. 1.6. "Harrison & Tyler" campaign emblem (1840). Woodcut. Prints and Photographs Division, Library of Congress, Washington, DC. "An untitled woodcut, bold in design, apparently created for use on broadsides or banners during the Whigs' 'log cabin' campaign of 1840. In front of a log cabin, a shirtsleeved William Henry Harrison welcomes a soldier, inviting him to rest and partake of a barrel of 'Hard Cider.' Nearby another soldier, already seated, drinks a glass of cider. On a staff at right is an American flag emblazoned with 'Harrison & Tyler.'" https://www.loc.gov/item/2008661359.

piece of Whig reverence for the self-made man. Through prudence, thrift, opportunism, and self-restraint, the Whigs told each other and a wry public, Harrison overcame his humble beginnings and achieved measured military success during the War of 1812 before settling down to execute the public will as a statesman. For Whigs, it did not matter much that this account was heavy on exaggeration and outright fabrication and light on hard facts; it was the vision of the world that they wanted to be true, the kind of America that they wanted to build. They argued—optimistically and perhaps naively—that all that separated the lowly from wealth and acclaim, aside from natural disparities in talent and ability, was hard work. The Whig theologian and polemicist Calvin Colton explained that America was "a country where men start from a humble origin, and from small beginnings gradually rise in the world, as the reward of merit and industry." And merit and industry qualified Whigs' understanding of equality itself. Thus, Whig men did not merely instruct their children in these values; they also lived or tried to live them as best they could.[69]

In some ways, the world that the Whigs wanted to build required a near impossibility: a calm, self-assured man who was equally at home in the country and in town, able to navigate the new world of factories, telegraphs, and lyceums as easily as he milked cows or mended fences. Antebellum men were often frustrated and confused by a world that seemed so radically different from the one they had known as boys. Indeed, Jackson's strongest support came from men who idealized the heroic artisan's resolute independence and determination to go it alone in the smaller social circles of trustworthy men and women known well to him. Old Hickory promised to protect his followers from the cold market world that they believed was seeking to exploit them, punish the haughty, the proud, and the evil by casting them down from the warm sanctuaries ill gained, as they saw things, through public corruption and the concentrated application of wealth, and, unlike the Whigs, leave them alone. It was a vision that was equal parts gloomy pluck and rose-colored nostalgia. Yet Whigs were often impatient with nostalgia because they believed that a vast, glorious future lay before those individuals who could control their passions and govern their will. An American middle-class society needed families full of self-made men and virtuous mothers to prosper and step out into the impersonal world. These men and women would raise children with a proper understanding of liberty and equality and support Whig efforts to secure the good life through education and reform. Finally, the stubborn presence of so many wrongheaded Jacksonian Democrats seeking office and power meant that Whig vigilance must never falter. Yet between the individual and the power of the state lies society. Whigs believed that churches, schools, and voluntary associations helped mitigate the worst tendencies of individuals, broadening their interests for the good of all. Social institutions were not bulwarks against the encroachment of exploitative forces beyond their control, as Democrats saw matters. Instead, they paved the way for a bright future.[70]

# 2

# Society

> Multiply your associations, and be free.
>
> Pierre-Joseph Proudhon

Individualism was an accomplished fact in antebellum America. To deny this truth was futile, so Whiggery focused instead on bending individualistic tendencies toward their middle-class vision of the greater social good because they rejected any sharp line dividing private and public. Daniel Webster observed: "What is true of private affairs is equally true of public affairs." Thus, Whigs looked to the future and saw two roads before all Americans. One led to morality, knowledge, prosperity, and progress. The other led to depravity, ignorance, ruin, and barbarism. Such a world was marked by "deep and pathetic complaints," John Pendleton Kennedy predicted, "of bankruptcies, beggary and ruin." Consequently, Whigs put their faith in social institutions such as churches, schools, and voluntary associations to secure the former and avoid the latter. These deep cultural ties were among the most powerful national links that middle-class people North or South shared. Whigs everywhere were optimistic about the bourgeois world that they might create but demanded much of individuals along the way. Americans might achieve marvels if they cultivated virtue, governed their will, practiced thrift, and embraced toil. But they might also slip back to barbarism should those efforts failed. Whigs believed that antebellum America's greatest challenge lay in convincing people to work together.[1]

Social institutions such as churches, schools, and voluntary associations were crucial because they helped produce broad-minded, morally reflective individuals. Churches played a key role by inculcating character and morality along middle-class, evangelical Protestant lines. By refining sentiments and elevating minds, Whigs such as Calvin Colton hoped "that these twins of heart and intellect might yet reap the advantages of this blessed era, and come together." The social cooperation that church attendance often encouraged was an added benefit as well. "The Whig lives in every State," Tennessee Whigs good-naturedly hoped in 1837. "He is not listed in sects by bounds, nor kept in them by prejudices; his mind is not contracted by systems, nor scared by bigots, it is open to God and nature; he is not attached to persons or factions, but to things, to justice, to liberty, to virtue, and to his country." Thus, Whigs also believed that universal education would foster a prosperous society by broadening and deepening people along these lines.[2]

Whigs contended that education rewarded diligence with opportunities for advancement and bourgeois affluence. "The whig party have ever contended for the adoption of those great National and State policies," Nashville Whigs' *Republican Banner* reminded readers. One such policy was "a scheme of education [in] which every child within it broad limits" could take part. As Whigs saw things, Americans also learned the rudiments of public life best in schools, where they were drawn into a shared middle-class culture larger than that of just their town or county. Finally, they supported voluntary associations as a means of bringing disconnected Americans together to achieve common goals. "The duration of the free institutions which bless our country," Webster argued in 1840, "depends upon habits of virtue and the prevalence of knowledge and of education." Support for these groups grew from Whig confidence in the strength of individuals united. At bottom, Whigs believed that these social institutions helped individuals navigate the modern world of strangers successfully. They hoped that cooperation would turn individualism toward the improvement of American society.[3]

## The Church

American religious experience changed during the antebellum period along with every other aspect of social life. The growing market economy, rapid demographic growth, geographic expansion, and transformations occurring in technology, transportation, and communication upended the old order. These changes were swift and deep. In a competitive world where whether one enjoyed wealth or fell into ruin often seemed capricious and fickle, religion offered a steady bulwark against the bewildering tide. Although the hidebound strictures of seminary training, reasoned apologetics, and a dispassionate examination of Protestant Christian theology lost their resonance for many, antebellum Americans responded in waves to a fiery, democratic religiosity where almost anyone could hear and heed God's call, where the King James Bible's redemptive message was plain to all who bothered to read the scriptures and a wrenching, emotional experience was required for salvation. American Protestantism always carried an evangelical vein, but the nineteenth century saw a special strain of evangelicalism emerge as the dominant form of spiritual expression. The camp meeting (see fig. 2.1), where thousands gathered in wooded areas to hear sermons, join in singing, pray, and cheer on or take part in Christian conversions and baptisms, illustrated this new vigor well. The vitality, dynamism, and overwhelming sense of activist energy that it unleashed characterized this evangelicalism above all. To be certain, school-trained clergy still mattered in the minds of many, but middle-class Whiggish folks' reading of authentic Christianity reinforced disciplined sobriety, thrift, and industriousness. Whigs were overwhelmingly evangelical Protestant, and they wanted their churches both to save their souls and to strengthen them to save the world.[4]

Whigs believed that churches infused character, encouraged virtue, and nurtured cooperation. As they saw things, character involved individual courage, honesty, integrity, and compassion. Additionally, Whiggery lionized virtues such as sobriety, thrift, and industry. Evangelical and, at least from the Whig point of view, compassionate middle-class Christianity fought to save the world from itself. Accordingly, Whigs understood religion's central role in society—beyond the theological work of saving souls—as instilling character and morality in isolated individuals. That church attendance encouraged social cooperation was another benefit. Whigs shared other evangelicals' longing for the millennium—the Christian belief that Jesus Christ's Second Coming, conquest of evil, and thousand-year reign on earth—and Whig preachers urged the faithful to perfect society itself to entice his return. For Whigs, finally, churches' most vital social role was the moral bridge that they provided, linking individuals together to pursue the common good. For their part, Democrats shared Whigs' commitment to Protestant Christianity, though most did not embrace their brand of evangelism. No doubt, many Jacksonians favored Christian moralism while offering a different reading of its proper application to social ills. Where Whigs saw opportunities for collaboration beyond hearth and home, Democrats saw churches as both protectors from and mediators of the impersonal world rising around them.

Fig. 2.1. Hugh Bridport (lithographer) and Alexander Rider (artist), *Camp-Meeting* ([Philadelphia]: Kennedy & Lucas Lithography, ca. 1829). Lithograph. Prints and Photographs Division, Library of Congress, Washington, DC. https://www.loc.gov/item/96510018.

As Whigs understood things, then, inculcating individual character was the most important social role that the church performed. The Mississippi Whig lawyer and politician Sergeant Smith Prentiss explained: "Good character always has been, and ever should be, a wall of strength around its possessor."[5] In the Whiggish view, character embodied the requisite middle-class principles necessary for individuals to make their way in the world. The Whig Presbyterian minister Lyman Beecher, perhaps one of the most famous antebellum evangelical reformers and cofounder of the American Temperance Society, linked the internal world of experienced faith and the external world of public witness: "This specific character of her [the church's] members is as indispensable to her chartered efficacy as her organized existence itself."[6] A Whig farmer in Tennessee agreed, arguing that "even the poorest boy in our country has something to trade upon" if he has "moral habits and religious principles." For Whigs, moral development pointed to success. "No man ever prospered in life and possessed the good will of society," the Vermont Whig newspaper *Bellow Falls Gazette* reminded readers in 1845, "without sustaining a good moral character." In the world that Whigs promised to build, character was first introduced in families, true, yet it was also developed and refined in churches.[7]

Churches reinforced Whigs' understanding of character by inculcating virtues. Whigs relished a biblical message of self-restraint, temperance, and effort. In 1842, a Whig minister in Chambersburg, Pennsylvania, comforted a newly widowed parishioner by urging her to "trust God and work hard."[8] On the face of it, such advice seems cold and unfeeling, but it accurately reflected the importance that Whigs placed on industry and perseverance. At an agricultural fair in Vermont, William Henry Seward argued: "Success, and even distinction and eminence, in any vocation, are proportioned to the measure of culture, training, industry, and perseverance brought into exercise." And the farmers present were familiar with similar themes from their churches and the columns of religious magazines. Indeed, themes of work, thrift, and prosperity, linked to specific notions of piety and reverence, appear in Whiggish sermons of the era repeatedly. "Shrink not from toil," one Whig religious pamphlet urged readers in 1851. Whigs' bourgeois reading of the gospel viewed laziness through narrowed eyes. "Toil and triumph," another Whig preacher thundered from the pulpit in 1831, "but be not deceived; God is not mocked; for whatsoever a man soweth, that shall he also reap."[9] America's Whigs preached a middle-class gospel of labor, striving, and self-control and considered affluence as the just reward for Godly living. This belief left them vulnerable to the charge that they were arguing that, just as God favored the hardworking with prosperity, he also punished the indolent with ruin. Whigs' critics argued that they believed that the poor deserved their lot. That is an unfair reading of their thinking, but Whiggish Americans certainly put a lot of faith in the idea that godly striving would lead to success. Whigs valued industry as a bedrock principle of middle-class success, and their churches reinforced this belief. Whigs appreciated labor more as a means and not necessarily as an edifying end. Like most American Protestants, they attached great importance to work and working but were among the first to internalize this sort of thinking as a near social creed. Across the antebellum United States, Whigs took the writings of Saint Paul to heart: "For even when we were with you, this we commanded you, that if any would not work, neither should he eat."[10]

There are important differences between working to meet one's immediate needs and working to accumulate wealth. On this point, Max Weber argued that, until the Protestant Reformation, intense Christian religious devotion and piety had often accompanied a rejection of worldly affairs, most notably the pursuit of wealth. But, after Luther's great dissent in 1517, both Protestant theology and social practice dignified work as sacred to God and charged individuals to seek out and embrace their life's work or "calling." The spirit of capitalism that Weber defined as the ideas and creeds infusing a cultural attitude of striving for profit and gain laid deep roots in the emerging mind of middle-class America. "In America, therefore, each finds easy ways, unknown elsewhere, to make his fortune or increase it," Alexis de Tocqueville noted in 1835. "Cupidity is always breathless there, and the human mind, distracted at every moment from pleasures of the imagination and works of intellect, gets carried away only in the pursuit of wealth." Tocqueville described the broad material outlook of most Whigs, though they might argue that he missed the underlying spirit of their push for middle-class material success.[11]

Whigs believed that striving was the path to thriving in both the pursuit of wealth and the hope of heaven. It was not material comfort for its own sake that they sought but the habits and inclinations that often led to success. They believed that God demanded effort's embrace. "A part of the sinner's penalty is labor," one Charleston Whiggish preacher reminded southern readers in 1849. He must "labor to acquire knowledge, labor to overcome sin, and to cultivate holiness, and labor to obtain the necessities and desires of our corporal being."[12] Constant labor and habits of industry and self-control were evidence, at least to Whigs' eyes, of upright morality. And their churches often confirmed this link. In 1835, a St. Louis Whig preacher urged young men across the Upper South and Middle West to be morally steadfast and hardworking. Industry and faith were complementary for Whigs because a true godly man must "strive to uphold his craft by every possible expedient." Failure to work hard likely meant in Whiggish eyes a lack of middle-class moral rigor. For their part, Jacksonian Democrats were unimpressed with Whig explanations of the point of working. Instead, they saw in Whig rhetoric sophistries lauding remorseless striving in which achievements were valued only for procuring wealth and acclaim. Jacksonians' worldview fixated on the local and the familiar as well as on a more sedate pace of life. Democrats often lamented the sense of being driven, at least in their rhetoric and polemic, while Whigs endured it more readily as the price of prosperity. This likely stemmed from the latter's sense of self-mastery and the former's feeling of deep social doubt. Consequently, Whigs' push for progress rang in Democrats' ears as the hollow cant of a fallen people driven by greed to carry their neighbors ever onward, on a journey with no end and no reward.[13]

Scriptural and social notions of thrift revealed subtle but important differences in outlook between the two warring political cultures. On the surface, all Americans tended to view thrift as virtuous. Yet, as with work and working, Whigs and Democrats did not agree on the deeper political meaning of thrift or the supposed larger social implications. "When thousands of minds at home are becoming soft and impressible," preached Daniel Dana, the Whiggish former president of Dartmouth College, "never was there a time, when the friends of Christianity were more imperiously called upon to rally round the standard of truth, to maintain, in their unimpaired vigor and purity, the peculiar doctrines of the gospel."[14] Whigs transformed their reading of these Christian values into the middle-class ideological substructure of a potent political vision. Across America they embraced thrift, industriousness, simplicity, and self-denial as middle-class alternatives to vain luxury or snobbery. For Dana and other Whigs, thrift became a marker of self-control and carried with it an implied utilitarian social function. Thrift, industry, religion, and education formed a potent alloy of Whig thinking about the proper pursuit of national prosperity. An 1847 Baltimore lithograph demonstrates their thinking well (see fig. 2.2).

The elements of thrift lead to the affluence that all desired. Although many Democrats might approve of thrifty self-control, they would reject a reformers' authority to coerce such behavior. Even in the direst of circumstances, Whig preachers argued, the truly Christian individual "will seek his greatest usefulness." Far from advocating that the faithful withdraw from society to contemplate and lament its complexities, Whigs called on them to embrace the world with humility and shoulder the load with their fellow men. As one Whig wrote: "He may not *see* the prosperity. But he will, in the end, experience good 'above what asks, or thinks.' His course, like that of the river, will be marked with verdure, and thrift, and beauty, and fruitfulness." Fruitfulness and energy were the point. As Whigs saw things, the secrets behind those who rise in the world were not secrets at all but "known to be the certain result of integrity, industry, and perseverance."[15] Striving should be turned to a moral purpose. Indeed, in 1835, St. Louis Whigs warned young men: "The prostitution of mind and of

Fig. 2.2. Robert Mayo, *Elements of National Thrift and Empire* (Baltimore: Edward Weber, 1847). Lithograph after Joseph Goldsborough Bruff. Prints and Photographs Division, Library of Congress, Washington, DC. https://www.loc.gov/item/2003680966.

talent, really affords a lesson on the moral turpitude of some men, which every ingenious mind must regard with disgust and horror." Everyone was either getting better or getting worse; moral stasis was impossible.[16]

Whig preachers and religious pamphleteers from Maine to Mississippi stressed social utility and a commitment to industry because churches bridged the gap between public and private. "Solitude is impractical, and society fatal," Emerson aptly pointed out, describing Whigs' social perspective well. "We must keep our head in one and our hands in the other." And Whigs looked to churches to help them do both. "Every citizen becomes better and wiser by the favor of God," urged the *American Whig Review* in 1845. "The same considerations make it certain that there is not a shadow of difference between that famous liberty 'of the just,' 'who live by faith,' and this liberty of the citizen, who makes free constitutions and just laws." Churches helped refine parishioners' perspective by broadening their sense of community. Indeed, for Whigs, private conscience made public justice possible.[17]

Thus, in Whigs' view, churches pursued charity work both to comply with Christian religious principles and to overcome modernity's isolating weakness. "Charity begins at home," New York Whigs reminded one another in 1836, yet it moved out into the wider communities through the church.[18] Beyond duty, moreover, this sort of work was exciting. "We used to be brought up to think that religion and dullness ought to be made synonymous," wrote another Whig reformer in 1848. "To be a Christian was to be dull, heavy, stupid and loggish, oyster-brained and frog-blooded." In contrast to this funereal brand of religion, Whig reform flowed from a bourgeois sense of hope. "Man alone, laughs. It is a peculiarly human attribute, human, humane, humanizing." The great drive for benevolence required a positive encouragement instead of dour browbeating, even if many Whigs often worried that their countrymen lacked proper self-control. Consequently, they urged reformers in their ranks to "resist the serious and indignant sprit; and see whether asperity and churlishness, or good humor and genial blithesomeness will do most for the humanity and happiness of the world." Broad denigration rarely won mass appeal in democratic countries.[19]

The benevolent empire of moral reform efforts such as temperance, common schools, hospitals, and Bible and tract societies was built on middle-class Christian hopes and fears. Whig worries concerning sloth, stupidity, and violence are obvious. Less apparent is the way in which social reform grew out of Whigs' religious aspirations, yet their confidence was stark. "I gave an address for Sabbath Union in support of the motion to supply the Valley with Sabbath-schools in two years," Lyman Beecher noted in an 1830 letter to his son. And the early returns were encouraging. "Arthur Tappan has promised $4000 in two years, and two individuals have guaranteed $5000 apiece. Nearly twenty thousand have been raised already in money, and agencies, and the right spirit is wide awake."[20] But Whig efforts to use churches to pursue broad moral causes was not limited to Beecher, Tappan, and a few schools in eastern Pennsylvania. In New York, for instance, Whigs "subscribed to the fund of the Asylum nearly $50,000."[21] Physicians, judges, merchants, and clergymen made up an overwhelming portion of the fund-raising, representing "a large portion of the intellectual and moral worth of our people."[22] These efforts were mirrored elsewhere by religious Whigs in Providence, Cincinnati, and even Chambersburg, Pennsylvania.

As middle-class Whiggish Americans saw things, connecting virtuous individuals to pursue the common good was the most important social role that churches performed. Whigs embraced a public role for churches that often made their opponents uncomfortable. "A few of our friends and not a few of our enemies appear to be alarmed at the idea of carrying temperance principles to the polls," relished Delaware Whigs in 1838. "Our friends are uneasy because of not understanding the resolution—our enemies because they do." Whig reformers connected a Christian virtue such as temperance with politics because many believed that alcohol was bad for republicanism. Even Whigs such as Henry Clay, who personally enjoyed an occasional nip, embraced this principle and would agree with the Whigs in Wilmington who urged: "It is time that the suffrages of a free people should be free from the control of whiskey."[23] Clay was no hard-line teetotaler, but he conceded the negative effects of broad social drinking. Consequently, Whigs' benevolence flowed from their desire to improve public life with the best of private conscience. They often brightly reassured one another: "It has purely been a labor of love." Their doubtful critics were not so sure.[24]

Whigs were modernists in that they believed that collaborating overcame isolated individuals' weakness in pursuing a middle-class future, with churches key opportunities. The *American Whig Review* stressed this principle in 1845, quoting William Blackstone: "The great end of society is to protect the weakness of individuals by the united strength of the community." Jacksonian Democrats saw the matter quite differently. As skeptics of the modernist ethos, most distrusted the entanglements of broad association outside their immediate circle of reliable friends and family. "We may not control a man's natural liberty even for the man's own good," argued Boston Jacksonian polemicists in 1838. In this view, the private sphere was sacred and inviolate. Any attempt to carry religion into the public sphere or, worse, politics was simply part of a covert attempt to control common men. Whigs disagreed. Right worship was a reliable base on which bourgeois benevolence and social organization could safely be built. Few social institutions, finally, demonstrated Whig thinking in this regard better than public schools. Like churches, schools drew individuals away from isolation, encouraging them to cooperate and work together.[25]

## The School

Beyond the church, education mattered because Whigs believed that schools reinforced morality, honesty, and persistence. "The mind is not only the object to be improved," Horace Mann stressed in 1851, "but it *is* the instrument to work with."[26] Whigs stressed how universal education ensured a prosperous society, and most argued that education rewarded diligence with opportunities for advancement and affluence. Education allowed all Americans, Whigs such as Maryland's John Pendleton Kennedy believed, "to improve their condition in an eminent degree."[27] Schools also taught students the basic principles of interaction and cooperation in public life. Whigs hoped that these lessons might bring about a larger, shared culture. At bottom, they argued that education or the lack thereof was intimately related to every good or evil that society desired or feared. Consequently, they fought for public schools in every state in the Union, albeit enjoying more success in western and northern states, where they held legislative majorities.

Whigs argued that, before all else, schools built citizens and taught individuals self-control. Certainly, many Jacksonians waxed eloquent about schools as well, but Whigs and Democrats had different things in mind when they talked about education. For those Democrats who supported public schools, education was another bulwark against the often faceless oppression of political, economic, and social forces beyond their control. It offered individuals the intellectual wherewithal to avoid getting taken advantage of in business among strangers or mislead by cunning politicians. On the other hand, Whigs saw something bigger and more important than individual well-being in universal education. Schools were crucial because they began the hard work of creating a robust American nation out of independent citizens and infusing the people with crucial values of self-control. Consequently, public schools and publicly funded education mattered far more to Whigs than to Democrats.[28]

Throughout the antebellum years, very few states offered universal, compulsory public education. Yet local churches and private individuals planted schools in a hodgepodge fashion across the growing young nation, typically more in the Northeast and Middle West than in the South. Generally, schoolmasters were left to their own devices, and the school's day-to-day activities were based on their training and preferences. Often, subscription based or funded by barter payments of food, drink, and lodging for the teacher, schools had to make a mishmash of students' ages, abilities, and attention work in a still rural world where most children attended school haphazardly and not at all during the warmer months, when they were needed to work their families' farms. Schoolhouses were usually small, discipline could be severe, and the pedagogical rigor offered often varied. Antebellum schools stressed the famous "the three Rs" (i.e., reading, writing, and arithmetic) through the study of history, geography, and mathematics. Oral examinations, rote memorization, and timed recitations were all typical. Whiggish American worked to bring order to the patchwork nature of local education both through a shared curriculum that everyone might follow and by trying to convince states, counties, or towns to pay for free schools for all their white children.[29]

Whigs' case for schooling began in their churches, and early public education efforts were expressly sectarian in content and curriculum. Consequently, the moral messages that families heard in the often-lengthy Sunday sermons were repeated and reinforced when the children reported to school on Monday morning. When a publication like the Whiggish *Christian Reflector* published a sermon arguing, for example, that "a great duty, which every Christian citizen owes to himself, to his children, and to his country, is to keep his mind well-informed respecting the constitution of the Commonwealth, and of the nation; respecting public men and public measures," the ideas expressed were often echoed in the dimly lit, musty schoolhouses of the countryside. "It [should be] the ardent wish of every patriot, philanthropist, and Christian, that 'the strong desire manifested to render this moral engine of social happiness and political security," Samuel Hall, another Whig from Boston, explained to prospective teachers in 1835, "as extensive, as complete and efficacious, as the vast resources of our intelligence and wealth will permit,' may not cease, till something effectual shall be accomplished." The schoolhouse had a vital role to play in the middle-class effort to win the future.[30]

Whigs grew increasingly impatient if anyone dared question such a proposition and often cast their frustration in terms of patriotism and nationalism. From their point of view, common schooling and public funding for education were not simply good ideas, to be tried and tinkered with as dollars and teachers became available. Instead, education was a social necessity. "It is the duty of every citizen to increase, to the best of his power, the means of public happiness in the nation," the Whiggish *Common School Assistant* challenged antebellum Americans in 1835.[31] From Whigs' point of view, those who refused to support common schools were complicit in social disorder and the violence that grew out of ignorance and a lack of self-control. Society therefore had a vital interest in moral development. "If children when young are not taught the evil of quarreling with each other and the advantages of mutual kindness, of governing their passions and controlling their appetites, is it not a plain dictate of common sense," Orville Taylor argued, "that when they grow to be men and women, they will continue their habitual propensities and [will be] vicious in their habits and quarrelsome members of society, ready to engage in riotous mobs and other combinations to disturb the peace and violate the rights of others?"[32] Whigs in Boston, New York, Philadelphia, Cincinnati, and New Orleans, along with countless others in places big and small, saw all of this as self-evident. "No man who has common sense, and who is possessed of only tolerable information, will venture, at the present day, to call in question the value of importance of education," argued a group of Lutheran Whigs in Pennsylvania who supported William Henry Harrison in 1840. "No one can be a true patriot or a sincere friend of the government under which he lives, who is opposed to this great interest." Consequently, schools were crucial because they taught children the fealty needed to preserve and protect the nation's interests.[33]

Whigs wanted more. They were not merely content to sprawl out geographically, remaining a sparsely settled, unlettered people clinging to a narrow, provincial view of life. Instead, education opened a middle-class road to the future. As the *Common School Journal* explained in 1846: "In schools are training the minds whose future action shall brighten or dim their country's glory." Consequently, Whig teachers often stressed the ends as much as the means when explaining the purpose of education. Yet it was not blind obedience to superior will or strength that Whigs valued but the development of integrity and character so that individuals would *want* to control their passions and appetites.[34]

Seen in this light, education was a lifelong process that was typically described in terms of work and achievement. "The young have the entire period of their activity before them," the *Quarterly Christian Spectator* advised in 1830, "and may be permitted to spend many years in works of Christian usefulness."[35] This endeavor carried tangible rewards, Whigs believed, but only if the effort extended beyond pews, lecture rooms, and schoolhouses. Like parenting, Whigs believed, schooling was no longer about breaking the individual's will but instead about teaching children to navigate a cold, impersonal world successfully. William Henry Seward carried "a deep conviction of the importance of education to all men, without regard to condition or circumstances." Whigs believed that American society needed broad, interpersonal trust and cooperation. True independence required it. "There are thousands of men around us, and here before us," Daniel Webster noted approvingly in 1851, "who till their own soil with their own hands; and others who earn their own livelihood by their own labor in the workshops and other places of industry." This sort of freedom privileged intellectual development. "But the school-house, I know, is among them. Education is among them. They read, and write, and think," Webster stressed. "Here, too, are women, educated, refined, and intelligent." Since the local ties of village, kin, and home were giving way to a modern world of strangers, mobility, and markets, society required some means of ensuring that individuals could be trusted with the wide latitude of political, social, and religious freedom fast becoming an accomplished fact in antebellum America. Schooling and education were part of the long-range middle-class development of soul, character, and personality, all meant to break down narrow localism and replace it with a new loyalty along Whiggish ideas of American nationalism.[36]

Accordingly, Whigs promoted education in every state in the Union. Pennsylvania Whigs demanded a public discussion of funding for common schools because education dealt with "questions of moral and social responsibility, of infinite moment to us and our posterity." Whigs believed that schools determined the future. And funding common schools was "of vast interest as connected with the moral and intellectual training of the children of the land—those who, when this generation of men shall have passed away, will succeed to public and social duties." Tennessee Whigs agreed with their Pittsburgh brethren, arguing that access to education "should be the common privilege of human nature." Moreover, the *American Whig Review* described Whigs' faith in common schooling, arguing: "One of the most glorious results of a free Government is the kindly influence it exerts in the development of Intellect. Under its institutions want of rank, fortune, or early scholastic training, opposes no insurmountable obstacles to advancement." Schools made possible the bourgeois hope to rise.[37]

Whigs insisted that education held out hope for individuals' rising to material affluence and social or political prominence, no matter how lowly or humble their origins. Few examples of these possibilities shone brighter than Benjamin Franklin. "If our object is improvement," insisted the *Literary Messenger*, "Franklin is one whose greatness should command our strictest scrutiny. Born in humble circumstances, without friends—without education—he raised himself to some of the highest stations in the calendar of our youthful history; and is perpetuated as a patriot, philosopher, and statesman." Whigs celebrated Franklin because they saw in his rise bourgeois principles lived and applied and hoped to emulate him. Indeed, in 1841, Maine Whig mechanics toasted "Benjamin Franklin, the mechanic, and philosopher; may every member of this association imitate his goodness and greatness."[38] Education was a prudent investment in the future. Like Franklin, Whigs believed that prosperous individuals would "waste neither time nor money but make the best use of both." Conversely, for Democrats, Franklin represented an example of the rugged, isolated individualism they admired. But how representative was Franklin's rise to wealth and fame, and how much does being representative matter?[39]

A growing body of scholarship suggests that those lucky few such as Benjamin Franklin, Mathew Carey, Abraham Lincoln, and Frederick Douglass were exceptions and that most Americans tended to live much as their parents had before them. Yet this insight only drives home the lasting power of the bourgeois idea that pluck, grit, and industry could bring remarkable success. True or not, widely possible or not, Americans wanted to believe it. Indeed, the hope of rising was a commonplace assumption in a bitterly partisan era, though, of course, Whigs and Democrats disagreed on the best ways to achieve it. Whigs saw collaboration as crucial, while Democrats did not trust that such endeavors would ever yield the benefits they promised.[40]

It is no myth that antebellum women used prevailing moral notions of domesticity, along with arguments for progress, to carve out a distinctive public niche in schools and other social organizations that was otherwise unavailable to them. As a number of scholars have stressed, white middle-class women performed crucial roles that allowed society to maintain order. As mothers, they protected children and began instilling the virtue and self-restraint needed to succeed in a world of strangers. As wives, they were expected to create a domestic refuge from the frenetic, impersonal world of business, commerce, and exchange. And, as homemakers, they managed household resources, modeling all the while Protestant optimism that eventually honest striving led to honest thriving. But women were not passive helpmeets, stoically accepting their roles and subsuming their ideas and imaginations to those of the men in their lives. Both as students and as teachers, women were offered by schools the chance to help win the future, and many, especially those of a Whiggish bent, took advantage of the opportunity. For their part, Whig men, serving as preachers, politicians, and editors, often took notice, lauding women's work in bold, often nationalistic language. "Professing to love our country, and to take an interest in the cause of human improvement," Boston's *American Magazine* warmly reminded readers in 1836 at the opening of a new female academy, "we rejoice to hear of, and to notice any new associations for promoting knowledge among the youth or our country." Although Whiggish women certainly did not need male approval to embrace what many viewed as a near-holy calling, that so many men did approve speaks to the importance of the school in Whig social thought.[41]

All these ideas and others besides are evident in Winslow Homer's 1871 painting *The Country School* (see fig. 2.3). Though created after the Civil War, Homer's work was in many ways representative of how Whigs conceived the antebellum school. His teacher is a white woman, dressed plainly but well, and seems warm and encouraging. The schoolhouse is clean, quiet, and simple, and the students represent a fairly diverse lot. Boys and girls, some with shoes and nicer clothes, others barefoot and a touch threadbare, they are united by their diligence in their lessons. The implication was clear. Schools offered a rough equality that privileged effort, merit, and achievement. Their rewards were open to all who mastered the core values of self-control, self-sacrifice, and industry.

Yet Whigs were not content simply to argue broadly for the social utility of common schools. Instead, they pushed for a national focus on education even as they tried to accommodate local concerns. The best schools "have aimed at a combination of local and general authority," the *American Annals of Education and Instruction* argued in 1834. "To place the schools exclusively under the local authorities, in their view, gives rise to 'a train of petty chicaneries' in regard to the management of the school, the choice of a teacher, and the influence exerted over him." Whigs saw the same corrosive tendencies in the vast web of state, county, and town

Fig. 2.3. Winslow Homer (American, 1836–1910), *The Country School* (1871), oil on canvas ($35\frac{7}{16} \times 48\frac{3}{4}$ inches). Saint Louis Art Museum, Museum Purchase 124:1944.

interests across the antebellum United States. While they accepted that local interests were important, they also worked to refashion this localism and bend it to national purposes. It is not surprising, then, that textbooks often mined national themes and held up for emulation heroes who could inspire children living in Albany, New York, as well as Atlanta, Georgia. First, schoolbooks and primers that Whigs lauded often emphasized the consolidating power, at least ideologically and socially, of the US Constitution. "That great instrument, which now governs more than twenty millions of people," hailed one American history primer, "and links in one common destiny thirty states, demands our purest affections, and our first and highest duty." Primers and school texts often used phrases such as *common purpose, national destiny,* and *shared glory,* sowing seeds of nationalism in the minds and hearts of readers.[42]

Middle-class Whiggish Americans looked to the founding era to justify their faith in the nationalizing purpose of education. William Grimshaw's popular American history textbook explained the glory of the 1787 Constitutional Convention with glittering, nationalistic language. People of the United States enjoyed "a constitution framed by their wisest and most virtuous men, and approved by themselves; embracing all that was valuable, and excluding everything that was found injurious." What made such greatness possible? Beyond the American people's shared constitutional heritage, itself a priceless patrimony, the founders were wise enough, at least from Whigs' perspective, to balance liberty with order. Most agreed that "the propitious smiles of Heaven could never be expected on a nation who disregarded the eternal rules of order and right, which Heaven itself had ordained." Discernment, conciliation, and self-mastery were, Whigs believed, hallmarks of a proper education and vital in the hard work of creating citizens. Many agreed with Tocqueville, who noted: "The century of blind devotions and instinctive virtues is already fleeing far from us, and I see the time approaching when freedom, pubic peace, and social order itself will not be able to do without enlightenment." Democrats might embrace many of these ideas as well, but they differed from Whigs on what each meant and implied. They also distrusted Whigs' nationalizing tendencies and the compulsory nature of Whig reform efforts. Education was a fine thing, most would concede in the abstract, but publicly funded schooling should go forward only if the states, or the counties, or the towns in question or the families within them wanted it to. Democrats did not accept Whigs' reading of the Constitution or trust their plans for common schools.[43]

## Voluntary Associations

Voluntary associations offered the best example of Whiggish attempts to *apply* those moral and social lessons in the shaping of a middle-class society. Whigs supported voluntary associations because they brought disconnected Americans together to achieve common goals. As Alexis de Tocqueville observed in 1831, the great mass of people "cannot take part in those associations for a long time without discovering how to maintain order among a great number of men and with what procedure one succeeds in getting them to advance in accord and methodically toward the same goal."[44] Such groups often reflected Whig confidence in the strength of individuals united. Lyceums, Bible and tract societies, and temperance organizations were all built on the bourgeois premise that individuals were made stronger by association and collaboration. And Whigs believed that cooperation would turn individualism toward the improvement of American society.

Many Whigs believed that the eyes of heaven were on them. Scripture promised that, before carrying the faithful to paradise, Jesus Christ would return for a thousand-year reign marked by widespread peace and joy. Yet that millennium would occur only, most supposed, if the world was perfected enough to entice his return. Thus, Whigs wove various religious and reform societies across the antebellum United States into an interconnected moral community. In this view, lyceums and public discussions gave antebellum adults—often with sparse formal schooling and limited education—an opportunity to develop their minds and manners and, more critically, to do so by association and collaboration. Likewise, Bible and tract societies made religious literature broadly available while also funding seminaries to educate young men called to God's service. And temperance reformers worked to free drunkards from the deadly grip of alcohol, offering refuge and rehabilitation for those individuals whose sense of self-mastery had broken down entirely, thereby benefiting these men's families and society. All these efforts would work together both to mitigate the social ambiguities of the modern world and to enable individuals to navigate the world of strangers, markets, and machines. "When [free citizens] are allowed to associate freely in all things," Whigs would echo Tocqueville, "in the end they see in association the universal, and so to speak the unique, means of which men can use to attain the different ends they propose for themselves." This is precisely the social and cultural conclusion that Whigs were counting on. "The habit of association is already formed," William Henry Seward explained, "as the interests of mutual intercourse are being formed." Indeed, Whigs preached what they practiced and spent their time and money on social causes they believed would secure the best kind of future.[45]

Lyceums formed a social bridge from school to community and offered a platform for public discussion of diverse subjects. "We live in an age distinguished for great benevolent exertion," Daniel Webster rejoiced in an 1840 speech before a group of Baltimore women, "in which the affluent are consecrating the means they possess by endowing colleges and academies, by uniting to build churches and support the cause of religion, and by establishing athenaeums, lyceums, and all other modes of popular instruction."[46] Indeed, Lyceums remained widely popular across America throughout the era. Yet associational and communitarian organizing, which undergirded the lyceums, was a cultural tenet of a decidedly middle-class Whiggish political economy. In 1838, Connecticut Whigs urged their neighbors to take part in lyceums: "No one who has not tried it, can for any just estimate of the interest which can, be produced in young minds."[47] In addition to cultivating a spirit of inquiry and improvement in youth, many Whigs simply enjoyed the social aspects of lyceums more generally. "It has for time been a standing question for debate in country Lyceums," Ohio Whigs conceded, "whether there is more pleasure in the anticipation than there this in the enjoyment of any given subject." Many Whigs simply relished getting out of their daily routine and discussing broad topics of varying degrees of importance.[48]

Were he sufficiently introspective, the Whiggish everyman might shake his head in wry bemusement over the content of some discussions, but he would also applaud the forum itself. Indeed, by 1850, approximately 400,000 Americans heard someone lecture at a lyceum every week. Middle-class Whigs enjoyed the opportunity to congregate and hash out the great issues of their day. At a New York lyceum series in 1840, local Whigs lined up a slate of intellectual heavyweights. The series, which included Theodore Frelinghuysen (speaking on the study of the Constitution of the United States in connection with early history) and Daniel Barnard (speaking on the spirit of American history), would be introduced by the former secretary of state and president and the current congressman from Massachusetts John Quincy Adams. Philadelphia Whigs celebrated a discounted textbook, moreover, because it "is designed to introduce this sublime study into the Domestic Circle, the Lyceums, and Common Schools of the country." Massachusetts's Whigs also noted that lyceums encourage "general cooperation among state, county, and town." Southern Whigs hosted lyceums in their towns and cities too, and they also sent away for printed addresses from Whiggish speakers, thinkers, and polemicists so that they could take part in the great discussions of America's past, present, and future. Thus, lyceums were part of a national conversation centered on improvement and "especially adapted to private learners."[49]

It was not simply a case of highly placed political and social thinkers talking to, for, and about one another in distant places. Instead, lyceums took place all across the antebellum United States on courthouse lawns, in churches, in school- and meetinghouses, and in villages, towns, and cities nationwide. "Such associations, it is well known," Pittsburgh's *Literary Messenger* reminded readers in 1841, "are established throughout Maine,

NOTICE.

A MEETING OF THE

Alton Lyceum,

Will be held this Evening, FRIDAY, NOVEMBER 29th, at the OLD COURT ROOM—over *Bowman, Neef & Co's.* Store; at which place the meetings of the Society will be held this Winter.

The public are respectfully invited to attend.

*By order of the Society.*

Fig. 2.4. Alton Lyceum, "Notice. A meeting of the Alton Lyceum, will be held this evening, Friday, November 29th, at the Old Court Room—over Bowman, Neef & Co's. store; at which place the meetings of the Society will be held this winter. The public are respectfully invited to attend. By order of the Society" (Alton, IL, 1840). Broadside. Printed Ephemera: Three Centuries of Broadsides and Other Printed Ephemera, Library of Congress, Washington, DC. https://www.loc.gov/item/rbpe.01603100.

New York, and Ohio [as well as North Carolina, Tennessee, Alabama, Kentucky, and Virginia], with the most cheering influence."[50] An 1840 broadside from Alton, Illinois, a sleepy river city squatting on the Mississippi just north of St. Louis, is typical of the notices that went up all over America (see fig. 2.4).

Even nasty weather could not dampen Whig enthusiasm for lyceums. "On Wednesday evening, notwithstanding the inclemency of the weather," the *New-Yorker* celebrated in 1840, "the spacious Broadway Tabernacle was filled to overflowing with citizens of all ages and conditions, listening with eager attention to the words of wisdom and power as they fell from the lips of the most wonderful of American Statesmen, the venerable JOHN

QUINCY ADAMS."[51] Similarly, Maine Whigs fought a bitter December snowstorm to debate whether capital punishment out to be abolished. Participation in lyceums brought American adults into a more national public dialogue and raised the prospects—or so Whigs hoped—of a more civil political culture. Given the acrid nature of the era's politics, this seems naive, even foolish, yet it also speaks to Whigs' faith in association and collaboration. Association broke down isolation and strengthened communities. Where Democrats would look to lyceums as a pragmatic way to strengthen individuals, Whigs stressed their potential for cooperative uplift.[52]

But how might Whigs promote broader opportunities for improvement for those unable or unwilling to attend a lyceum? One answer was the wide dissemination of the King James Bible. Placing a Protestant Bible in the hands of every man, woman, and child across the growing United States—and, indeed, across the wider world—was a dream of many evangelical reformers. Throughout the antebellum era, moreover, there were few benevolent societies that enjoyed the widespread popularity and success of the American Bible Society. For example, in 1830, some 238,000 Bibles were distributed across the United States.[53] By 1850, the society had increased those efforts by nearly 30 percent and broadened its evangelism to include translations in Ojibwa, Choctaw, Mohawk, and Delaware as well as Chinese, Arabic, Syriac, Gaelic, and even West African Grebo. John Jay, DeWitt Clinton, John Quincy Adams, and James Fennimore Cooper all played prominent roles in the early leadership and promotion of the society, and the *American Whig Review* and the *United States Magazine, and Democratic Review* both lauded its efforts. Yet the aims that Whigs and Democrats sought with the distribution of scripture often differed considerably.[54]

For their part, Democrats saw the broad dissemination of God's word as added rampart meant to protect isolated individuals from the cruel, impersonal world. Given the boom-bust nature of economic growth throughout the era and the punishing daily labor that nearly all antebellum Americans endured in some form throughout their lives, resorting to scripture's succor makes sense. Whigs saw things differently—or, perhaps, more broadly. Certainly, they would grant, God's word offered strength through difficult times, but, for Whiggish Americans, religion was about more than that. The urge to spread the word of God across the county flowed from their middle-class desire to cultivate individual virtue and increase social cohesion. And, given their reading of America's national mission, the process was part of the purpose because distributing Bibles encouraged education, morality, and restraint. Although public education often remained spotty and limited, Whigs saw Bible study as an effective counter to popular newspapers, pamphlets, and broadsides meant to trivialize the important and sensationalize the inane. "The reading of the age is fragmentary," groaned the *New York Evangelist.* "What is read, must be short—short articles, brief items—something of which the eye can take in the beginning and the end at the same glance; something which can be caught up in an odd moment, and be dispatched in a brief space." It is perhaps ironic that Whiggish conceptions of the self-made man privileged a sense of industry and work that often came at the expense of deliberative leisure.[55]

Yet spreading God's word encouraged a hope that regular Bible study would encourage deeper thinking and moral cultivation. "As of individuals, so perhaps it may be said of a people," the *American Whig Review* noted in 1849, "that they come to the appreciation of a good by slow degrees." Studying scripture refined American coarseness and fostered appreciation for the lovely, good, and true. And deliberation clarified thinking, improving society one introspective person at a time. "There is no luck in it," noted Emerson, describing many Whigs' aspirations for clarity. "It proceeds by Fate. Every scripture is given by the inspiration of God. Every composition proceeds out of a greater or less depth of thought, and this is the measure of its effect."[56] Whiggery privileged the pursuit of excellence, both individual and social. "Good and true books are but as the rarer shells," Philadelphia Whigs reminded readers from Charleston to Chicago in 1851, "and voyages and travels having passed on beyond the interest of mere discovery, are to be estimated by those deeper qualities which make civilized nations truly acquainted with each other." What book represented the very best of Western civilization and, thus, the United States, Whigs demanded, more than God's Holy Bible?[57]

More than the social utility of reading the Bible, the process for spreading the word was, at least for Whigs, a monument to effective national organization, grassroots execution, and an iron-willed commitment to a bourgeois future. Indeed, one Whiggish Tennessean from Nashville sent half his monthly profits from a successful racetrack to the American

Bible Society. "And believing as I do that nothing tends more to the improvement of the moral condition of man than the general and universal dissemination of the word of God," he wrote the society's local chapter, "I cannot but wish success to your efforts."[58] In this vein, the society's tactics offered a telling example of the Whig approach to creating a more perfect society. First, scholars have shown that early on its managers eschewed the largely voluntary network of county and town auxiliaries, each with a wide degree of local autonomy, in favor of a more centralized system of traveling agents and factories.[59] That may seem like an obvious development to modern readers, but it represented a startling innovation for antebellum Americans, whose daily lives tended to be dominated by the local. To be sure, local Bible societies remained a vibrant part of antebellum evangelical culture, and nationally mind reformers were clever enough to encourage their efforts. But, far more than their Jacksonian neighbors, Whigs tended to favor a more regular, centralized approach. In 1851, New York managers were able to plan for a "missionary to Santa Fe, in regard to the moral condition of New Mexico," as well as celebrate "that the preparation of the Old Testament in the Chinese language is progressing satisfactorily."[60] They created effective campaign propaganda and literature such as a handsome receipt (see fig. 2.5) that acknowledged financial support with divine provenance. Ostensibly just a record of money received, this receipt drive home the society's message by placing an angel holding an open Bible among the clouds, rays of light breaking through the darkness. Subscribers' cash went toward an organized and cooperative effort to bring God's light to a world languishing in darkness. Along similar lines, Cincinnati Whigs reminded one another that in 1844 they raised almost $24,000 to spread the gospel. "Of this amount," these Queen City reformers chided their neighbors across the Ohio River, "between seventeen and eighteen thousand was collected in the *free* states."[61]

Thus, Whigs' embrace of a more nationally minded outlook led to a mixed strategy that left most big decisions to Boston, New York, Philadelphia, or Cincinnati while tapping local enthusiasm, markets, and manpower. On this point, as they did with schools, Whiggish women loomed large. In 1835, New Haven's *Religious Intelligencer* published a lengthy update on a missionary's efforts spreading God's word in Texas at the request of several Whig women, "especially those who furnished him with Bibles and other religious books for distribution, and those benevolent ladies who

Fig. 2.5. Alfred Jones (engraver) and John William Casilear (artist), "This certifies that by the payment of [blank] dollars [blank] has been constituted a [blank] of life of the American & Foreign Bible Society / J. W. Casilear; Alfred Jones" (ca. 1850–1867). Engraving. Prints and Photographs Division, Library of Congress, Washington, DC. "Print shows an angel among clouds, holding an open bible illuminated by rays of light breaking through the clouds." https://www.loc.gov/item/2015647080.

contributed to supply this mission."[62] Indeed, it was often women like these who performed the exhausting work of knocking on doors in urban slums with Bibles and tracts in hand, visiting cabins and homesteads in the mountain South and Middle West to urge occupants to attend church and send their children to school, or lending the grace and elegance of their presence to social gatherings and often their money as well.

For many antebellum Americans, groups promoting temperance reform became nearly as popular as Bible societies, though Whiggish and Jacksonian Americans often differed on the proper scope and purpose of such organizations. All seemingly agreed that Americans drank too much, and they were probably right. Indeed, by 1830, American men, women, and even some children polished off an average of five gallons of rum, gin, brandy, or whiskey every year, not to mention the additional drams of beer, wine, and various hard ciders.[63] For Jacksonians, temperance was a cause that fired the hearts of some while leaving others cold and disinterested. Excessive drinking could become a problem, most conceded, but so too could state-sponsored efforts to control it. One Democratic temperance reformer reminded his more zealous Whig counterparts: "A majority of the people are not ready to sanction a law prohibiting the sale of intoxicating drinks."[64] Persuade, cajole, or wheedle, Jacksonians allowed, but they remained deeply suspicious of arguments for social control from distant legislatures.[65]

Whigs believed that such arguments underestimated the deeper social danger of alcoholism and drunkenness. In 1842, Hartford Whigs steeled their resolve for "the unwearied labors in the cause of Temperance."[66] Beyond the moral concerns that excessive drinking raised, Whigs pointed to pragmatic worries as well. From their point of view, temperance societies were crucial for helping individuals enslaved to drink develop self-mastery and a needed work ethic. "The alarming prevalence of intemperance," New York Whigs agreed, "and the consequent increase of crime, pauperism and taxation, call upon all virtuous citizens to combine their counsels, to arrest the dreadful burning tide."[67] Men who stayed habitually drunk were not likely to keep steady hours at any sort of job or vocation, and, when they did, the quality of their work must logically suffer. In 1837, Cincinnati Whigs argued, perhaps tongue-in-cheek, that reliance on alcohol was part of the reason the Van Buren administration governed so poorly: "Some of the higher executive officers at Washington are, and have been, notorious drunkards . . . habitually affected by ardent spirits—drunk at least once a week." Worse, alcohol stirred the savage tendencies lurking inside everyone and fueled all manner of crime, including assault, robbery, rape, and murder. A nation of drunkards could not be trusted to build a future worth having.[68]

Whiggish women agreed because they shared Whiggish men's perspective privileging work, striving, and achievement. Consequently, they often took pride in the size, scope, and duration of their social-outreach efforts. For example, "while others groan because they have to work hard for their bread," the *Ladies Repository* reminded readers, "we say that work is full of pleasure, of profit, and of materials for self-improvement."[69] Whig women were often bold and outspoken in the way in which they supported and carried forward these ideas. "We must not look idly on, but plead," Ohio women urged one another, "plead even as the woman of the unjust judge, and we may succeed where men have failed." These women believed that they might be more successful than men in these efforts because of their natural virtue, which made them better equipped to win the day in moral causes. The stakes were high. "The homes of loved ones are spoiled; the lowly, the great, and the gifted are slain, and their living curses warn us that the same destroyer is among us, beside our pleasant homes, along the pathway of our youth, beside our mills, our streams, and desolates many others as well."[70] Despite their diligence and sincerity, Whig men often failed to halt the rising tide of drunkenness threatening to drown America's middle-class future. It often fell to Whiggish women, then, to step into the breach.[71]

Temperance and Bible societies, along with lyceums, schools, and churches, were all part of a larger social effort to perfect society along middle-class lines. Support for these groups grew from Whig confidence in the strength of individuals united. A world of strangers required these social institutions to help isolated individuals find happiness, contentment, and success. "The doctrine of self-interest well understood perhaps prevents some men from mounting far above the ordinary level of humanity," Whigs would concede along with Tocqueville. "Consider some individuals, they are lowered. View the species, it is elevated." Whigs sought to break down or at least mitigate the more degenerative tendencies of localism and replace them with new nationally minded loyalties and perspectives. Theirs was a gospel of self-restraint, improvement, and collaboration. "Release man from the contexts of community and you get not freedom and rights," they would echo one modern scholar, "but intolerable aloneness and subjection to demoniac fears and passions." In a similar manner, their ideas for the proper size, scope, and purpose of the state were geared toward individual and social progress and an eye on the future. If society's greatest purpose was to answer individuals' weakness through associated effort, then, the *American Whig Review* argued, "the principle use of government, is to direct that united strength in the most effectual manner." Whiggery embraced a spacious reading of state action to win the future.[72]

# 3

# The State

> The State is our neighbors; our neighbors are the State.
>
> Ralph Waldo Emerson

The Whigs' understanding of America held an expansive view of state power. Whigs' desire to strengthen social bonds and encourage widespread prosperity led them to support a broader reading of constitutional authority than did their Jacksonian neighbors. "The legitimate object of government," Abraham Lincoln famously pointed out in 1854, "is to do for a community of people, whatever they need to have done, but can not do, *at all,* or can not, *so well do,* for themselves—in their separate, and individual capacities." Yet Whigs were not statists in the modern sense. Indeed, in the same speech Lincoln further argued: "In all that the people can individually do as well for themselves, government ought not to interfere."[1] Thus, Whigs' support for public works was qualified by their insistence on individual virtue and self-control. At bottom they believed in the bedrock principle of self-reliance and tended to see wealth and poverty as the logical rewards of thrift and sloth, respectively.

Whigs' understanding of political power began with the people, broadly considered, and was infused with their skepticism of the executive. Executive power attracted men of "irregular ambition," Daniel Webster warned in 1840, "destitute of all true patriotism, and a love of power, reckless of the means of its gratification."[2] Whigs trusted legislatures more than executives because they trusted their aggregate commitment to republican rule more and believed that only the wisest should fill its councils. Executive office stank of arbitrary power, which Whigs deeply feared, but legislatures offered valid opportunities for collaborative progress. "Virginians do not rush out into that extravagant confidence in men," Webster noted, using Whiggish political thinking to describe all Old Dominion voters and partisan logic ironically to strike a bipartisan chord. "They are for restraining power by law; they are for hedging in and strictly guarding all who exercise it. They look upon all who are in office as limited agents, and will not repose too much trust in any."[3] Bias binds and blinds, and most Whigs probably agreed that Webster's views should be shared by all. And, because Whigs believed that the best men ought to fill these offices, they trusted them to promote the common good.

Whigs also argued that their political program was better suited to the new world of commerce, credit, and industry than were the minimalist ideas cherished by Democrats. Most Whigs agreed with John Quincy Adams's observation: "The great object of civil government is the improvement of the condition of those who are parties to the social compact."[4] Whig theories of political power bent toward the future, not the past. They looked to government to promote development through corporations, banks, tariffs, and internal improvements. According to Calvin Colton, government was "an enterprise in humanity and benevolence."[5] Whigs embraced a vibrant, varied political culture. While their worries flowed from a partisan shudder at an unwanted future, it was not merely worry that defined them. Instead, their hopes also informed their understanding of political power, the rule of law, and the proper scope of state or public action.

## Power

Antebellum America was in many ways a golden age of widespread political interest. This was due to two major reasons. First, as the United States expanded west, the new states forming beyond the Appalachians and, later, the Mississippi River extended voting rights to virtually all adult white men to attract settlement. No doubt the promise of cheap land helped lure pioneers too. Only a few free black men and propertied widows could vote during these years, it is true, but Americans still enjoyed one of the broadest franchises in the world. Next, antebellum Americans debated important issues in the elections and legislative sessions held from 1828 through the Whigs' fall in 1854. Americans strongly disagreed about the proper direction for the emerging market economy: what substantive role, if any, the federal government should play in its development; what place should immigrants have in a nation steadily sprawling across the plains; the pace, depth, breadth, and prudence of territorial expansion; and, above all, the fate of slavery in the new territories. Big issues that lots of people cared about drew big interest. Political debate was not closeted off away from common people. Instead, it was almost a spectator sport, drawing large crowds all over America in places both big and small. Politicians expected broad public participation, with the people listening closely to what was being said, criticizing or questioning what they did not like, heckling, cheering and booing, drinking, smoking, and swearing. As a result, the canvass often resembled a country fair. George Caleb Bingham's 1853 painting *Stump Speaking* (see fig. 1.3) reflects the intimacy of this sort of political style well. Bingham shows two politicians campaigning for votes in a nondescript rural town. Their audience is composed of men of diverse backgrounds and social standings. Some listen carefully to the speaker; others seek diversion around a watermelon wagon, chat, drink, and struggle to stay awake. In a letter to a friend, the Whig painter described the candidates: "In my orator I have endeavored to personify a wiry politician, grown gray in the pursuit of office and the service of party. His influence upon the crowd is quite manifest, but I have placed behind him a shrewd clear-headed opponent, who is busy taking notes, and who will, when his turn comes, make sophisms fly like cobwebs before the housekeeper's broom." This was a scene that was repeated all across the antebellum United States throughout the era. Rival newspapers printed opposing slates, and voters clipped the lists and marked their favored candidates before going to the polling place, where ballots were cast in the open, where everyone could see your choice. Heckling, drinking, and sometimes even violence could be expected. It was big and loud and messy, like the country that it represented.[6]

Beneath the hurly-burly lay contested notions of power. Like virtually all Americans, middle-class Whigs believed that political power rested ultimately with the people. In the broadest sense, everyone agreed with the argument in George Washington's first inaugural address: "The preservation of the sacred fire of liberty, and the destiny of the republican model of government, are justly considered as deeply, perhaps as finally staked, on the experiment entrusted to the hands of the American people."[7] This principle dominated American political thought during the antebellum era, and it was well understood that public officials held their posts at the people's pleasure. Yet Whigs also argued that the people's pleasure must be expressed in an orderly manner. In fact, most Whigs sought to strengthen the ties

Fig. 3.1. George Caleb Bingham (American, 1811–1879), *Stump Speaking* (1853–1854), oil on canvas (42½ × 58 inches). Saint Louis Art Museum, Gift of Bank of America 43:2001.

between the American people and their government. In his famous 1830 speech "Second Reply to South Carolina Senator, Robert Hayne," Daniel Webster dismissed Hayne's argument that the states held ultimate power in maintaining or ending the Union. "Sir, the opinion which the honorable gentleman maintains is a notion founded in a total misapprehension, in my judgment," he admonished the Senate, "of the origin of this government, and of the foundation on which it stands. I hold it to be a popular government, erected by the people; those who administer it, responsible to the people."[8] Whigs across the country agreed, urging all Americans to cling to their government and the laws that formed its bedrock base. Abraham Lincoln hoped that "reverence for the laws, [would] be breathed by every American mother, to the lisping babe, that prattles on her lap."[9] William Henry Seward believed: "The agency of institutions of self-government is indispensable to the accomplishment of these sublime purposes. Such institutions can only be maintained by an educated and enlightened people."[10]

But who were *the people*, precisely? The idea was contested and evolving throughout the antebellum era. In the widest, most generous sense of the term, all American citizens together constituted the people. However, pure political power (i.e., the ability to vote or hold office) in Jacksonian America was far more limited. Power in these terms privileged white, Protestant men. Even so, the franchise was similarly restricted in most democratic countries, and, for its white population at least, America remained one of the freest nations in the world. By the end of the 1830s, property qualifications for voting were abolished across most of the United States, and Americans turned out in record numbers to vote in elections. No matter their partisan inclinations, most Americans believed that who won offices mattered because the state reflected the popular will in action.[11]

Legislation, jurisprudence, and executive power were, in this view, supposed to take into account the expressed wishes of the electorate, but they were also supposed to act in the best interests of the wider community. "It is essential not only to the rightful action but to the stability of the government," William Henry Seward noted in 1840, "that the will of the people, when clearly expressed, should be obeyed by their representatives."[12] Whigs built their view of statecraft on an expansive reading of America's potential because the bourgeoisie sought success above all. "The elevation of the people, we repeat," the *American Whig Review* stressed, "is the growing principle of the Whigs."[13] The will of the people gave legitimacy to their efforts. Yet disputes arose as to when and how the people expressed their will most clearly. What is more, Whigs and Jacksonians often disagreed on which was more important, the people's expressed wishes or their best interests.

The heart of the matter was trust. Most Jacksonian Democrats staunchly defended the right of constituents to instruct their elected officials how to vote, for instance, because they distrusted government. Indeed, the lifelong Democrat George Bancroft argued: "They who deny the right of instruction, deify the will of the representative, or temporary agent, and refusing to the people the right of paramount judgment, surrender the government to arbitrary caprice, the desperate ambition, the bigotry or selfishness of an individual." The problem was the effects of power on human nature. Jacksonians found the argument that governments could safely expand their power to meet the needs of the people naive or misguided because of the way that power corrupted the human soul. Most Democrats thought that power beguiled even the purest of hearts once safely ensconced in office. "He is all at once wiser in the affairs of his neighbors than they are themselves," the *New York Evening Post* acidly remarked in 1836. "He sees that they do not manage their own business properly; his fingers itch to arrange it for them, and his head teams with admirable and useful schemes of legislation for obliging them to attend to their own interests." Jacksonians were certain that such scheming would not end. Legislators in distant capitals would ceaselessly seek new ways to tell free-born Americans how best to live their own lives unless carefully watched by a diligent electorate.[14]

Not surprisingly, Whigs disagreed. Conceding Democrats' point about the darker tendencies of human nature, they were still far more inclined to trust state power and government action. First, they believed in restricting high offices to the best men, to the wisest and most knowledgeable of the community. By this they did not necessarily mean that the wealthiest ought to serve by default. Instead, they urged those men with the widest sense of the community and the deepest understanding of the proper uses of law to stand for office. The *American Whig Review* clarified this perspective in 1849: "A party that means to endure, must ground itself upon the physical hopes and necessities of the middle classes of men, those whose property and whose affections are engaged in permanent industry."[15] If middle-class Whiggery was built on a broader sense of nationalism and a bigger conception of the community, then Whigs also believed that only America's most broadly minded men were worthy of guiding the ship of state.

In this vein, Whiggish Americans saw the right of instruction in more general terms than did Democrats. "The Whigs, with Republicans of all times," declared Thurlow Weed's *Albany Evening Journal* from New York in 1840, "maintain the duty of every Representative to shape his official action in general conformity with the wishes of his constituents."[16] Yet Whigs harbored a middle-class trust in their elected leaders, one based on common commitment to bourgeois virtues that Democrats did not share. Indeed, Boston Whigs credited their triumph in the 1840 presidential election to the people weighing and measuring the Democrats, who were then found wanting: "They have looked upon the present administration, in its administrative character, as low-minded and corrupt, as deficient in both capacity and integrity, and therefore as unfit to be entrusted with the management of public affairs."[17] Whigs' self-confidence fostered their political optimism. Consequently, they did not fear the state because they trusted their capacity to elect the best men to lead it. "It is in the character of the officers," Daniel Webster declared in 1840, "and not in the strength of bars and vaults that we must look for the security of the public treasure." The Whig reading of individualism highly valued self-control and the lifelong cultivation of virtue in public and private life. Baltimore Whigs stressed these points in defending the New Jerseyan Theodore Frelinghuysen's merits as a potential vice president in 1844. "He brings to the discharge of all his duties soundness of judgment, steadiness of purpose, and habits and principles of strictest integrity." Frelinghuysen's embrace of middle-class virtues meant that he could be trusted: "His views are liberal and enlightened." And crucial to Whigs: "He is beyond the control of mere selfish or partisan influence." Whigs' vision of the future was optimistic, but it was also qualified by the need for virtue and self-control. Families, churches, and schools shaped and strengthened American character, forging a stable, connected society from a fidgety mass of isolated individuals. And from that society the state emerged. Thus, it is fair to suggest that Whig confidence carried a disclaimer. Americans could trust the state *if* the people were wise enough to elect virtuous men to its counsels and offices.[18]

Beyond issues of trust and merit, in antebellum America *the people* often also became code for *political orthodoxy.* Party leaders supposedly spoke for the true interests of the people, while their opponents were hacks or demagogues seeking personal gain at public expense. In 1844, a group of Rhode Island Whigs explained their party's perspective on Jacksonians' penchant for raucous, antiestablishment rabble-rousing in the stark terms of true patriotism. "The wild spirit of insubordination to established authority," they argued, "of determined disobedience to public law is everywhere so manifest and alarming as to awaken serious apprehensions in the minds of all *considerate* and *patriotic* men."[19] Theirs was not simply a partisan stance or one perspective among many, these Ocean State Whigs implied, but the correct way of seeing things. If others disagreed, then they must be inconsiderate and unpatriotic, apostates of the worst sort. "Let the dwellers in the whole country see and feel that, whatever may be their personal convictions," New York Whigs agreed in 1841, "or whatever course of conduct their passions may prompt, the power of LAW is still above them, is *supreme* in the land." Ideological tribalism meshed well with party organization, and parties offered members the comfort and trust of the tribe or clan. Understood in these terms, politics was not simply a game of horse race and electioneering for offices, where candidates held varying opinions while broadly agreeing on ultimate national goals. The stakes were high because it was a clash of opposing worldviews and differing moral outlooks. If the prize meant control of America's future, then who held power and who should hold power became questions of crucial importance.[20]

Although the franchise and access to state and federal offices were restricted to white men, middle-class Whig political culture was also built on a broader understanding of the people. Whig women not only attended political rallies, stump speeches, and barbecues; they also grew frustrated when they were excluded. "Should a man be afraid of being seen with a woman who is not his wife, I should commend his modesty," one woman wrote in to *Godey's Lady's Book* in 1831 after her husband failed to take her to a local rally supporting common schools. "But what impertinent whim can make him ashamed of his own wife?" Women were a *vibrant,* vital corps of moral and social activism within middle-class Whiggery, and they took their duties seriously. Indeed, ladies like those in Felix Darley's *Two Women Standing over Seated Reading Women* (see fig. 3.2) were a dynamic part of Whig political culture. Their faces hidden, as most women themselves often were for much of recorded history, these women nonetheless illustrate the bourgeois faith in literacy, education, and community that was the lifeblood of the world that the Whigs promised to build. Antebellum women proved stalwart supporters of the Whig cause and were active in pushing that cause forward.[21]

In the months leading up to the 1844 nominating convention, Whig women in Baltimore, New York, Trenton, and even Dover City, Delaware, made banners, prepared food, browbeat wavering moderates, and above all celebrated Henry Clay. "The white rose of Pennsylvania defends the fame of Henry Clay!" one defiant white satin banner read. And the women presenting it reminded men: "The fair reward the brave!"[22] Whig women did not vote or hold office, it is true, yet their presence and their money mattered. In 1840, at a gathering of Whig women in Richmond, Virginia, Daniel Webster joked: "If both the saint and sinner, and all the ladies, too, are against Mr. Van Buren, what prospect can he possibly have of success?" Whiggish women doggedly demanded public action on issues such as universal education,

Fig. 3.2. Felix Octavius Carr Darley, [*Two Women Standing over Seated Reading Woman*] (between 1840 and 1888). Drawing. Prints and Photographs Division, Library of Congress, Washington, DC. https://www.loc.gov/item/2010715563.

hospital reform, and abolition. This sort of power was subtler than that exercised by men, perhaps, but it was still politically formidable.[23]

Although middle-class Whiggery offered women a public political role, Whigs also carried a more conservative skepticism about certain groups' fitness to hold electoral power. Initially, their worries lingered over the virtue of working-class whites at the ballot box, but, as the era wore on, their anxieties came to rest on the waves of foreign-born, Roman Catholic Irish and German immigrants pouring into New York, Boston, and Baltimore. One angry Whig polemicist from Boston argued: "The perverse and apparently innate lawlessness of the Irish made it a matter of enormous difficulty to govern them mildly and effectively." But that was only the beginning of the problem. "Hundreds of thousands flock to America—disturbing their adopted country with their incorrigible turbulence, inflaming it by their insane delusions, and spreading through the length and breadth of the land mental and moral poison of the most subtle and degrading kind." Whigs thought these the wrong sort of people to trust with political power, and throughout the era they believed in their bones that Democrats manipulated Catholic immigrants for partisan gain. Naturalization was too easily obtained, they feared. And immigrants too soon became voters and "as such [were] sought for, flattered, and cajoled," usually by Jacksonians, they grumbled, "their prejudices . . . humored or adopted." They worried that priest-ridden Catholic immigrants pouring into America during the antebellum years would fail to practice the self-control needed to avoid the worst tendencies of individualism.[24]

The name *Whig* was a historical nod toward a deeply felt fear of executive power. Drawing on America's recent Revolutionary experience and its longer heritage of country-party political culture, American Whigs first organized as a sprawling middle-class response to what they felt were the first drumbeats of monarchy that Andrew Jackson's election to the presidency in 1828 represented. Consequently, the term *Whig* was meant to echo Revolutionary Whiggish thinkers on both sides of the Atlantic, such as Edmund Burke and George Mason as well as those from the Glorious Revolution of 1688. In the view of the nascent Whigs, Jackson's ascension hardly constituted proof of American democracy reaching full flower, at least as his supporters foolishly believed. Instead, they were dismayed to see the American people prove themselves so convincingly inept after being trusted with the broad use of power.[25]

For Whiggish Americans, the election of Andrew Jackson to the presidency heralded the triumph of the wrong sort of people. For friend and foe alike, the name *Jackson* hung in the air like a challenge, and he represented everything Whigs abhorred. His deep passions, dark jealousies, petty hatreds, and baleful ignorance should be obvious to all not held in thrall by his cult of personality or in debt to his political machine. Old Hickory represented something far more important and ominous, at least for Whigs, than just the prospects of what they hoped would be a failed presidency. "The ungodly were now in the ascendancy," Jackson's greatest modern champion observed, "and those who walked not in their counsels had little but Scripture for consolation." What had the old general done, Whigs wondered, to make anyone with sound judgment believe that he was worthy of such high office? After his reelection in 1832, Whig worry often gave way to angry consternation. "Except an enormous fabric of executive power for himself," Henry Clay coldly argued from the Senate floor in 1834, "the president has built up nothing, constructed nothing, and will leave no enduring monument of his administration. He goes for destruction, universal destruction; and it seems to be his greatest ambition to efface and obliterate every trace of the wisdom of his predecessors." Jackson represented liberty taken too far, democracy run amok. Worse, "King Andrew" and a cabal of intriguers around him used his fame to inflame the people and cause them to vote against their own best interests. Whigs also argued that Democrats used violence and intimidation to sway elections. "We cannot sufficiently express our abhorrence to the system of lawless violence and outrage," Philadelphia Whigs seethed in 1834, "adopted by the friends of Gen. Jackson, to deter the aged, infirm and timid from going to the polls, and to wreak their vengeance upon those who did not vote according to their wishes." Whig argued that Jacksonians could rarely engage in vigorous debates that challenged their partisan dogma.[26]

For Whigs this was democratic power used against the very people it was meant to serve, perverting and twisting notions of liberty to enthrone the few at the expense of the many. American Whigs sought wisdom in the counsel of the Whigs of old and most admired Edmund Burke. "While the Reformer is certain to be applauded if successful, because his object is definite and clear to everyone," the *American Whig Review* reminded readers in 1852, "the Conservative, whose influence is felt rather than seen, must content himself with but a small measure of that public approbation which he feels to be his due." Whigs felt kinship with Burke because "he was ever the advocate of prudence" and like them "was never understood." And on all the issues that mattered, Whigs argued, Burke was right. From urging reconciliation with the American colonies during the 1770s, to standing up to British oppression and corruption in India in the 1780s, to protecting England from bloody Jacobin revolutions in the 1790s, again and again history vindicated the volatile statesman from Dublin. "Yet all the services of Burke to his country never won him its entire regard." Whigs felt a similar lack of appreciation in the antebellum United States. They too endured "disappointed aspirations, broken hopes, long years of altercation and unavailing struggle."[27]

Time and again Whigs echoed Burke's stubborn argument to Charles-Jean-François Depont: "The Liberty I mean is social freedom. It is that state in which Liberty is secured by equality of Restraint." Jackson's politics were built on mob rule, and mobocracy was the very opposite of self-restraint. And would the mob ultimately share in the spoils their rage helped secure? Whigs scoffed. Not likely. "[Liberty] is not solitary, unconnected, individual, selfish Liberty. As if Man was to regulate the whole of his Conduct by his own will."[28] Whiggery itself was based on connecting individuals and weaving them into a strong, national fabric that would beat back localism and tamp down political selfishness. Whigs viewed self-restraint as the foundation for the proper use of political power. "Modern Locofocoism [a Whig pejorative for Democrats meaning 'incendiary' or 'radical'] is a creature of adventure," warned the *American Whig Review*, "and like a soldier of fortune, prospers best in confusion. It follows no uniform path, for it has no settled aim." Over and over, Whig candidates for executive office assured voters of their willingness to be restrained by legislatures and courts once in office. William Henry Harrison spent nearly half of his 8,445-word inaugural address promising fealty to the principle that Congress should enact laws and presidents should content themselves with seeing them carried out.[29]

In this line of thinking, Whigs' middle-class institutional conservatism became apparent because they believed that innovation and change should be slow and deliberate. "The Whig party is the really conservative party of the country," New York Whigs agreed. "It intelligently prefers the tried to the untried, the certain to the uncertain, the safe to the hazardous." And few things were as slow, deliberative, or predictable as antebellum legislative debate. "The immediate welfare of the people and their permanent prosperity will be better promoted by a steady adherence to the settled policy of the state," Harrison urged the country in 1840, "with economy and retrenchment in its prosecution, and by the preservation of institutions intimately connected with the policy and with the various individual interests of our fellow citizens."[30] Whigs argued that the vigilant maintenance of legislative power was crucial in protecting America's republican experiment from executive despotism.

For Whigs, then, the image *King Andrew I* (see fig. 3.3) was not simply electioneering claptrap or the clever use of charged rhetoric to score cheap points at the polls. While their fears of monarchy were overblown and did

Fig. 3.3. *King Andrew the First* ([New York?], 1833). Lithograph. Prints and Photographs Division, Library of Congress, Washington, DC. "A caricature of Andrew Jackson as a despotic monarch, probably issued during the Fall of 1833 in response to the President's September order to remove federal deposits from the Bank of the United States. The print is dated a year earlier by Weitenkampf and related to Jackson's controversial veto of Congress's bill to recharter the Bank in July 1832. However, the charge, implicit in the print, of Jackson's exceeding the President's constitutional power . . . was most widely advanced in connection not with the veto but with the 1833 removal order, on which the President was strongly criticized for acting without congressional approval. Jackson, in regal costume, stands before a throne in a frontal pose reminiscent of a playing-card king. He holds a 'veto' in his left hand and a scepter in his right. The Federal Constitution and the arms of Pennsylvania (the United States Bank was located in Philadelphia) lie in tatters under his feet. A book 'Judiciary of the U[nited] States' lies nearby. Around the border of the print are the words 'Of Veto Memory', 'Born to Command' and 'Had I Been Consulted.'" https://www.loc.gov/item/2008661753.

not accurately reflect Democratic views, they undergirded a portion of their political passion. Fear does not need rational appraisal to bind sentiment. Instead, a caricatured distortion of one's opponents' supposedly worst qualities carries the lodestone of dread that often proves powerful. It does not matter that Democrats did not really want to hoist a bumpkin monarchy on a credulous American Republic. What matters is that most Whigs *believed* that they did and often voted accordingly. It was a powerful symbol that offered a telling window into the often-overwhelming anxiety many Whigs felt when confronted with what they considered the horror of Jackson's creeping tyranny. This charge was not fair or just, but it grew out of partisan suspicions, which are rarely fair or just. It did not matter that this foreboding was rooted more in imagined slights than in actual abuses of power. Indeed, in many ways, that made it worse. The political imagination seemed almost infinite in its ability to conjure both fear and loathing. So it was for Whigs with Andrew Jackson.[31]

As *King Andrew I* demonstrates, Whigs indeed objected to the actual policies and ideas of Jackson and his supporters as well. From the spoils system rewarding cronies with political offices to the quixotic war on the Second Bank of the United States, they had plenty to fill their lists of why Jackson was unfit for the station he held. But their worries cut deeper still. In 1839, in a speech before the Virginia state party convention, Benjamin Watkins Leigh, a Whig from Richmond, described his party's central fear of unchecked executive power and its consequences for the future. "[Presidents Jackson and Van Buren] have wrought a practical change in the political institutions of the country most pernicious in itself," Leigh reminded them, "and fraught, unless it be timely counteracted, with the utmost danger to the very being of republican government." Jackson preened and strutted his hour across the national stage and would be heard no more, but Whigs worried that the political heresies he represented could poison American republicanism forever. "The clouds of public misfortune thicken to a tempest," John Quincy Adams warned a group of young Whigs in Boston in 1845. "Your trial is approaching. The spirit of freedom and the spirit of slavery are drawing together for the deadly conflict of arms." Whigs believed that Andrew Jackson was responsible. The cult of personality that had elected him, the distracted, reckless use of power to punish enemies and reward friends, the intolerable arrogance of a demagogue secure in his position because he had hoodwinked too many voters—these things kindled a frustration among Whigs that teetered toward ossified hate. This was the new language of American politics, and it was ironic that Andrew Jackson first endured its broadsides, for few Americans understood hate so well as Jackson himself.[32]

In this vein, Whigs from Massachusetts to Maryland blasted Jackson's use of the presidential veto as the imposition of one man's will over that of the people. The *American Whig Review* vented this frustration, arguing: "The veto power was anti-republican, exceedingly liable to be abused, and in its abuse throwing such undue influence into the hands of the Executive as to endanger our free institutions." Though constitutional, vetoes had been rare in previous administrations. Indeed, Old Hickory issued more vetoes than any president from George Washington to Andrew Johnson—and more than his six predecessors combined. Moreover, of the thirty-three vetoes issued from Jackson to Lincoln, all came from the desk of Democratic presidents. Even if the Jacksonian apostate, John Tyler, and his ten vetoes are unjustly added to the Whig ledger, Democrats still dominated with twenty-three.[33] To Whigs, this offered clear proof of a radical departure from settled precedent and represented a dangerous rejection of the broader community's wisdom. Perhaps the most famous instance occurred in May 1830, when Jackson vetoed federal funding for the Maysville Road in Kentucky, a proposed turnpike from Lexington to Maysville designed to link up with the larger national system of transportation and communication. Since this road was going to be a part of the larger national road, Whigs judged it an innocuous and beneficial use of federal money.

Shocking no one, Andrew Jackson disagreed. No doubt relishing the opportunity to inconvenience and embarrass Henry Clay, he nonetheless staked his objections to the Maysville Road on higher ideological ground. The road was unconstitutional, he explained, because its entire length, and thus its benefits, ran only in Kentucky. As he and his supporters saw things, funding the road was a risky federal intrusion into local affairs. If Kentuckians wanted a turnpike, let them pay for it.

Whigs were unmoved by Jackson's logic. Nicholas D. Coleman, a southern congressman from Kentucky, made their case. "But gentleman say, every inch of the Maysville Road is in the State of Kentucky. How can it be national?" he admitted, acknowledging the president's argument that the road benefited only Kentucky. "I answer, every inch of the Delaware Canal, sixteen miles in length, is in the State of New Jersey; and every inch of the Louisville Canal is in one county; nay, I believe in one city. How can they be national? Yet, Congress have subscribed for stock in both of them." The argument that the road was purely local was specious at best. And Kentucky's Whigs charged Democrats with duplicity and petty cronyism. "Jackson men are not to be trusted," the *Louisville Journal* coldly argued in 1830 just before Christmas. "Their devotion to a superannuated old man has swallowed up all their feelings, powers, and faculties, and in him they live, move, and have their being." Whigs grew disgusted with Democrats because they seemed to put their faith in the judgment of one man and substituted loyalty to his cause for fealty to the will and concern for the welfare of the community. This blind, parochial loyalty frustrated Whigs because to their eyes it represented creeping monarchy and was anathema to American republicanism. Old Hickory's crushing electoral successes only twisted the knife deeper.[34]

For his part, Henry Clay saw the Maysville Road veto as a false, overreaching application of political power born of one man's smoldering hatreds and his party's sycophantic, cowardly fear of the future. "My enemies flatter themselves that those systems [i.e., roads, turnpikes, canals, banks, and credit] may be overthrown by my destruction," Clay coldly derided his Democratic detractors in an 1830 speech given before mechanics and artisans in Cincinnati. "Vain and impotent hope! Long, long after I am gone, whilst the lofty hills encompass this fair city, those systems will invigorate the industry and animate the hopes of the farmer, the mechanic, the manufacturer and all other classes of our country-men."[35] In a moment of striking clairvoyance, Clay understood that middle-class Whiggery's most enduring legacies probably would not come at the ballot box. Instead, they would be etched in the marrow and sinew of American society as it progressed into the future.

In stark contrast to their distrust of executive power, Whigs placed great faith in state and national legislatures. For Whigs, this flowed from their belief that legislatures most closely mirrored the broad will of the people because their members were drawn from small, local districts and thus reflected the diversity of the American polity. As the *American Whig Review* noted in 1845, Whigs believed that placing their trust in legislatures was "none other than a Moral Power." Legislatures were forced by their makeup to discuss, deliberate, and compromise. Further, it was virtually impossible for them to impose controversial policies by fiat because of the presence of opposition. Conversely, unilateral executive action seemed to Whig eyes "utterly destructive of that nationality which belongs to, and forms the greatest strength of the Whig party."[36]

Whigs' self-assurance made them more willing to trust candidates once in office, so long as they followed a Whiggish reading of the proper uses of power. There was a bit of middle-class naïveté at work because of their faith, sometimes blind, in public institutions. If Americans had virtue enough to install the wisest men in high office, then the people had little to fear from corruption, incompetence, or despotism—big ifs in any age. Yet Whigs believed that they lost elections only when Americans were seduced by demagogues or gave in to worries about their neighbors, about the economy, or about the future. Of course, Democrats boasted a steady record of electoral success throughout the age of Jackson, but those victories lead Whigs not to distrust governments per se but instead to question the virtue of the people electing them. To Whig eyes, Jacksonians had no positive policy to recommend them. They tapped into powerful anxieties about the modern world and translated that fear into ballot-box success. They seemed to countenance no higher purpose for government than maintaining the common defense and preventing future calamities. Democrats championed a politics of fear. The Whigs' America held out great hope for the possibilities of public action and championed a much broader reading of the true purpose of state power.[37]

## Purpose

During the age of Jackson and Clay, few questions generated so much debate and disagreement between Whigs and Democrats as the proper scope of government. Many of their disagreements flowed from different understandings of American nationalism and public obligations. As Whigs understood things, uniting the distant parts of the country into one community was the aim of good government. "We do not impose geographical limits to our patriotic feeling or regard," Daniel Webster observed. "We do not follow rivers and mountains and lines of latitude to find boundaries beyond which public improvements do not benefit us." Webster spoke for most Whigs, who often sought to turn the question from one of *could* to one of *should*. "I have never seen any more difficulty in erecting lighthouses on the lakes than on the ocean," he continued, "in improving the harbors of inland seas, than if they were within the ebb and flow of the tide; or in removing obstructions in the vast streams of the West, more than in any work to facilitate commerce on the Atlantic coast."[38] For the Whiggish Americans, the most fundamental purpose of the federal constitution and the government it created was to make *one* people out of the many social and material interests dividing antebellum America.

Thus, Whigs tended to see state action in far more flexible, middle-class terms than did Democrats. They oriented their politics toward the future. They believed that their policies were designed to reform the present in ways that were faithful to the past so that all Americans might enjoy a prosperous future. As William Henry Seward explained in 1839, the American System and the larger Whig program were the best ways to achieve these goals because they would secure "the continual advance by millions in the value of real estate, the increase in quantity and value of agricultural productions and manufactured fabrics, the establishment and enlargement of inland commerce, and of foreign trade, economy in the expense, saving of time, and increase in amount of travel, augmentation of population, unbounded prosperity and increase of rising villages, cities, and towns, and all the consequent advantages to morality, piety, and knowledge." Seward's vision was boundless. It spoke to the longings within Whigs' hearts and their faith that their ideas, properly applied, would answer them.[39]

Henry Clay and his Whigs spent nearly three decades explaining, promoting, and defending the American System as the best use of public power because they believed that it would strengthen national unity and increase overall prosperity. In 1832, Clay pointed to positive changes in American life that he thought the modest tariff of 1824 had created to bolster the Whig case. "On a general survey," Clay stressed, "we behold cultivation extended, the arts flourishing, the face of the country improved, our people fully and profitably employed, and the public countenance exhibiting tranquility, contentment, and happiness."[40] Whigs like Clay further argued that the federal government and the various states should support internal improvements such as canals, toll roads, and railroads to link the various sections of the country. Finally, Whigs supported a national bank to regulate the money supply and provide sturdy, reliable credit. In this way, merchants and industrialists in the commercial Northeast would have access to capital to fund business expansion and absorb risk as well as federal protection from foreign competition.

The American System encouraged local development, instead of demographic diffusion. "The general operation of the establishments is to check emigration from the settled to the unsettled parts of the country," the *North American Review* explained Whigs' hopes, "to increase the population, and with it the wealth and comforts of the former, and to raise the standard of civilization and morals throughout the whole."[41] If Americans stayed in or near their hometowns instead of moving west and south seeking prosperity elsewhere, then the quality of life for all people would rise. In Henry Clay's mind, his public legacy rested firmly on the American System and its partisan recipe for future prosperity. Farmers and planters in the West and South would sell their cotton, hemp, foodstuffs, and other raw materials to factories and finishing houses in New England, using canals, roads, and railroads paid for by Congress or the several states, and in turn purchase finished products from these same or similar northern merchants with credit provided by the national bank. Everyone would be connected to everyone else. It was an elegant program for national prosperity through linked markets, shared morals, and mutual exchange.[42]

Jacksonian Democrats did not see it that way. In the American System, Democrats instead discovered a vast, sinister scheme bent on exploiting, extorting, and enslaving them. "Jacksonians desired the peace and unity of an idealized past," Lawrence F. Kohl has pointed out, "not the ceaseless conflict of a capitalist future." Democrats were wary of changes in demographics, industry, work, and the very pace of daily life. "But," Kohl continued, "while Whiggish institutions and attitudes prevailed [in the long run], Jacksonians were taught the virtues of competition rather than cooperation, resistance rather than reconciliation, and destruction rather than creation." The picking and choosing of winners and losers cut Democrats like William Leggett to the quick because they always assumed that they would be the losers. "It [i.e., the state] may one day legislate exclusively for the farmer," he warned, "the next for the mechanic, and the third for the manufacturer, who all thus become the mere puppets of legislative cobbling and tinkering, instead of independent citizens, relying on their own resources for their prosperity." The Whig program robbed Americans of their industriousness, Democrats believed, and enthroned *the state* as the final arbiter of liberty, comfort, and security. To Democratic eyes, then, the American System was objectionable because Whigs proposed to use public power to protect one section of the American economy and force the rest of the country to comply, whether they wanted to or not. As Democrats saw it, Whig ideas were not simply wrong; they were deceptive, dangerous, and immoral.[43]

Whigs dismissed Democratic concerns, viewing any policy that might increase individuals' opportunities to secure material affluence with near political reverence. By self-control individuals might govern their passions, and by religious instruction and broader education they might deepen their virtue and widen their knowledge. "A people thus enriched will not abandon the system to which they owe their wealth," Seward argued, "because the agents by whom it has been conducted may have erred, or may even have been unfaithful; nor will they be stopped in their career by obstacles which time must diminish and enterprise will overcome."[44] The virtuous, educated citizen would enjoy the just fruits of prosperity and, as Whigs in Boston, Baltimore, Charleston, and Columbus agreed, would support public programs to help his fellow men achieve the same. "The elevation of the people," the *American Whig Review* stressed, "is the growing principle of the Whigs." For all the interest in congressional debates, moreover, America's federal government remained small throughout the antebellum era. State governments and local municipalities pushed the American System forward.[45]

Whigs hoped to tie the country together through improved infrastructure. And they grew tired of Democratic cries for elbow room and respite from progress. "Our Country is a country of busy men," the Baltimore Whig John P. Kennedy reminded a packed hall in New York in 1833. "Everywhere the incessant murmur and gush of business tells of a generation intent upon aggrandizing a vast and scattered empire." Winning a thriving future required cooperation and shared sacrifice on a vast scale. But Whigs urged their fellow Americans to look at what had already been achieved and continue to support those efforts. "That the subject [i.e., internal improvements etc.] is one of great importance to the prosperity of Nashville, none will deny," Tennessee Whigs agreed, urging their fellow citizens to help Nashville live up to its self-styled sobriquet "the Athens of the South" and fund a turnpike. "We therefore trust that our Citizens, at a general and full Town meeting, will promptly give the authority necessary to ensure the speedy execution of this highly desirable piece of internal improvement." For his part, Kennedy predicted that, if Americans in 1823 had traveled abroad for ten years, they would be astonished on their return at the prosperity generated by the modest investment in canals and roads. "You will find huts grown into comfortable houses, hamlets into villages, villages into cities, and cities into great and gorgeous marts." For Whigs, north, south, and west, improvement was the point. "No man in America is contented to be poor," the *American Whig Review* pointed out, "or expects to continue so."[46]

The term *internal improvements* carries an unfortunate parliamentary coldness that minimizes its antebellum importance. Lost in bureaucratic translation is the sheer excitement of new possibilities, the astonishing sense of change each project represented for those involved. One Whiggish New England pamphleteer captured this sentiment well when reflecting on railroads in 1851: "The brevity of human life is forcibly illustrated in the rapidity with which man becomes accustomed to every great revolution, either in civil order, in commerce, or in the economy of the household." For Whigs like him, the commercial changes of the antebellum years were matched only by how readily Americans accepted them. "This is exemplified by the recent application of steam to locomotion. We are in the transition period, when traveling thirty miles in an hour is ceasing to excite surprise," he ruefully shook his head. "The children of the present day will never appreciate the improvement."[47] Whigs not only embraced these developments; they worked to speed them up. In 1847, the *Ohio State Journal* urged Whigs to remember always that they belonged to "that great national party in which are centered all our hopes for the peace, prosperity and deliverance of the nation."[48] At the same time, Whigs often lamented the tendency of subsequent generations to forget the toil required to secure their affluence. The Whig political culture tended to take the long view of progress, but Whigs called for continuing character reform because they worried that comfort brought complacency, which in turn eroded habits of self-control and industry.[49]

Despite such worries, Whigs such as John Pendleton Kennedy firmly believed that theirs was a glorious future and had little patience with any disagreement. "It is unmeaning cant—nay worse—it is pernicious heresy," Kennedy thundered in 1833, "to defend what is called the 'let-us-alone' policy in the affairs of nations. Individual astuteness may be a safe guide in individual concerns; but it will never [or should never] shape or control the circumstances of the state."[50] According to Edward Everett, Whigs objected to the idea "that [ governance] involves the narrow view which is becoming too fashionable of the objects of Governments, as if it had no higher or further purpose than the mere restraining of one man from committing violence on another."[51] For those who believed in the Whigs' America far more was possible.

The state did not exist simply to protect property and administer justice; rather, public power ought to promote the public good. "We believe," New York Whigs stressed in 1838, "that Education, Morality, and the securing of any good which may be more feasibly attained through the action of the community than of the individuals, are within the proper sphere of its operations and exertions." And, as Whigs understood their world, a close observation of public improvements tracked the development of societies from barbarism to civility. "The barbarian, for instance, is simply content with the foot-path," New Orleans Whigs argued in 1848. "In the next degree of humanity we find the high road; next, come the turnpike and canal; and then, within the area of civilization and intellectual life, are the locomotive, propelled onward by the perfection of science, and the magnetic telegraph, robbing the lightning of its swiftness, and rendering its touch powerful to enlighten and not to destroy." And Whigs imagined a future full of astonishing achievements. "We must not forget that the railroad is but one step in the ascending staircase," Connecticut Whigs stressed, "on which the race is mounting, guiding and cheered by heavenly voices. We only mark the beginning of wonders which shall cooperate with the divine purpose in the redemption of man, and the restoration of a ruined world."[52]

An example of this perspective in action was the national push for canals. While the famous Erie Canal looms large in scholarship on antebellum era internal improvements, other canal projects shed light on the Whigs' view of state power rightly applied. The Louisville and Portland Canal just south of Louisville, Kentucky, is one such example. As one Boston travel pamphlet explained: "Louisville stands high among our western cities for culture and refinement, [and] is extensively resorted to by merchants from the river towns above and below, and from the interior of the adjacent States, as an eligible wholesale market for dry goods and groceries." Yet, for all its business and sophistication, the so-called Gateway to the South had a geography problem. "The greatest falls in the Ohio River are just below this city; which are caused by a bed of limestone extending across the river, over which the waters pour with a broken and irregular current, for a distance of two miles, making a descent of 22 feet, and, excepting one or two months during the periods of highest flood, entirely intercepting the passage of loaded boats up and down the river."[53]

For those building the Whigs' America, the answer was a canal. At a cost of $1 million, local businessmen, with a little help from the federal government, built a waterway that was "between two and three miles, 50 feet wide at the surface, and overcoming 22½ feet of fall by four locks, sufficiently capacious to admit steamboats of the largest size."[54] And the canal was a success, paying for itself in the first decade of operation, something that Whigs saw as national in impact. "The country will be benefitted by this freedom to our commerce," *Niles' Weekly Register* promised in 1835.[55] Beyond Louisville, from 1830 through 1850, Whigs celebrated other successful canal projects such as the Illinois and Michigan, connecting the Great Lakes with the Mississippi River, and the Chesapeake and Ohio, which linked Pittsburgh and the Appalachian Mountains to mid-Atlantic commercial centers. Indeed, as both maps 3.1 and 3.2 demonstrate, the Whiggish push for expanded infrastructure continued apace throughout the age of Jackson and Clay.[56]

As Whigs saw things, therefore, internal improvements like canals and, indeed, railroads and turnpikes were not simply sound uses of public money but necessities for winning the right kind of future. They believed that this was bigger than electoral wins and losses. In 1848, the *American Whigs Review* urged Whigs running for office at every level of government across the country to hold fast to their ideals, especially government promotion of internal improvements: "The trial of men's virtue never comes but when they are called on to maintain their principles at some sacrifice." Public works were expensive, and not all of them proved profitable. "There have doubtless been many gross errors committed in the devising and constructing of work of Internal Improvement," the *New-Yorker* conceded in 1840. But even mistakes and malfeasance such as railroads running over budget and financiers absconding with revenue before significant work was completed were useful if lessons were learned: "These errors will serve as beacons against similar mistakes in the future." Thus, gritty persistence was necessary because Whigs often endured vicious broadsides from Democrats who were convinced that public improvements were little more than speculative efforts to bribe the people with their own money. Worse, when such efforts failed—and many did—the taxpayers were left with the bill.[57]

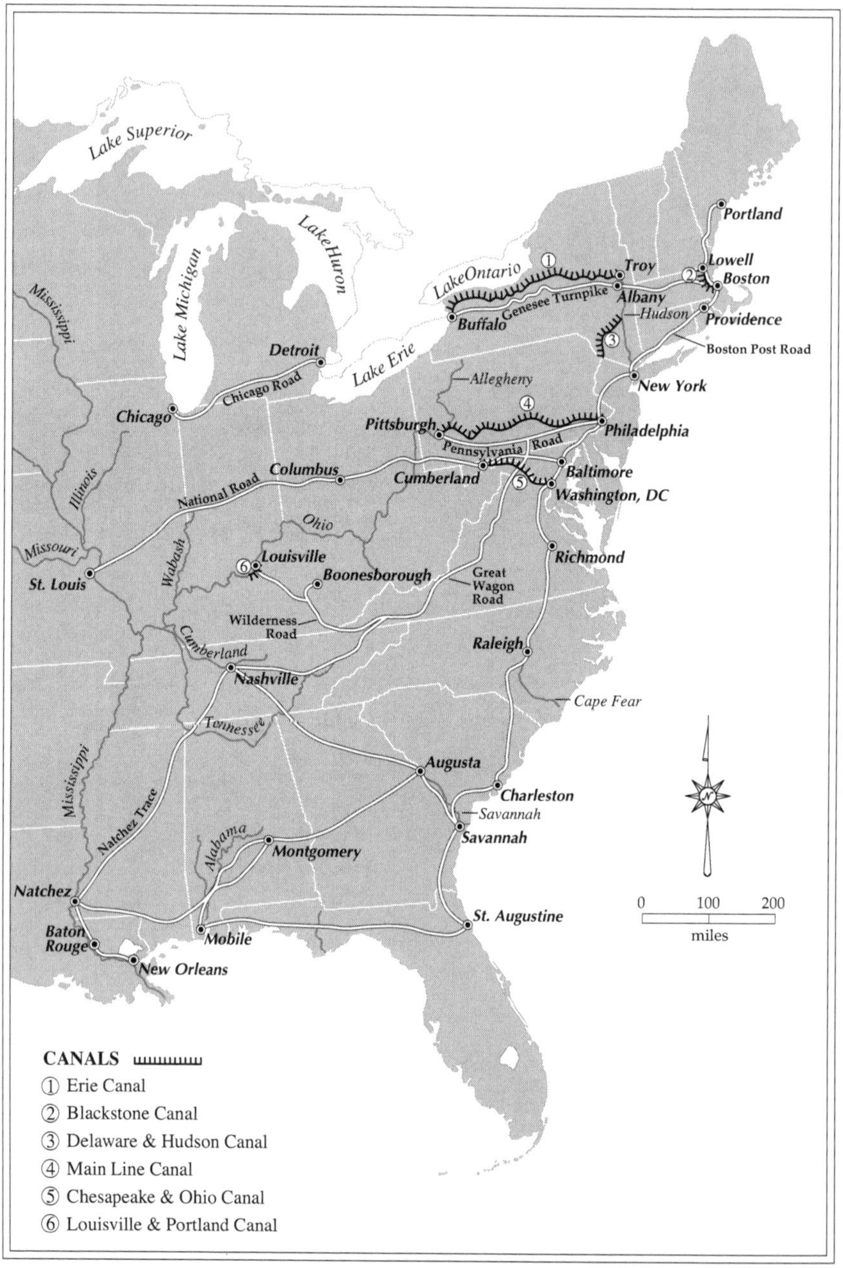


Map 3.1. Major roads and canal routes in the 1830s.

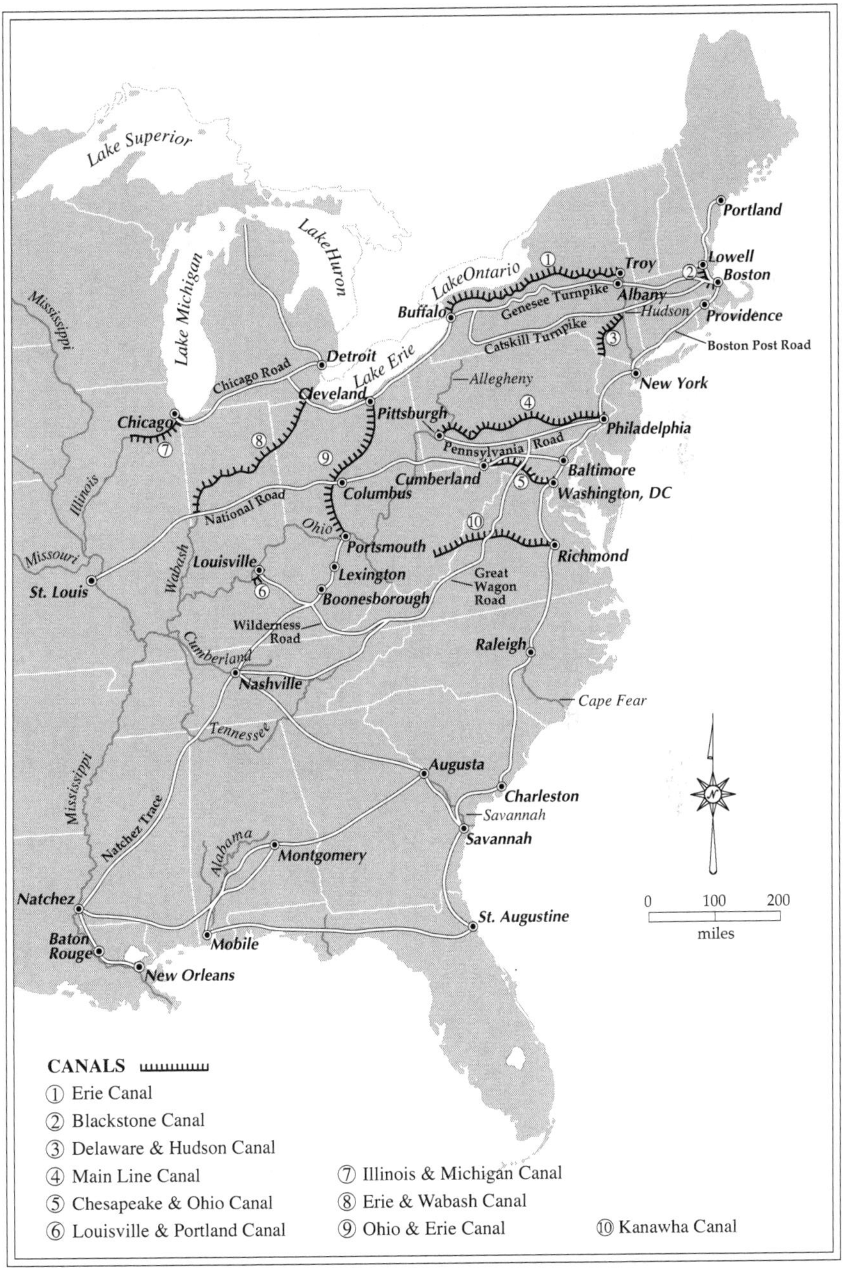


Map 3.2. Major roads and canal routes in the 1850s.

Indeed, Democrats dismissed the Whig program as the calculated sophistry of the wealthy, languid few seeking to rob the toil-weary many. "The property of the American farmer has not been acquired by the dark maneuvers of financiering," the *United States Magazine, and Democratic Review* reminded Jacksonian readers in 1840. "It has been wrought from the soil by hard labor in the face of the day."[58] In Democratic eyes, Whiggery was the political creed of the lazy schemer, who looked to governments to provide him what he refused to earn through honest toil.

Whigs found such thinking narrow and inane. Modernity had arrived, whether Americans welcomed it or not. It was pointless, Whigs argued, even dangerous, to resist the rising tide of the modern world. Far better to ensure that American society could not merely endure but prosper. "The destiny of these principles has not yet been completed," stressed the *American Whig Review,* defending middle-class Whiggish ideas of a more active government, "and to sacrifice any one of them at the present time, on any pretext, is willful and suicidal madness."[59] Whigs argued that it was little more than vain hope that America would or could continue as a primarily agrarian nation. Industry was its future, and public improvements were the best means to secure that future.

Indeed, Whigs wholly rejected the notion that industry and agriculture were somehow at odds. In their view, these pursuits were complementary. Massachusetts Whigs reminded voters that they "regard[ed] the great interests of agriculture, commerce, and manufactures as so inseparably connected that national measures injurious to either are injurious to all."[60] Whigs favored internal improvements because they wanted to strengthen the bonds of community. William Henry Seward spoke for most Whigs when he explained: "Internal improvement regards the highest possible cultivation of every part of the state, and the perfect development of its resources; the widest possible extension of the territory which can be made tributary to its markets, and the greatest possible diminution of the cost of transportation of persons and property." It was not a matter of securing the prosperity of some at the expense of others. Whiggish Americans imagined a world where virtuous and hardworking men and women might rise to affluence. Consequently, Whigs aggressively pushed for state action to help overcome the limits of geography. As Seward put it: "All such improvements, therefore, rightfully engage the public attention, and will doubtless receive from the legislature the discriminating favor due to their respective merits." As Whigs saw things, infrastructure connected communities, building a greater, shared common culture for all.[61]

Whig support for corporations revealed similar thinking. The Whig vision of America rejected the prevailing view among most Democrats that corporations merely funneled the country's wealth into the hands of a few speculators and capitalists. Instead, Whigs considered public sanction for business an encouragement to the wealthy to take risks and make investments that often benefited a wide swath of people. As Boston Whigs in 1836 saw it, corporations gave common men of modest means the opportunity to "originate and carry on undertakings which, without the power, credit and faculties derived from such acts [i.e., states granting corporate charters], would either not be undertaken at all, or only by individuals of great wealth for their sole benefit." Far from enthroning aristocracy, Daniel Webster explained in 1844, corporations "rather exhibit a convenient and in every respect, desirable mode of investment for all who have, or by the labor can acquire, anything to invest!"[62]

To illustrate the democratic character of corporations, Webster pointed to the Merrimac Mills in Lowell, Massachusetts. Of 390 proprietors, 46 were merchants, 68 women, 52 retirees, 80 administrators, 23 lawyers, 18 physicians, 3 literary institutions, 15 farmers, 40 secretaries, clerks, and students, and 45 mechanics and machinists. Further, the 45 mechanics alone owned $60,000 in stock. To Whig eyes, this impressive figure confirmed the wisdom of legislatures granting corporate charters. Whigs' support for banks and banking drew on their understanding of economic development. Jacksonian Democrats, however, viewed banks and the credit system with distrust and contempt. Few issues illustrated the moral and ideological gap between Whigs and Democrats regarding the purpose of state power more starkly, then, than their wars over banking. Perhaps no such row was more famous or consequential than Andrew Jackson's famous war on the Second Bank of the United States. Indeed, the national bank's destruction motivated middle-class minded Americans to form the Whig Party itself.

Whiggish Americans were almost destined to dislike Andrew Jackson and the values that he seemed to represent. Carried into power in 1828 on a wave of support from new men in new states in the West and the South, Jackson did not so much advocate one set of policies over another as he championed a new political style, a crass appeal to passion and anxiety. That

Fig. 3.4. Robert Cruikshank, *President's Levee; or, All Creation Going to the White House* (London: Saunders & Otley 1841). Aquatint. Prints and Photographs Division, Library of Congress, Washington, DC. "Crowd in front of White House during Andrew Jackson's first inaugural reception in 1829." https://www.loc.gov/item/96521704.

Jackson's first inauguration devolved into a drunken party of well-wishers trashing the White House, as Robert Cruikshank's 1841 *President's Levee* (fig. 3.4) demonstrates, did little to ease Whig suspicions. Cruikshank's dagger-edged satire mocked Jackson as a bumpkin king at the head of a drunken mob (e.g., *levee* in this context echoed the elaborate morning rituals of the French king Louis XIV). As the Supreme Court justice Joseph Story pointed out, speaking for many: "The reign of King Mob seemed triumphant."[63]

Jackson's first term saw its share of rollicking controversies, such as the forced removal of Native Americans from Georgia despite a contrary ruling by John Marshall's Supreme Court, the implementation of the spoils system to reward supporters with public posts while punishing enemies, and the call to end the Electoral College. Of course, where Whigs saw mobs run amok, Democrats saw the state sticking up for the little guy, using its power to confront the growing power of capitalist interests. Yet, for all the heated rhetoric, these dustups paled when compared to the vitriol and acrimony generated by Jackson's war on the national bank.

The antebellum banking system helped establish America as a truly independent nation, as several scholars have shown, because banks supplied a medium of exchange in the form of banknotes and deposits for a young economy that was chronically strangled by shortages of specie (actual gold or silver), money, and credit. Banks also sparked industry, which helped create wealth and an affluent standard of living for many. Consequently, Whigs viewed them as an essential part of their wider system of publicly funded commercial infrastructure. Like schools, bridges, roads, canals, river clearing, and harbor improvement, Whiggish Americans believed that banks would benefit everyone.

Adaptability was antebellum American banks' most important feature. One important study has argued: "One measure of the financial sector's value is how and to what extent it evolves with changing economic conditions. Put in place to perform certain functions under one set of economic circumstances, how did it alter its behavior and service the needs of borrowers as circumstances changed?"[64] One of the chief benefits of the American political system was that each state could and did establish banking systems that reflected local needs and tastes while also enjoying the support, strength, and stability of a national financial institution in the First and later the Second Bank of the United States. Consequently, the flexibility of America's formal banking rules and informal commercial constraints encouraged economic risk taking, which fostered innovation and created opportunities. Further, the various state banking systems reflected their states' particular climate, geography, population density, culture, industrial activity, and agricultural strengths and weaknesses. While each state's banks might take a different form, their overall purpose was the same: to provide the state's citizens with stable currency, flexible credit, and investment capital to promote economic growth.

Above it all sat the Second Bank of the United States (see fig. 3.5). Chartered by Congress for twenty years in 1816, it replaced its predecessor, the First Bank of the United States, which the Jeffersonians had allowed to die in 1811 because they did not believe that the US Constitution allowed such an institution to exist. The Second Bank enjoyed $35 million in capital, far more than the $10 million allotted to the First Bank. The bank's influence was also far greater than that of its forerunner. Indeed, the Second Bank of the United States ultimately boasted twenty-five branches across the growing country, more than triple those of the first bank. The Second

Fig. 3.5. Cephas G. Childs (engraver), *Bank of the United States* (Philadelphia: C. G. Childs, ca. 1828). Engraving after a drawing by Geo. Strickland. Prints and Photographs Division, Library of Congress, Washington, DC. https://www.loc.gov/item/2018654849.

Bank's extensive network also supported America's westward expansion and its economic growth, as several scholars have shown, by extending credit to merchants and farmers, thus financing trade over longer distances and industrial production and agricultural output, and also by moving the money supply around the new country. The bank did not set monetary policy or regulate, hold the reserves of, or act as a lender of last resort for all other financial institutions. "Nonetheless," as Andrew Hill notes, "its prominence as one of the largest US corporations and its branches' broad geographic position in the expanding economy allowed it to conduct a rudimentary monetary policy." Its notes also provided a strong national currency because they were backed by considerable gold reserves.[65]

How did it work? In the course of doing business, the Second Bank of the United States collected the state banks' notes. When its managers wanted to slow growth down, it presented the notes for payment in gold or silver, which shrank the state banks' reserves, curtailing their ability to lend.

Conversely, if its managers wanted to speed growth up, it would simply hold on to the state banks' notes, increasing their reserves, and allowing them to lend more money. Generally, the Second Bank used its power well, balancing liquidity and stability in the growing market economy.[66]

Of course, not everyone saw it that way. Like the millions who regarded him as their champion, Old Hickory saw the world as a vast struggle between the privileged few and the exploited many. Few institutions in antebellum America stank of privilege more than the Second Bank of the United States. Thus, in 1829, when Jackson pointed out that "the charter of the Bank of the United States [would expire] in 1836, and its stock holders [would] most probably apply for a renewal of their privileges," he was not looking to save the institution. He had come to Congress not to debate the matter but to lay out his case for the bank's destruction. "Both the constitutionality and the expediency of the law creating this bank are well questioned by a large portion of our fellow citizens," he coldly informed the gathered members, "and it must be admitted by all that it has failed." Jackson and those who shared his perspective distrusted the national banks because, in their view, it embodied the abuse of power. It was true, as Jackson claimed, that the Bank of the United States *did* enjoy distant, complex, and immense power. "Its operations are so extended and so much detailed," Democratic Virginians growled, "that the eyes of Argus could not reach them." To Jacksonian eyes, the national bank was the ultimate monument to entrenched privilege.[67]

Of course, it is matter of deep historical irony that a figure like Andrew Jackson could ever feel like an outsider. A former general, the conqueror of Alabama's Creeks and the proud Seminoles, the Yankee conquistador of Spanish Florida, a US congressman and senator, and an enormously wealthy planter from Tennessee, he never quite felt like he had arrived. What more he could have done after winning the White House twice no one could say, but he clung to grudges and practiced politics like he practiced war. It was all about destruction, his or his enemies'.

Beyond question, in 1829, the Second Bank of the United States was a powerful commercial institution, one with national reach through its regulatory power and political support. Most Democrats revered Jackson precisely because he "renounced the support of the Bank of the United States, the grand reservoir of the moneyed influence in America, and with it the whole mercenary system." To be fair, "the grand reservoir" was deep. With its capital limit of $35 million, the Second Bank was one of the wealthiest institutions in the country. Worse, at least to the Democratic eyes, 20 percent of that capital, or $7.5 million, belonged to the federal government. Jacksonians viewed the bank's size, wealth, and power with deep suspicion. One Democrat toasted it, warning: "It divides itself like a Polypus, and at each division a monster is created, which, like a Vampyre, preys on the vitals of the Republic." As sole fiscal agent of the United States, the bank held and transferred all US deposits, handled all payments and receipts for all government contracts and transactions, and processed all tax payments. It was also required to pay the government $1.5 million each year as a bonus for using public funds, interest free, in its various private ventures.[68]

The bank's fall is a story quickly told. Andrew Jackson took a hard stance after 1829, refusing to recharter it despite repeated attempts by Nicholas Biddle, the bank's president, to broker a compromise. Henry Clay urged Biddle to submit the recharter request to Congress in 1832 (an election year), calculating that the Jacksonians would blink. Biddle was up for a fight. "This worthy President thinks that because he has scalped Indians and imprisoned Judges, he is to have his way with the Bank," he later described his resolve. "He is mistaken."[69] Given the national bank's popularity, the valuable services it provided, and the seeming imprudence of risking controversy during an election year, this seemed like sound strategy.

Unfortunately for Biddle and the bank, Henry Clay was wrong. Though Congress rechartered the bank in 1832, Jackson vetoed the bill. "It is to be regretted that the rich and powerful too often bend the acts of government to their selfish purposes," he explained. "There are no necessary evils in government. Its evils exist only in its abuses. If it would confine itself to equal protection, and, as Heaven does its rains, shower its favors alike on the high and the low, the rich and the poor, it would be an unqualified blessing. In the act before me there seems to be a wide and unnecessary departure from these just principles." Democrats agreed with Jackson and supported his challenge, often depicting his struggle as grappling with a literal monster (see fig. 3.6). Whigs tried to make 1832's presidential election a referendum on the bank but lost in stinging fashion to Jackson's political machine and popular appeal. Worse, in a fit of pique, Biddle brought on a financial crisis by calling in the bank's loans, ironically proving Jackson's claim that the bank held too much power. "The Bank, Mr. Van Buren, is trying to kill me," he told his wily secretary of state in

Fig. 3.6. Henry R. Robinson, *General Jackson Slaying the Many Headed Monster* (New York: H. R. Robinson, 1836). Lithograph. Prints and Photographs Divisions, Library of Congress, Washington, DC. "A satire on Andrew Jackson's campaign to destroy the Bank of the United States and its support among state banks. Jackson, Martin Van Buren, and Jack Downing struggle against a snake with heads representing the states. Jackson (on the left) raises a cane marked 'Veto' and says, 'Biddle thou Monster Avaunt!! avaount I say! or by the Great Eternal I'll cleave thee to the earth, aye thee and thy four and twenty satellites. Matty if thou art true . . . come on. if thou art false, may the venomous monster turn his dire fang upon thee . . .' Van Buren: 'Well done General, Major Jack Downing, Adams, Clay, well done all. I dislike dissentions beyond every thing, for it often compels a man to play a double part, were it only for his own safety. Policy, policy is my motto, but intrigues I cannot countenance.' Downing (dropping his axe): 'Now now you nasty varmint, be you imperishable? I swan Gineral that are beats all I reckon, that's the horrible wiper wot wommits wenemous heads I guess . . .' The largest of the heads is president of the Bank Nicholas Biddle's, which wears a top hat labeled 'Penn' (i.e. Pennsylvania) and '$35,000,000.' This refers to the rechartering of the Bank by the Pennsylvania legislature in defiance of the administration's efforts to destroy it." https://www.loc.gov/item/2008661279.

1832, "but I shall *kill it.*" And kill it he did. By October1833, Jackson had removed the federal government's deposits, and the bank was liquidated by 1841. As with most things in his public life, Andrew Jackson won.[70]

Yet the consequences of the bank's destruction lingered. Whigs did not believe in the sincerity of Democrats' attack on the bank. They saw not principles in action but power misused. Daniel Webster spoke for most Whigs when he reminded the Senate in 1832: "Sir, no President and no public man ever before advanced such doctrines in the face of the nation."[71] Democrats had struck at a vital American institution, and, in killing the bank, they also wounded public trust. Perhaps antebellum America's great foreign observer, Alexis de Tocqueville, agreed. "Do you think that the people could discern the reasons for his opinion amid the twists and turns of such a difficult question when experienced men hesitated?" he pondered in describing Jackson's victory. "Not at all. But the bank is a great establishment that has an independent existence; the people, who destroy or raise all powers, can do nothing about it, which astonishes them. In the midst of the universal movement of society, the sight of this unmovable point shocks them, and they want to see if they cannot get it going like the rest."[72] For their part, Whigs wondered what limits existed? Jacksonians wrongheaded conceptions of the purpose and scope of state power might lead them to strike the sun if it insulted them. Far from demonizing wealth or those who pursued it, then, Whigs believed that government's purpose was to protect property, punish criminals, and unleash the risk-taking, innovative energy of the broad mass of people so that they might rise too.[73]

For middle-class Whigs, Jacksonians' war on the national bank was disastrous because it stirred one class of Americans against another for political gain. Daniel Webster defended banking as a public good, arguing: "Banks, everywhere, and especially with us, are made for the borrowers. They are made for the good of the many, and not for the good of the few." Casting bankers, merchants, and other businessmen as vultures or parasites reaping huge profits at the supposed expense of common Americans was corrosive to the bonds of social capital needed to win the future. "It is the *poor* man who is *benefited* in the highest degree by the *credit system,*" the *Albany Evening Journal* argued in 1840, "because it is the *poor who need credit.*" Thus, setting one class against another was wrong on the merits. Yes, some wealthy men prospered through banking, speculation, and credit, sometimes through duplicity, malfeasance, or stupidity. And, yes, many men of modest means were ruined by fickle changes in distant markets that often had little to do with their own individual virtue or industry.[74]

Still, Whigs argued that no outcome among the myriad financial possibilities playing out across antebellum America occurred in a vacuum. Banking and finance were linked to labor and agriculture. John Pendleton Kennedy argued that Whig policies most benefited the common man by "identifying him with the prosperity and happiness of the nation, by causing him to feel that in promoting that prosperity he promotes his own." Society was no machine composed of interchangeable parts that governments could grease, repair, or remove without consequences, and the institutions that Jacksonians attacked promoted prosperity. "Sustain the position of American capital and labor," Calvin Colton urged, "that every man may be secure of the fair reward of his exertions, however humble his birth and calling." Whigs further argued that, taken in the aggregate, far more Americans enjoyed rising incomes and higher standards of living thanks to the opportunities provided by "monster" banks and their allies in business and capital investment than would have without them. On this point, their views of the proper application of state power came back to a bourgeois understanding of promoting and preserving community.[75]

At bottom, the Whigs' America was an ongoing attempt to create a better world, one built on social institutions such as churches, schools, and voluntary associations, yet Whigs looked to the state to help American individuals prosper and thrive. They sought to break down or at least mitigate the more degenerative tendencies of localism and replace them with new nationally minded loyalties and perspectives. They embraced a political gospel of self-restraint, improvement, and collaboration. Their faith in social institutions could also blind them to their potential abuses. Money and power made awfully cozy bedfellows, and the virtuous did not always manage either. Yet Whigs clung to their belief that, in the long run, their middle-class vision would win out and create better lives for more people.

In Whigs' view, finally, the state grew from American society, which was itself dependent on virtuous middle-class families. "The family, religious association, and local community," Whigs might echo one modern scholar, "are essentially prior to the individual and are the indispensable supports of belief and conduct."[76] Thus, even when sharp disagreements arose, they argued, public deliberation and discussion remained socially useful because they drew disconnected individuals together in a community of the mind. Their understanding of the proper size, scope, and purpose of the state was meant to foster individual and social progress with an eye on the future. Though they admired America's founding generation, by and large they wanted to leave the past behind.

## 4

# The Past

> In such condition, there is no place for Industry . . . no account of Time; no Arts; no Letters; no Society; and which is worst of all, continual fear, and danger of violent death; And the life of man solitary, poor, nasty, brutish, and short.
>
> Thomas Hobbes

American Whigs were forward looking, valuing progress over nostalgia. Yet Whigs also represented America's first middle-class political culture, and their shared need for prudence meant that the past still mattered. However, when they considered the deep past, they typically did not ponder America's colonial experience. Instead, they looked back to the Middle Ages and saw a barbaric world. For them, the past's barbarism meant a lack of self-control, prudence, and restraint. They often longed for community in an age of individualism, but they were not nostalgic for thatch-hutted villages, privileged aristocrats, dissolute clergy, or lordly kings.

Whigs did not share Democrats' dreams of a simpler time because, owing to their attitudes toward the past, they saw in it a world that was everything they did not want to be. Consequently, they believed that contemporary life in antebellum America was better along almost every line of comparison. Whigs saw history as a progressive story of improvement in the human condition. They were not nostalgic, but they were often sentimental, and their sentimentality was most poignant concerning America's underlying purpose and meaning. In the United States in the three decades before the Civil War, they argued, individualism came of age, and Americans' grand experiment in self-government offered the world something new, something important, and, most vital of all, something good. The past was, on that view, best understood as the slow, steady building of a bourgeois society based on legitimate authority. In the founding of the

United States, Whigs saw the defeat of barbarism, the firm establishment of the rule of law, and the triumph of self-determinism.

## Barbarism

When Whigs considered the deep past, they often looked to the Middle Ages.[1] The further back their minds wandered, the more barbarous a world they saw. But what does it mean to say that something is barbaric or barbarous? At its most essential, the charge of barbarism indicted past peoples in terms of both taste and behavior.[2] While the past certainly boasted men and women committed to faith, hope, love, courage, and justice, middle-class Whigs believed that most also lacked temperance and prudence, which they argued made the other virtues work.[3] Further, Whig political culture was built on a bourgeois or middle-class worldview. Thus, given their outlook, temperament, and manners, Whigs' attitudes toward the past confirmed their belief that the slow, steady movement of people in Western civilizations—namely, Great Britain and the independent United States—from the countryside to the town was a good thing, so long as those shifts were accompanied by the cultivation of appropriate virtues. Indeed, as Whigs saw it, without prudence and temperance, the piling of people into cities only exacerbated problems of disorder. Consequently, they valued the development of a middle-class mind-set above all. And, because the past was neither prudent nor temperate, it was barbarous.

Antebellum America was not divided into city Whigs and country Democrats, at least not in the way many scholars suggest. Indeed, the United States remained an overwhelmingly rural place until after the Civil War, and no political party could be competitive if its base resided solely in towns or in cities. Thus, it was a shared worldview or outlook that mattered most. No matter where they lived, most Whigs exemplified the bourgeois tendency to link their interests through associations and institutions and work together to develop their villages into towns and their towns into cities. Conversely, most Jacksonian Democrats tended to long for the freedom that they believed individual farms and country estates provided and the rustic trust that they argued city life compromised. Whigs believed that Jacksonian nostalgia was pointless. Plain middle-class prudence told them it was better to build for the future than to pine for the past.[4]

But what was prudence? Most Whigs agreed that prudence meant practical wisdom and good judgment. In the deepest sense, middle-class prudence was built on the ancient Greek notion of *phronesis,* or φρόνησις, which meant "wisdom," "sensibility," "discretion," and "pragmatism."[5] But *prudence* was a virtue in the old, rich sense of the word and carried a value beyond mere commonsense practicality. "Prudence is the virtue of the senses," Emerson reminded readers in 1841. "It is the science of appearances."[6] Thus, the vast majority of antebellum Whigs, most of whom had no knowledge of Greek ethical philosophy or any inclination to learn, still admired prudence. For example, what Horace Greeley objected to when it came to the Reverend Edward Irving in 1840 was that he "sinned so enormously against prudence, and indeed against all sanity of mind." Indeed, Whigs believed that foresight, caution, planning, and a practical understanding of what was possible, especially in politics and society, were all part of a proper middle-class mind-set. "How grateful is the task of watching and noting the evidences of returning prosperity," Baltimore Whigs noted, interpreting Martin Van Buren's defeat with this understanding in mind, "after so many years of painful duty in recording the losses, disasters, and causes for gloom which an imprudent course had subjected us to." Prudent people strove for self-improvement through study, reflection, and restraint. To Whig eyes, Jacksonians were mired in the worst aspects of the past because they seemed to flout all these principles with abandon. The development of societies where free individuals exercised self-control and practiced prudence was vital to Whigs' progressive understanding of history.[7]

In stark contrast to their hopeful reading of the future, Whigs first believed that the past was barbaric because people living during the Middle Ages were not prudent. Civil life in these dead centuries was marred by "dark passion and debasing crimes," Sarah Josepha Hale argued in 1840, and a lack restraint that "destroy[s] the fine edge of the soul, and eat[s] it, like a corroding cancer." Such people bore the "mark of rudeness and incivilization," nodded another Whig polemicist in 1841. "A purely savage people live only in the present moment. The satisfactions of immediate wants, the enjoyment of the passing hour, make up the sum total of their existence." In the centuries after Rome crumbled, then, Whigs thought that men and women yielded to the basest instincts of human nature, with nothing but a licentious clergy and a libertine aristocracy to curb their excesses with the fear of hell or the lash.[8]

Shuffling along from field to parish and back again during those dark centuries, Europeans were ignorant and ignominious. In this sense, *barbarism* meant "existing outside time." Barbarous people lived only in the present, thinking little of the past and almost nothing of the future. Of them Whigs believed: "They have no monuments, and they leave none. To them, the deeds of forefathers, the exploits of other times, the good or the evil that marked an earlier day, afford no examples and impart no instruction."[9] Time simply happens to these sorts of people, and such an experience left no sense of history, purpose, or meaning with which to understand the broader world. This was a world of immediacy, one based on violence, war, stupidity, sloth, pleasure, and poverty. "Amid these scenes of horror," a Whig editor in New York informed readers in 1838, "intemperance, dissipation, and profligacy were carried to the highest pitch. Forests sprung up and covered entire districts; and wolves, and other beasts of prey took possession of the deserted haunts of men."[10] For Whigs, the deep past was a barbaric wilderness where the great mass of men obeyed only the carnal laws of lust and power and no fixed principles guided their behavior. Indeed, one of their chief complaints about their Democratic opponents was that they seemed to want to drag America back to the cruel vagaries of bygone eras. Louisville Whigs scoffed in 1849: "Locofoco principles have perpetually shifted and changed about like the combinations of the kaleidoscope, presenting a series of unexpected views, first one thing and its opposite, until they have by turns smiled and frowned on or reflected almost every possible line of policy." Worse, Jacksonian Democrats seemed happy about it.[11]

As Whigs understood things, beating back barbarism was about steady development along broad lines of morality and intellect, not simply raising living standards or securing technological and industrial advances. "How many youthful minds," Henry Clay pondered while celebrating American education, "have been rescued from ignorance, vice, and ruin?" It was about the way in which people saw their world. American Whigs certainly believed that everyday life was improving, especially when compared with the past. To disagree on this point, Whigs like Calvin Colton believed, was "to oppose the march of the civilization." Paradoxically, they also believed that the very individualism that was breaking down the past's parochial narrowness was also eroding the bonds of community that held societies together. Democrats were "avaricious, selfish, and mean," Connecticut Whigs urged one another in 1843: "It is seen in the meanness of their dwelling, in the parsimoniousness of their style of living, the niggardliness of their public improvement, the want of regard for that which constitutes the ultimatum, the refinement of society." Whig sentimentalism mirrored Jacksonian nostalgia in its shared longing for community. The crucial difference was that Jacksonians pined for a lost world that would not return while Whigs yearned for a future yet to occur.[12]

Whigs' reading of history depended on their belief that white middle-class America marked the culmination of the centuries-long rise of the individualistic bourgeoisie. American prosperity represented "true greatness," Horace Greeley explained in 1840, and was the world's "beau ideal, the height of sublimity, the union of grandeur and repose." Along with most antebellum Americans, Whigs believed that the Western world turned toward modernity with the Protestant Reformation. Accordingly, they rarely viewed the years before the English break with Rome favorably. "Rude, rustic, and misshapen," claimed the Whiggish *National Magazine* in 1839, "the middle ages have little to boast of." Even more striking still, when Whigs wrote, talked, or thought about this era, they often did so in terms of darkness and light. Catholic priestcraft and popular superstition—often interchangeable in Whig thinking about the past—conspired to hold the world in darkness.[13]

*Medieval* even served as a byword for graft, corruption, greed, and the abuses of patronage in antebellum Whig political rhetoric. Edward Williams Clay, a New York Whig, satirized this view in his 1852 lithograph *The Seven Stages of the Office Seeker* (see fig. 4.1). A biting mockery of the Whig belief that Democrats abused patronage through corruption in New York State politics, *The Seven Stages* is based on the medieval theme "the life and ages of man." Famously detailed in Shakespeare's *As You Like It*, the ages in the life of a medieval man included the infant, the schoolboy, the lover, the soldier, the justice, the Pantalone, and the dotard, the latter staggered under the prospect of death. As the character Jacques explains:

> All the world's a stage,
> And all the men and women merely players.
> They have their exits and their entrances,
> And one man in his time plays many parts,
> His acts being seven ages. (2.7.146)

Fig. 4.1. J. Childs (lithographer) and Edward Williams Clay (artist). *The Seven Stages of the Office Seeker* ([New York]: J. Childs, [1852]). Lithograph. Prints and Photographs Division, Library of Congress, Washington, DC. "A satire on patronage and corruption in New York State politics, based on the medieval theme, perpetuated in American folk art, of the 'life and ages of man.' Here the seven stages are illustrated as key points in the life and career of a political hack. At each stage the figure occupies a different step of a pyramid, under which is shown his metaphorical counterpart in the animal kingdom. According to Elizabeth Sears the compositional device of a stepped pyramid is used in this context as early as the sixteenth century. Here, the author gives a corresponding epigram for each stage. Clay, a Whig, appears to incorporate in his rendition of the theme an indictment of the patronage policies of the Democrats in New York, controlled almost continuously since 1828 by presidents loyal to that party. Former Democratic governor of New York and later president Martin Van Buren appears as 'the Govenor' in vignette number three, 'Begging for Office.' Under Van Buren's administration, the Custom House, here the office seeker's center of power, was the focus of Democratic corruption in New York City. The seven stages proceed from left to right. 1. 'Treating'—the candidate in a saloon toasts supporters. 'He proves to thirsty loafers he's the man, / And drowns their judgment in the flowing can.' Below, a fox eyes a cock on a fence. 2. 'Stumping'—the candidate is surrounded by supporters, before a banner 'Regular Nominations' and a weather vane crowned by a liberty cap. 'Then on the Stump he takes his station, / The purest patriot in the nation.' Below, a fox at a lectern or pulpit is cheered by geese. 3. 'Begging for Office'—'Next we see him stand before the Govenor's face, / And crouching like a spaniel for a place.' A begging dog appears below. 4. 'In Office'—The candidate strides past the U.S. Custom House oblivious of two supplicant gentlemen. 'His object gained, he spurns the common herd, / Nor deigns to applicants a single word.' Here is portrayed a turkey in full plumage, two rural cottages beyond. 5. 'Out of Office'—Hands in pockets he walks in a storm. 'But now alas! are Fortune's favors fled; / Too lazy grown he scorns to work for bread.' Below appears a scrawny dog in a barren landscape. 6. 'Exit'—The office seeker hangs from a tree. 'A hanger on, twas thus his life he past. / And ends his days by hanging on at last.' Below are a skull and crossbones and a carriage bound for 'Potter's Field.' 7. 'Coroner's Inquest'—'Now twelve wise men, accounting for his death, / Show how a rope may stop a mortal's breath.' Several men in an interior ponder the unfortunate's body. Below, a group of owls crowd around a dead horse." https://www.loc.gov/item/2004665351.

In Clay's 1852 satire, the seven stages are shown as crucial moments in the life and career of a political hack. At each stage, the huckster dwells on a different step of a pyramid while, underneath, his metaphoric twin in the animal kingdom is shown. Clay was a partisan Whig and, in his take on the medieval theme, offered a scorching indictment of Democrats' patronage policies in New York, controlled almost continuously since 1828 by men loyal to Jackson's party. Indeed, the former Democratic governor of New York (and later president) Martin Van Buren appears as the Governor in the third vignette, "Begging for Office." Under Van Buren's administration, the customhouse, shown here as the office seeker's center of power, was, in Whig eyes anyway, the focus of Democratic corruption in New York City. The medieval world's barbarism offered political codes for satire that Whigs appreciated on many levels.

Religion offered another potent source for Whig political rhetoric because Whigs believed that the Protestant Reformation represented a positive break with barbarism. If not for Luther's principled dissent and the rise of reformed Christianity, the *American Whig Review* explained, "the world would not yet have witnessed the lapse of the dark ages." Whigs dismissed the Catholic hierarchy—both the clergy and the nobility—as indifferent to profligacy and hedonism because these things made people easier to control. Again and again, Whigs described this age as one of darkness, savagery, and night. But for the dawn of Protestant Christianity and the English settlement of the New World, Whigs believed, "the somber shadows would still have rested over mankind and the lore of early ages been unrescued from the womb of the past."[14] And, in Whigs' view, this stunting of human potential was among the past's most grievous sins.

Whigs tied the emergence of values such as restraint, discretion, and discipline to the rise of Protestantism. They valued progress in stark terms and did not want to go backward. "The battle for the souls of the world," said New York Whigs in 1841, "lies between the Roman Catholic and the Protestant."[15] Along with the varieties of European Enlightenment that followed, the sixteenth-century Protestant dissent unleashed individualism on the world. For Whigs, this was an admirable achievement. Where in the world, many asked, were people prospering and Protestants or Protestant values not ascendant? "The Czar is fully occupied in keeping the barbarous nations beneath him still barbarized," one Boston Whig editor wryly reveled in a heady rush of Anglo-American xenophobia. "The oriental empire is already gone to its grave, and a few hundred British troops master the Pacha of Egypt. Brahminist, Buddhist, and Mahometan alike bend before the Saxon Protestant."[16] Whigs gloried in these achievements and saw in them evidence that Americans shared in the promise of history's ever onward and upward trajectory. "And do we hear mean talk of the revival of Popery?" Whigs scoffed. In Whiggish eyes, Catholics remained trapped in the clutches of a dark medieval past, and the Church of Rome offered the world little beyond a return to barbarism. Before Americans would kneel before barbarous priests, "THOR may as soon try to revive."[17]

Whigs believed that past people's lack of prudence was also demonstrated by their failure to cultivate manners and propriety. Calvin Colton spoke for most Whigs, arguing that violence and "war [were] the trade of barbarians." Aggression was the central trait of savages. "The brutes that lack discourse of reason are without [manners]," the *American Whig Review* agreed in 1848. They seek to interact only "through the various blind instinct [*sic*] with which they are endowed." The Whigs' view held that individuals who would not or could not react to their world with anything save brute aggression belonged in the past: "They have no presiding consciousness, no sense of position, no respect for character, no ideas of propriety, grace, or beauty." All these ills stemmed first from a lack of self-control. As Whigs understood it, this was the world of the Middle Ages, and Americans must not regress. In this sense, at least, Whigs sought freedom from the past.[18]

Of course, a glaring example of historical irony was the accommodation that typically forward-looking Whigs made for black chattel slavery. Certainly, Whiggish Americans felt a deep disquiet with the obvious barbarity that slavery required. Abraham Lincoln explained in 1854: "My ancient faith teaches me that 'all men are created equal;' and that there can be no moral right in connection with one man's making a slave of another." Far more than Democrats, Whigs pondered abolition's possibilities, and many searched for a way out that did not end in either race or civil war. "Slavery is founded in the selfishness of man's nature—opposition to it is in his love of justice," Mr. Lincoln quietly urged his audience in Peoria, Illinois, concerned with the growing violence in Kansas and Nebraska. "These principles are an eternal antagonism; and when brought into collision so fiercely, as slavery extension brings them, shocks, and throes, and convulsions must ceaselessly follow. Repeal the Missouri Compromise—repeal all compromises—repeal the declaration of independence—repeal all past history, you still can not repeal human nature. It still will be the abundance of man's heart, that slavery extension is wrong; and out of the abundance of his heart, his mouth will continue to speak."[19] Yet slavery endured throughout the era, for the most part with Whigs' acceptance and, at least among the southern Whigs, their hardy support.

In many ways, Georgia's Alexander Stephens demonstrated the southern Whig view of slavery well. In most respects, Stephens was a typical middle-class Whig, North or South. Born in east-central Georgia, near the South Carolina state line, he supported public funding for education, infrastructure, and strong banks and opposed the Mexican-American War. Although he condemned the slave trade and balked at the idea that slavery was a positive good, he reflected most Whiggish southerners' views on race control. Southern whites refused to countenance any social system that did not guarantee their racial supremacy. "It was inconceivable to him that any system other than slavery could ensure social stability in the South," one of his better biographers points out. "'Truth,' he had stated in one 1845 speech, 'is fixed, indelible, immutable, and eternal.' Black inferiority and subordination to the white race, albeit regrettable, were 'stern necessity' because for Stephens they were eternal truths."[20] Accommodating people like Stephens was essential for any antebellum political party that hoped to enjoy any sort of national success. Thus, the need for unity meant that contradictory, often uncomfortable compromises were required.

How could a political vision that was so concerned with barbarism tolerate such an obvious strand of it in their midst? As was his wont, Lincoln tried to reconcile this inconsistency in his moving eulogy to his fallen political hero Henry Clay after the great Kentuckian died in 1852. "He [Clay] ever was, on principle and in feeling, opposed to slavery," the Illinois Whig noted. "The very earliest, and one of the latest public efforts of his life, separated by a period of more than fifty years, were both made in favor of gradual emancipation of the slaves in Kentucky." Whigs like Lincoln and Clay supported emancipation schemes that would end the peculiar institution slowly, over time. "He did not perceive," Lincoln continued, "that on a question of human right, the negroes were to be excepted from the human race." In contrast to many Democrats, Whigs did not carve out some lower rung on the evolutionary ladder to explain away slavery in terms of ridiculous pseudoscience. "And yet Mr. Clay was the owner of slaves," Lincoln conceded. "Cast into life where slavery was already widely spread and deeply seated, he did not perceive, as I think no wise man has perceived, how it could be at once eradicated, without producing a greater evil, even to the cause of human liberty itself. His feeling and his judgment, therefore, ever led him to oppose both extremes of opinion on the subject."[21] Clay mirrored most Whiggish thinking in his belief that any movement against slavery that vowed immediate liberation would spark a civil war. Therefore, Whigs looked the other way from the barbarism in their midst to maintain the Union, in the hope that, come what may, later generations would somehow find the wisdom, courage, and resolve that they lacked to extend the full meaning of America's founding creed to *all* its children.

In the broadest sense, Whigs did not merely want to escape the past. Instead, Whiggery promised to conquer it as well. The dread of barbarism was a crucial part of Whiggish Americans' understanding of themselves. To be bourgeois meant, by definition, *not* to be savage. It meant that a man or a woman wanted to be and was prudent, temperate, and self-controlled.[22] Whiggery became the political creed of Americans who embraced modernity's possibilities and rejected the romantic pastoralism of their Democratic neighbors. Whigs believed that Democrats failed to grasp the true meaning of the United States, which in their view was a land where order tempered liberty and material development and moral development were within the reach of all who were willing to work for them.

Barbarism's influence on Whiggish thinking about the past is also evident in the art that Whigs enjoyed. Like political speeches and religious sermons, art often tells us as much about the audience as it does about the artist. For example, Thomas Cole's series of paintings *The Course of Empire* (1833–1836) offers a poignant window into a cyclic understanding of history that appealed to many antebellum Americans. As Cole himself explained: "The philosophy of my subject is drawn from the history of the past, wherein we see how nations have risen from the savage state to that of power and glory, and then fallen, and become extinct." Like most of his countrymen, Cole linked the fate of nations to the character of their people and believed his *Course of Empire* was ultimately about human nature. As he wrote a friend about the idea behind the paintings: "A series of pictures might be painted that should illustrate the history of a natural scene, as well as be an epitome of Man,—showing the natural changes of landscape, and those effected by man in his progress from barbarism to civilization—to

Fig. 4.2. Thomas Cole, *Course of Empire: The Arcadian or Pastoral State* (second in the series) (1834), oil on canvas (39¼ x 63¼ inches), negative #6046c, ID 1858. 2, Gift of the New York Gallery of Fine Arts New York Gallery of the Fine Arts. Digital image created by Oppenheimer Editions.

luxury—to the vicious state, or state of destruction—and to the state of ruin and desolation."[23] Cole intended his audience to view the paintings as one piece. More than Whigs, Democrats tended to share Cole's cyclic understanding of the past. As they saw it, rapid commercial development only hastened civilization's self-wrought destruction. Consequently, they fought to maintain Thomas Jefferson's vision of an agrarian yeoman American Republic—represented by Cole in the second painting in the *Course of Empire* series, *The Arcadian or Pastoral State* (see fig. 4.2)—in the face of modernity's rising tide.[24] Whigs countered that that was impossible. The modern world was not simply a development that could be endured or ignored; it was an ongoing social, political, cultural, economic, and moral transformation of the way in which people thought, acted, and related to each other. Americans were not simply part of modernity; they had helped bring it about. And for Whigs that was a good thing.

Whiggish people looked to build, maintain, and improve America as demonstrated in the third painting in the *Course of Empire* series, *The Consummation of Empire* (see fig. 4.3). Whigs would agree with Cole himself,

Fig. 4.3. Thomas Cole, *Course of Empire: Consummation* (third in the series) (1836), oil on canvas (51¼ x 76 inches), negative #6047c; ID 1858.3; Gift of the New York Gallery of Fine Arts New York Gallery of the Fine Arts. Digital image created by Oppenheimer Editions.

who, in explaining the painting's purpose, noted: "The third must be a noonday,—a great city girding the bay, gorgeous piles of architecture, bridges, aqueducts, temples—the port crowded with vessels—splendid processions, &c.—all that can be combined to show the fullness of prosperity."[25] In summoning visions of ancient Rome, Whigs were embracing a partisan vision of American destiny, one in which "all that can be combined to show the fullness of prosperity" existed in ordered harmony. Whigs argued that history did not necessarily have to be cyclic *if* Americans committed themselves to bourgeois principles of prudence and self-control. Democrats did not believe that Whig plans would conquer history. Instead, they worried that Whigs worked to hasten the triumph of wealth, working to enthrone a new plutocracy that would be every bit as arbitrary, capricious, and cruel as the worst examples of the near and distant past. The human journey from the darkness of barbarism to the light of civilization was a progressive story that culminated, Whigs insisted past such objections, with the founding of the United States.

America existed to conquer the worst of the past. It is difficult to overstate the optimism Whigs felt in this regard. So far as it went, Democrats shared Whigs' robust love for the founding generation too. Yet Whigs' bourgeois desire for self-mastery was important because it offered a clear break from the past's barbaric disorder. Indeed, Whigs saw a direct link between the historical prevalence of monarchy and the social instability of past peoples. It was the king's laws, courts, and soldiers that maintained social order, prevented widespread violence, and protected property because a barbarous people could not be trusted to control their appetites or master their vices. Crucial to Whigs' view of history, then, was their fear of monarchy and Catholic priestcraft and their almost sacred understanding of the American nation.

## Authority

A deep distrust of executive power formed the heart of the political culture of the Whigs. This suspicion grew out of their attitudes toward the past and their disdain for what they saw as illegitimate authority. In general, authority in antebellum America was trustworthy precisely because it privileged valid republican power. Consequently, Whigs derided unearned privileges such as those enjoyed by hereditary aristocracies or corrupt clerics because they believed that power, prestige, and wealth ought to reflect merit. In a general way, Democrats might have agreed, but they feared that these tendencies were more likely to rise out of corrupt moneyed interests than a few priests or an occasional vigorous presidency. Conversely, the name *Whig* itself was a deliberate effort to clothe Whiggish partisanship in the country-party rhetoric of the American Revolution. For Whigs, the past proved that the potential for political abuse rose in direct proportion to the amount of power conferred, and they argued that those tendencies were best checked by cooperation and vigilance.

Thus, Whigs did not trust any one individual to wield broad power safely. Instead, they stressed the importance of legislatures as the true guardians of American republicanism. As they saw things, the past offered numerous examples of the latent tyranny endemic to undeserved privilege. Aristocracy and priestcraft were the most obvious. Both were objectionable because they controlled people's lives in ways that Whigs believed were antiquated, and, thus, neither belonged in America.

Whigs' scorn for monarchy was an overwhelming part of their initial opposition to Andrew Jackson and his successor, Martin Van Buren. Whigs usually grounded their dissent in a partisan reading of the past. "Republics do not degenerate into Aristocracies," the *Ohio State Journal* pointed out in 1842, "but into Monarchies. Aristocracy comes afterwards, as a necessary appendage." History's cycle might be broken in America but only if the cycles were properly recognized. Thus: "Jackson and Van Buren were the first who undertook to form the will of the people, and control their representatives." Whigs were certain that they would not be the last. Consequently, Henry Clay and most notable Whigs of the era often reminded voters of the warnings that they believed history offered regarding the dangers of illegitimate executive power. At a dinner party in his hometown of Lexington, Kentucky, Clay hit this theme early and often. "If . . . the Chief Magistrate, as soon as he is clothed with power, proceeds to exercise it so as to minister to his passions, and to gratify his favorites," he argued, clearly referring to Andrew Jackson, "that Chief Magistrate, for the time being, is in fact, if not in form, a monarch." The reason? "In a monarchy, all power and authority, all offices and honors, proceed from the monarch. His interests, his caprices and his passions, influence and control the destinies of the kingdom." Clay believed that America's glory was in throwing off just this sort of yoke, and his view was typical of the era's most important Whig statesmen. Indeed, Daniel Webster echoed the Great Compromiser when in 1847 he explained that monarchists were always "those who hold that violence is strength." In contrast to republics, then, monarchies did not rely on the consent of the governed. Instead, Whigs believed, history demonstrated kings' use of swift, arbitrary violence to keep the masses in line. Most troubling for them, therefore, was Jackson's bloody personal history and comfort with arbitrary power, which seemed to echo the very worst of the past.[26]

These views were not limited to prominent Whig politicians. Indeed, Whigs' historical fear of illegitimate authority appeared in state and local newspapers as well as in national magazines and periodicals. "It cannot but be clear to every observing man," Ohio Whigs explained in 1838, "that the main point of difference between the Administration and the Opposition is on the subject of Executive power." These hardy Buckeyes worried that the precedents established by Andrew Jackson and his chosen successor, Martin Van Buren, were following the disturbing trend of historical despotism. "Taking advantage of public distress," Columbus Whigs agreed with their brethren in Troy, "he [i.e., Jackson] forced them to submit to his will in one thing, and thereby purchased the power of dictating another." From rewarding lackeys and punishing foes, to using power for power's sake, as Whigs saw matters Jackson was guilty of all the worst offenses of kings. They believed that the past spoke out against him. "It is the old strife in short," the Ohio *Investigator and Expositor* explained, "Whig and Tory, the People vs. the Monarch,—the People holding *on,* the Monarch *taking* hold." These Ohioans were not alone.[27]

Across the country, many bourgeois Whigs of the 1830s looked to the past and wondered whether they were worthy of their namesakes. Horace Greeley's *New-Yorker* argued that bold talk ought to inform bold action, asking: "Who would dare to leap on the moss-grown and frowning ramparts of Monarchy, and pluck down its blood-red flag?" And in 1840 the *American Monthly Magazine* also gave thanks to God while predicting the fall of the "Jackson Dynasty," urging Whigs: "We cannot doubt that, though hours of gloom may intervene, the dawn of our political regeneration is at hand." This rhetoric carried the tone and tenor of religious deliverance as Whigs across the country celebrated the symbolic toppling of Jacksonian "monarchs." Whigs played on this theme early and often in their campaign polemics and posters in the 1840 race for the White House. In *The North Bend Farmer and His Visitors* (see fig. 4.4), a highly partisan distortion of the supposedly insidious Democratic love of wealth, power, and influence is set against an image of the allegedly plain-living Whig presidential candidate, William Henry Harrison. In Whig eyes, the insidious and high-living Van Buren and his henchmen suffer by comparison to Harrison, who is portrayed in buckskins and standing near a plough on his Ohio farm. The monarchical party is fancier, wealthier, and more effete than poor Harrison, but his virtues are those of thrift, industry, and prudence. It did not matter to most Whigs that his background was actually rooted in Virginia affluence and that Van Buren worked his way up from his father's modest inn in Kinderhook, New York, to the presidency. Nor did they pause to consider that most Democrats did not really want to create an American monarchy, despite their personal attachments to Andrew Jackson. No, what mattered to Whiggish Americans was that Van Buren was their great antagonist's chosen successor, a prince in the line of succession who savored partisan politics and on whose overthrow hung the fate of American liberty and freedom. Overwrought, sometimes hysterical partisan politics did not begin in the age of Jackson and Clay—and certainly did not end there either. Whigs relished Van Buren's 1840 defeat because, to them, it meant rolling back monarchy. The *American Whig Review* was similarly rhapsodic after Zachary Taylor won the White House in 1848, rejoicing: "The spirit of monarchy has been exorcised from the body politic, and the Republic has been made whole." In habits, outlook, and imagination, middle-class Whigs shared a historical opposition to executive encroachment. What was it about monarchy that specifically drew Whigs ire?[28]

First, Whigs objected to the arbitrariness of monarchy. "The whigs of 1840 stand where the republicans of 1798 stood," Henry Clay explained to a throng of onlookers in Hanover, Virginia, just after Independence Day in 1840, "battling for liberty, for the people, for free institutions, against power, against executive encroachments, against monarchy." Power in these terms was the antithesis of everything Whigs believed the founding generation fought and sacrificed to build. "We are republicans," a New York Whig editor agreed. "We do not want a monarchy disguised under republican forms." Whigs thought that that meant a government "free from arbitrary interposition and the corrupt blandishments of the Executive." Democrats might counter that executive power had to be strong to limit the corrupting influence of concentrated wealth. In contrast, Whigs believed that executives were more susceptible to corruption than were legislatures because power was concentrated in far fewer hands.[29]

As Whigs viewed the past, kings always vaguely pointed to heaven's sanction to justify their power. "Time was when the divine right of kings was the fundamental axiom in the political creed," the *American Quarterly Review* reminded readers in 1834. "'I am the state,' was then the self-consequent boast of the monarch." Whigs balked at this idea because human nature was so flawed. Once secure on his throne, to whom would such a ruler answer? "Holding his authority, not at the will of the people, nor for them on the grounds of expediency, but by the ordinance of God, in and for his own person, [the King] looked upon himself as the source and final cause of all his maxims or policy and measures of government." To Whig eyes, that was too much power with which to trust any one man. In a republic, moreover, the people were everything. In a monarchy, the monarch was everything.[30]

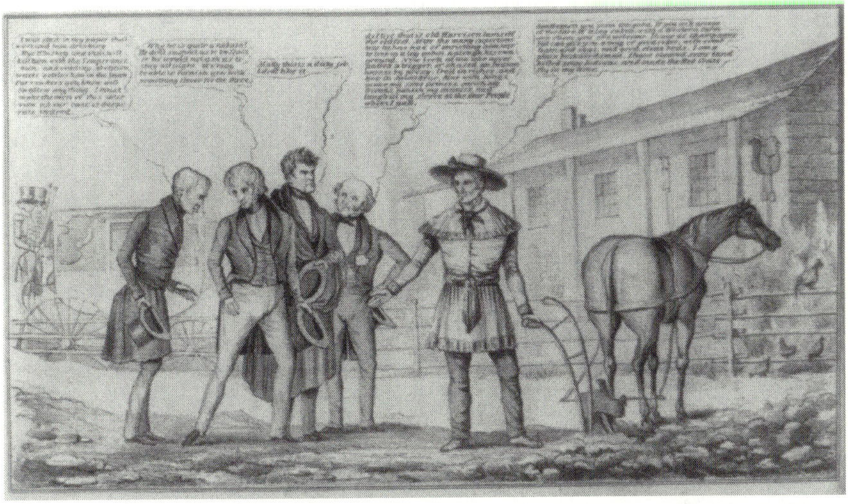

Fig. 4.4. Henry Dacre and Henry R. Robinson, *The North Bend Farmer and His Visitors* (New York and Washington, DC: H. R. Robinson, 1840). Lithograph. Prints and Photographs Division, Library of Congress, Washington, DC. "A slanderous portrayal of Democratic tactics against Whig presidential candidate William Henry Harrison. The supposedly insidious and high-living Van Buren and his minions suffer by comparison to the Whig candidate, here portrayed as rustic and plainspoken. Harrison is shown dressed in buckskins and standing near a plough on his Ohio farm. A contingent of Democrats have arrived in an elegant coach at left. The visitors are (left to right) Francis Preston Blair, Amos Kendall, John Calhoun, and Martin Van Buren. Blair remarks to Kendall, 'I will state in my paper that we found him drinking Rye Whiskey and that will kill him with the Temperance men and reading Abolition tracts settles him in the South. Our readers you know will swallow anything. I must make the most of this interview as our case is desperate indeed.' Kendall responds, 'Why he is quite a natural. He dont suspect us to be Spies . . . We may be able to furnish you with something clever for the Globe [i.e., Blair's newspaper the *Washington Globe*].' Calhoun protests to Van Buren, 'Matty this is a dirty job. I don't like it.' Van Buren says, 'As I live that is old Harrison himself the old fool. After the many opportunities he has had of enriching himself to live in a log cabin and plough his own ground. Now look at me who never pulled a trigger, or chased an Indian unless by proxy: I roll in riches, and live in splendour, dine with kings, make my sons princes, enrich my friends, punish my enemies, and laugh in my sleeve at the dear People whom I gull.' Harrison greets them with, 'Gentlemen you seem fatigued, If you will accept of the fare of a log cabin, with a Western farmer's cheer, you are welcome. I have no champagne but can give you a mug of good cider, with some ham and eggs, and good clean beds. I am a plain backwoodsman, I have cleared some land, killed some Indians, and made the Red Coats fly in my time.'" https://www.loc.gov/item/2008661371.

American Whigs were more excited about the future than afraid of it. Their understanding of the past undergirded their belief that human nature tended to be violent, stupid, and self-serving when left alone. That is why they often refused to leave people alone. They promoted voluntary associations such as temperance societies, lyceums, and literary clubs because they wanted to bring people together and encourage self-improvement. They were not grumpy cynics who dismissed mankind as hopeless; rather, they argued that history showed that individual restraint was crucial to a good society. Whigs had a broad, old sense of community and believed that the state should promote individuals' and broader groups' efforts to work together. Indeed, their historical appreciation for human weakness and their need to seek improvement also led them to embrace conviviality, comity, and compromise. "Let him who elevates himself above humanity," most Whigs would agree with Henry Clay, "above its weaknesses, its infirmities, its wants, its necessities, say, if he pleases, I never will compromise, but let no one who is not above the frailties of our common nature disdain compromise."[31] In a broad way, Whigs' entire political program can be understood as a vast, hopeful effort to knit isolated Americans together on the basis of their reading of the past. They were deeply optimistic about America's possibilities, so long as individual Americans developed self-control. Ultimately, Whiggery appealed to those Americans seeking achievement, community, and meaning through collaborative effort and self-control in a world growing more and more impersonal.

# 5

# The Future

"For I know the plans I have for you," declares the Lord, "plans to prosper you and not to harm you, plans to give you hope and a future."

Jer. 29:11 (NIV)

Tomorrow lurks in us, the latency to be all that was not achieved before.

Loren Eiseley

Whig attitudes toward the future were infused with deep optimism. Most Whigs agreed with Calvin Colton that America represented "the very greatest hope that the world has for future progress." Consequently, all aspects of Whig political culture culminated in an outlook that was forward-looking and self-assured. Skeptical of the past's barbarism and false authority, Whig middle-class confidence in the future was almost boundless. New York Whigs, for instance, believed that America offered a "broad and unobstructed path to prosperity and honor," while their Virginia brethren celebrated that "the nation at large was in possession of such immense wealth" and that "we at this moment stand fair and equal with all nations, and have nothing to oppress of even annoy us from abroad."[1] Indeed, it is difficult to overstate Whiggish faith in America's prospects.

If self-interest was enlightened and individuals nurtured trust and practiced cooperation, then Whigs believed that America's possibilities were limitless. Further, Whigs argued that their political program made a prosperous future possible. "The unquestionable operation of all these things has been not only to increase property," Daniel Webster stressed, "but to equalize it, to diffuse, to scatter its advantages among the many, and to give content, cheerfulness, and animation to all classes of the social system." Whigs believed that their ideas opened bourgeois opportunities to attain knowledge, develop virtue, and amass wealth for all who would work for them. Thus, William Henry Seward spoke for many when he argued that Whiggery was ultimately about, among other things, "augmentation of population, unbounded prosperity and increase of rising villages, cities, and towns, and all the consequent advantages to morality, piety, and knowledge."[2]

Yet Whigs also understood that a thriving future was not guaranteed. The basic problems of individualism remained. Absent virtue, self-interest shriveled to selfishness, and developing trust so that isolated individuals might work together for the common good was difficult. Therefore, if the past's greatest challenge was lingering barbarism, then Whigs believed that the future was most threatened by a narrow understanding of individualism. Egotism, in this view, "has a heart of stone incased in iron," Whig women in Cincinnati noted in 1848. "It robs its own grave, sells its own bones to the doctors, and its soul to the devil."[3] Whigs argued that America's future was bright but fragile. Consequently, the Whigs' America stressed cooperation built on trust to mitigate individuals' selfish tendencies. Whigs rejected the cynicism of their detractors. They believed that America's future would be prosperous, contented, and happy because of their ideas.

## Enlightened Self-Interest

Individualism's defeat of the communitarian past was broad, deep, and decisive. Thus, middle-class Whig attitudes about the future were concerned with bending its consequences to the greater social good, and Whig political culture was built for this purpose above all. Most Whigs believed that self-interest was not necessarily bad if it was enlightened and refined by middle-class moral habits such as self-control, thrift, and industry. Further, Whigs celebrated success while rejecting Democrats' reading of self-interest as too narrow. In this way, the general Whig perspective was to see the sacrifices of the moment in a larger context in which the individual and society would ultimately benefit. And, in the Whig view, modern American society would eventually become the envy of the world.

Self-interest was not inherently evil so long as it was properly understood. For Whigs, enlightened self-interest was *not* selfishness. "Selfishness is a passionate and exaggerated love of self," Alexis de Tocqueville explained in his seminal *Democracy in America,* "that brings man to relate

Fig. 5.1. Théodore Chassériau, [*Portrait of Alexis de Tocqueville*] (1901). Prints and Photographs Division, Library of Congress, Washington, DC. "Print shows portrait of Alexis de Tocqueville after 1848 lithograph by Theodore Chasseriau." https://www.loc.gov/item/96509612.

everything to himself alone and prefer himself to everything."[4] (For a portrait of Tocqueville, see fig. 5.1.) This shortsighted understanding of self-interest was individualism's greatest danger because it destroyed public virtue one man at a time. "But all the world knows that this is ill nature," Calvin Colton noted in 1833, speaking for most Whigs. Middle-class Whigs like Colton believed that this was sinister because to prosper American society must produce individuals whose commitment to self-interest would not drown in egotism. "With the selfish man, the great regard to measures is, 'How will they affect me?' Boston Whigs pointed out in 1833. "'How will they bear upon my reputation, my interest, my family, my prospects and happiness?'" Philadelphia Whigs agreed, lamenting in 1849: "It is strange, and as pitiful as strange, that human selfishness can so harden the heart." In the future, Whigs argued that only an enlightened understanding of self-interest would mitigate these profligate tendencies.[5]

In contrast to selfishness, then, enlightened self-interest drew individuals back into society through the pull of steady habits. "The doctrine of self-interest well understood [or enlightened self-interest] does not produce great devotion," Tocqueville stressed, "but it suggests little sacrifices each day; by itself it cannot make a man virtuous; but it forms a multitude of citizens who are regulated, temperate, moderate, farsighted, masters of themselves; and if it does not lead directly to virtue through the will, it brings them near to it insensibly through habits." It was these bourgeois habits that Whigs sought to develop in individual Americans and, through them, American society. "Marvelously accommodating to the weaknesses of men, [enlightened self-interest] obtains a great empire with ease, and preserves it without difficulty because it turns personal interest against itself, and to direct the passions, it makes use of the spur that excites them."[6]

An important reason that Whigs championed public institutions such as churches, charities, and lyceums was their tendency to reform and enlighten self-interest. Churches were important because they cultivated individual virtue. The future required a broader understanding of self-interest, true, yet daily sacrifices need not preclude daily contentment. "We have frequently taken occasion to contend," Utica, New York, Whigs reminded their neighbors in 1840, "that virtue produces present happiness, and vice present misery." The virtuous habits strengthened in churches made day-to-day life better because those who practiced them avoided the daily pitfalls of drunkenness, violence, and insolvency. Boston Whigs lamented that religious people too often described virtue as a benefit unfortunately most enjoyed after death: "They make it appear as if, in this world, it was a deformity rather than a loveliness; an injury rather than a benefit." Practicing virtue now made life better now.[7]

In this vein, Whigs championed temperance reform to benefit both individual antebellum Americans and future society. Intemperance was bad for individuals because, according to New York Whigs, it "intercepts the light of the sun of righteousness, and brutifies the soul, and denies the God that is above." Drunkards could not have enlightened self-interest because their bondage to alcohol blinded them to all other concerns. Horace Greeley pointed out that drunkenness made a man "a boisterous demon, a terror to his family, and nuisance and burden to society." A future enslaved to substance abuse was a dark and bloody ground. Temperance helped save individuals from their own worst tendencies. "Who can doubt that citizens growing up under such regulations," Greeley pointed out, "would be more industrious, intelligent, enterprising, and patriotic." In the Whig view, then, temperance required sacrifices of the moment for long-term benefit for all. "Every man, therefore," Cincinnati Whigs urged in 1837, "every community, every nation, that will adopt this principle, will be defended from all dangers of drunkenness and attendant evils."[8]

These efforts were not about bourgeoisie condescension or material guilt. Instead, participation by individual Whigs in benevolent societies broadened their perspectives and enlightened what they felt was their legitimate self-interest. "It is the entire abandonment of selfish considerations for the sake of others' good," Boston Whig reformers noted, offering a rose-colored explanation of their efforts in 1841.[9] Democrats often supported these efforts too, but their support reflected their own understanding of self-interest, which privileged autonomy and self-determinism over collaboration. They also worried that broad temperance efforts too often browbeat those reluctant to agree. To be fair, there was a bit of truth to this last criticism. "They are the noisy, reckless, bullying minority," the *United States Review* angrily noted, "who constantly attempt to ever-crow peaceable men, and force silence through fear of unpopularity."[10] In this view, reformers often masked social control with the admirable pursuit of reform. Whigs disagreed because they saw reform efforts in broader terms.

Consequently, Whigs argued that, if Americans practiced enlightened self-interest along middle-class lines, they would enjoy a bright future. In this vein, Mississippi's Sergeant Prentiss spoke for many Whigs in 1840 when he boldly declared: "American industry and enterprise have subdued the wilderness and caused it to rejoice and blossom as the rose."[11] Indeed, Whigs took it as an article of faith that their policies encouraged prosperity for all hardworking Americans. Moreover, the *American Whig Review* argued that Whig policies arose "out of Enlightened and Liberal Democracy" and that from them "come Enterprise and Bold Nationality." Industry and national fidelity were important because they nurtured "a country loved & labor honored," which led to "National glory—National achievement in every art, Union and internal peace, [the] distribution of wealth,—universal employment."[12] At bottom, then, Whig attitudes toward the future championed middle-class values such as striving, success, and achievement.

Along with this view, Whigs believed that enlightened self-interest was not material selfishness and embraced success without apology. "In

Kentucky," Henry Clay argued from the floor of the Senate in 1832, "almost every manufactory known to me, is in the hands of enterprising and self-made men, who have acquired whatever wealth they possess by patient and diligent labor."[13] The insistence on personal effort and individual industry underlay Whig understandings of enlightened self-interest. In 1847, for example, New York Whigs explained: "The man who by the force of early habit 'learns to labor and to wait;' who lives from day to day by the exercise, in his sphere, of his hands or head, and seeks to improve himself, acquires for himself that *property of soul,* which has always upheld . . . the self-made man."[14] That is, he was not selfish but virtuous. Enlightened self-interest was about self-reliance and substance. Petersburg, Virginia, Whigs pointed out that successful men were typically of "plain, unassuming, straight-forward character." In addition, Whigs believed that their efforts made success more likely for more people.[15]

Democrats were not so optimistic. In their view, Whigs gamed the system to cheat the common man out of his just portion. According to the staunch Kentucky Democrat Amos Kendall, Whigs wanted to "convert [the] government into a heartless aristocracy, in which the people are to be transferred, cheated, taxed, and oppressed, that a few may revel on the spoils of the many."[16] Moreover, Whig democratic pretensions were subterfuge meant to flatter and deceive in order to secure electoral success and nothing more. "It suits the designs of the Federal Whigs, on the near approach of an election, to affect wonderful tenderness for the rights and well-being of the PEOPLE," Virginia Democrats seethed in 1840. Whiggish populism was, in these Virginia Democrats' view, ironic because, as they saw things, it was "the People, whom all the political tenets and practices of [the Whigs] have a tendency to degrade, and whom, whenever in the possession of power, the same party has never failed to abuse and oppress."[17] Democrats believed that Whig talk of enlightened self-interest was little more than hogwash. Whigs dismissed such criticism as missing the point in a dogged partisan effort to avoid change. They often had little sympathy for Democratic worries because they doubted that such fears were earnest, that they mattered, or that they were in good faith.

Whigs' advocacy for the physically disabled and mentally ill points to their concern with modernity's collateral damage. These efforts spoke to both their faith in broader self-interest and their belief that none should be left behind. It is not surprising that Whigs carried their frenetic, bourgeois sense of work to their charitable efforts and political pursuits, but it is striking how often they worried about the psychological consequences affecting those who failed to practice self-mastery. At the heights of progressive achievement, moreover, individuals' psychological footing often became the least certain. "The triumphs of mind seem best calculated to elicit our admiration of others, or the increased reverence of ourselves," Sarah Hale warned in 1833. "Little do we reflect that the time may come when this intelligence may fail us, or that, striving after things beyond its reach and comprehension, it may burst the confines of reason and launch us on the shoreless ocean of insanity."[18] Democratic polemicists largely agreed, noting in 1855: "The highest genius seems most nearly to border on madness."[19] As Whigs understood things, however, or perhaps hoped, insanity, at least the sort that developed over time, was preventable, and their understanding of its underlying causes spoke to their larger concerns with individual character and social capital.

For the future that Whigs wanted, active, regular work was the first step toward preventing the mind from succumbing to strain and anxiety. For Whigs, too much leisure was not only materially damaging but also psychologically dangerous. A strong middle-class Protestant work ethic, therefore, prepared individuals to weather the storms of uncertain times: "There will be good hope that if disappointments and misfortunes come they will not crush the spirit, but on the contrary purify and strengthen it."[20]

Whigs and Jacksonians agreed on the general makeup of the mind and the broad understanding of madness as an illness but differed in both causes and treatment. Asylums represented the Whig effort to use public power to correct private ills and bring damaged individuals back into collaborative society. For Democrats, unbounded ambitions and material striving were also evidence of emerging psychosis, while Whigs often cited the predominance of an ungovernable, solitary will. The *American Whig Review* pointed to unseemly solitude and passions run wild in a poem aptly titled "Madness":

> I felt like some lone house, (if such could feel,)
> Deserted, naked, and for ever void;
> While in the charnel chambers of my soul
> Distorted fantasies, like dungeon rats,

Grew bold in solitude, and peeping out,
Thrilled every nerve with loathsome rioting.
Thought, healthy Thought, had fled away, and I
Was face to face to with Madness![21]

No individual could thrill "every nerve" in idle reverie, Whigs argued, and not expect to pay a psychological cost. The Illinois Whig Abraham Lincoln also indulged the poet's license from time to time, often working through his own struggles with melancholy and depression in poignant verse. Indeed, after visiting his childhood home and encountering again a young man trapped in the throes of madness, he wrote:

But here's an object more of dread
Than ought the grave contains—
A human form with reason fled,
While wretched life remains.[22]

Lincoln and the broader middle-class Whiggish worldview he represented viewed insanity with a cold shudder because they placed such a high social premium on self-control and self-mastery.

For their part, Jacksonians argued that, beyond grief or melancholy, the anxiety generated by Whigs' ceaseless striving more than excessive idleness drove many Americans to the brink of madness. Insanity and mental instability in the antebellum United States had much to do, wrote one Democratic physician in 1840, with "the varied and increasing temptations to embark in the wildest schemes of speculation; the sudden accumulation and loss of fortune; . . . the fierce strifes of the predominating passions of ambition and avarice."[23] In a future where prosperity seemed within the reach of all who would work hard enough to seize it, failure was a bitter blow to self-esteem and social reputation. While it dates to later in the nineteenth century, a Gilded Age portrait by Allan McLane Hamilton of a young New York woman stricken with melancholia attonita (see fig. 5.2) bore out many Jacksonian fears concerning the future that Whigs were building. According to the *American Heritage Medical Dictionary,* she suffered from a "catatonic state in schizophrenia that is characterized by immobility and muscular rigidity." The number of men and women suffering from this or other psychological disorders only increased as the century

Fig. 5.2. *Melancholia Attonita.* Allan McLane Hamilton, *Types of Insanity: An Illustrated guide in the Physical Diagnosis of Mental Disease* (New York : William Wood, 1883), pl. 3. Prints and Photographs Division, Library of Congress, Washington, DC. "Head-and-shoulders portrait of a woman with melancholia attonita." https://www.loc.gov/item/96522292.

wore on, as did the number of people seeking, and in many cases suffering from, treatment in hospitals and asylums.[24] In Democratic eyes, Whigs' push for a working, striving, achieving populace directly contributed to these rising instances of melancholy, depression, insanity, and suicide. Finally, Democrats rejected the notion that individuals' mental instability was anything more than an unfortunate private matter.

Ultimately, Whigs winced when Jacksonians implied that, when they stared down the face of madness, they saw the self-made man unmade by society. Whiggish Americans put their faith in middle-class social institutions such as churches, schools, and voluntary associations, but Whigs also worked through asylums and hospitals to help American individuals prosper and thrive. They sought to break down or at least mitigate the more desperate tendencies of individualism and replace them with new, broader perspectives.

Whigs and Democrats understood self-interest differently because their understanding of individualism differed. Democrats stressed individuals over associations because they feared collaborative efforts to control them. Thus, if individuals prospered according to their pluck, grit, and perseverance, then they failed along precisely the same lines. "You ask me what I think of 'hard times'?" a Massachusetts Jacksonian fumed in 1843. "Think—why I think that as a nation we are in the same predicament as the frog in the fable, who tried to swell to the size of the ox, and finally, without attaining its object, 'bursted.'" As Democrats saw it, moreover, most failed because they foolishly followed Whig ideas of credit and speculation. "The immorality of the acts [i.e., Whigs' American System]," stressed the *United States Magazine, and Democratic Review* in November of the same year, "has been fully proved by the ruin of the old Credit System." In this view, neither society nor the state bore any legitimate responsibility to relieve self-made ruin. Democrats' reading of self-interest was constricted, holding that men supposedly rose or fell on the strengths of their merits alone. Ultimately, they relied on no one to succeed and could not legitimately impose on others to mitigate failure.[25]

Whigs disagreed because, in their view, this narrow reading of individualism was the future's central danger. If most Whigs believed that success was a just reward for virtuous effort, then most also rejected "a reason in the man" for failure, supporting instead a wide array of public and private relief efforts.[26] "To give relief," William Henry Seward argued in 1834, "will revive languishing commerce, agriculture, and manufactures." It will also "recall confidence and prosperity everywhere throughout this land."[27] For Whigs, it was a problem of circumscribed possibility. Without public relief, the impetus to work for improvement was gone. "[Debtors and bankrupts] can have not inducement to strive or toil," New York Whigs noted in 1840, "because they cannot hope to enjoy the fruits of their labor; while the wasteful process of snatching it from them inopportunely and converting it to the use of others forbids all hope that it will ever satisfy their indebtedness or sensibly benefit their creditors." Yet Whigs rejected the notion that their support of these measures was about subsidizing bad behavior.[28]

Instead, in the Whig view, a prosperous future was contingent on cultivating virtues such as prudence, temperance, and industry. In 1829, Henry Clay argued that America's future was dependent on developing "the greatest public virtue."[29] For Whigs like Clay, therefore, the future was not simply about the remorseless pursuit of wealth. "To a certain extent, it is of course the duty of every man to acquire property," confirmed a Boston Whig, "but not for the sake of property itself, nor for the love of gain. When carried to this extent, the pursuit of wealth becomes a disease."[30] The love of gain for its own sake threatened the values that Whigs considered necessary to achieve success. "Many of the difficulties in life which men have to struggle with arise from their sumptuous modes of living," Philadelphia Whigs agreed in 1848, "and the excessive trading of a part of the community to make themselves suddenly rich." This was a false authority of another sort that led to a wrong ordering of things and, ultimately, came down to the crucial moral difference between doing good and doing well.[31]

Whigs needed to believe that their material pursuits were about more than comfort and security because the line between wealth and worth was not always clear. "Virtue, honesty, happiness, all these, and whatever else that is pure and lovely," Whig women in Massachusetts warned in 1844, "must be sacrificed at the shrine of Mammon."[32] Whigs' worry was stark in this respect because much of their political perspective turned on the supposed benefits of widespread affluence. Rightly understood, Whigs hoped, future prosperity was about more than wealth, and a good man was more than his financial solvency. In the end, the *American Monthly Magazine* stressed in 1834: "True passion for money, the mere desire to accumulate . . . is . . . demoralizing and debasing in itself." Whigs argued that their efforts were bigger than that, with wider benefits for more people: "The search after competence is unquestionably one of the best springs of action in community, at least it is one whose good effects is [*sic*] apparent in the industry, the *employment,* and consequently the morals and happiness, of the greater proportion of society."[33]

Whigs argued that momentary individual sacrifices were justified because, ultimately, society as a whole would benefit. "The prudent, penniless beginner in the world, labors for wages awhile, saves a surplus with which to buy tools or land, for himself," Abraham Lincoln noted, still championing this perspective near the close of the antebellum years, "then labors on his own account another while, and at length hires another new beginner to help him. This, say its advocates, is free labor—the just and generous, and prosperous system, which opens the way for all—gives hope to all, and energy, and progress, and improvement of condition to all."[34] Whigs' attitudes toward the future embraced this understanding of enlightened self-interest as near political gospel. They needed to believe that the sturdy comforts of middle-class living were worth the cost needed to secure them—but only if uplift was tempered by virtue. Americans often give "too exclusive devotion," the *American Whig Review* worried in 1851, "to the narrow circle of [one's] own operations."[35] Individualism, autonomy, liberty—these were all enviable achievements. But unchecked selfishness carried social consequences that would only worsen over time.

Beyond a narrow reading of self-interest, then, Whigs worried that the future faced a challenge of trust. If distrust became widespread, the costs were both far-reaching and harmful. "Then not only is trust in such and such a man destroyed," Tocqueville explained Whiggish doubt in this regard, "but their taste for believing *any* man whatsoever. Each therefore withdraws narrowly into himself and claims to judge the world from there." For their part, Democrats worried that, the more broadly they trusted, the more vulnerable they became. In contrast, Whigs argued that social trust was crucial to building a prosperous future. It was "not the cause of any one state," Baltimore's *Niles' National Register* pointed out 1844, "but the cause of our common liberty, of our common country, of good government." A middle-class future was built on their faith that America offered the world a better tomorrow, so long as succeeding generations practiced enlightened self-interest and embraced daily virtues to make it so.[36]

## Trust

Along with cultivating an enlightened understanding of self-interest, Whigs tried to generate widespread trust. Trust was important because, without it, Americans would never work together, and that would have been disastrous because, Whigs thought, mutual cooperation was the surest means of reconnecting isolated individuals in order that they might pursue the common good. In this vein, Whigs argued, Americans must not allow a self-interested, sometimes selfish society to undermine the necessary trust in men and institutions. For their part, Jacksonians did not trust elites, politicians, or associations because they were never convinced that the interests of the people would be served. To Democratic ears, moreover, Whig rhetoric about "the common good" masked efforts by the powerful to rob and exploit the people. Whigs disagreed. They wanted individual Americans to work together to prevent their shared future from crumbling into ruin. To facilitate these efforts, Whigs worked to induce trust.

Trust was essential because it was about the "firm belief in the reliability, truth, ability, or strength of someone or something."[37] Consequently, it involves both logic and emotion. Logically, trust requires individuals to discern the dependability of others to do the things they say they will and mean the things they say they mean. Here, the past was prologue, offering clues to previous dealings, truthfulness, and the fulfillment of obligations. Yet, in a world of strangers, that sort of knowledge was often unavailable. This was why trust was also an emotional exercise, leaving the trusting open to possible mistreatment and abuse. Whigs believed that these risks only rose as society grew more impersonal and a stringent reading of individualism grew starker. Tocqueville observed that it was this tendency "that disposes each citizen to isolate himself from the mass of those like him and to withdraw to one side with his family and friends."[38] Without shared social trust, therefore, individual Americans would associate with only an ever-shrinking circle of like-minded confidants because they would doubt both the motives and the integrity of those with whom they disagreed.

Trust required faith, and faith of any sort was chancy. If trust was mislaid, then the trusting hazarded fraud, deceit, and disappointment. Further, there is a blindness about trust that is unsettling. Indeed, the King James Bible that most antebellum Americans read confirmed this discomfort, celebrating it as right religion. "Now faith is the substance of things hoped for," it explained, "the evidence of things not seen" (Heb. 11:1 [AV]). Unsettling or not, trust was Whigs believed vital because, without it, society would not be social. One Brooklyn Whig minister argued that trust was "the proof of faith": "It implies not merely the belief of a thing, but the risking of something on that belief—a venture that will be wholly lost, if our confidence is misplaced." Broken trust was poisonous to social comity because it left feelings of gullibility and foolishness. And there was the rub. Antebellum America was becoming a world of strangers, rapid movement, and cultural change. In the face of such deeply felt upheaval, suspicion seemed shrewd counsel.[39]

Thus, wary Democrats considered Whig arguments for the extension of trust either naive or sinister. They worried that, the more broadly they trusted, the more vulnerable they became. In 1840, Virginia Democrats saw a world full of "suppleness, crooked insincerity and revolting insensibility to shame."[40] These inclinations seemed most pronounced among Whigs. Jacksonians in Michigan worried that the Whigs' ultimate goal was "to force us into submission and make us wear the yoke of political bondage." Democrats asked Whigs to leave them alone, and they put their faith in the past above all. "Men satisfied with their own condition," as John L. O'Sullivan's *United States Magazine, and Democratic Review* explained this perspective in 1852, "dreading the risk and hazards of an uncertain future, cleave strongly and tenaciously to the examples and precepts of the past, as affording the only safe guides and true rules for the conduct and action and their people or government." Whigs urged people to trust men they did not know and often did not respect in order to take the country to places that were not clear.[41]

Accordingly, Democrats often railed against corporations and banks because they did not trust them. "In our country," the *United States Magazine, and Democratic Review* nervously pointed out, "wealth has more power than in any other."[42] Corporations and banks wielded dangerous plutocratic privileges that, unchecked, would grow with time. Worse, the wealthy enjoyed deliberative benefits that strengthened their position at the expense of everyone else. "They have time to work head-work and lay deep plans," dismayed Ohio Democrats conceded in 1840, "while the poorer class are obliged to be at their daily labor."[43] Where Whigs might see the opportunity for collaborative middle-class development—in this instance public education—Jacksonians saw only chances for further coercion and control. What benefit could people enjoy as a result of such efforts if their poverty precluded them for taking part? Far better, most felt, to resist Whig siren songs and let each be responsible for his own lot.

Whigs disagreed because they feared that, if distrust became the rule, the consequences would be both far-reaching and bad. Distrust, in this view, destroyed social harmony. Democrats themselves admitted as much, though they believed the disruption justified. "When endeavoring to nullify and to remove customs, sanctioned by the authority of hereditary power, or to abolish long existing institutions," the *United States Magazine, and Democratic Review* conceded, "humane efforts are frequently retarded from the distrust in those systems which it is promoted to substitute."[44] Democrats and Whigs believed the challenge to be so important because the stakes were so high.

Whigs were unimpressed with Democrats' distrust because they found it narrow and argued that this sort of suspicion flowed from inherent weakness, not strength. "Any attempt to divide the people into classes, distinguished by birth, by wealth or poverty, or by profession, or occupation," Alabama Whigs declared in 1840, "is subversive of the true principles of our political institutions; and it ought to be discountenanced."[45] Jacksonian scorched-earth rhetoric made compromise difficult, Boston Whigs argued in 1837, creating "a spirit of incurable distrust"; any politicians whose success is built on the sum of voters' fears "will be looked upon as men . . . whom no promises can bind."[46] To Whig eyes, Democrats practiced an ostrich brand of politics that substituted shrill reactionary brinksmanship for thoughtful deliberation. "The locofoco pot of discord is seething," Nashville Whigs noted in 1843. "It salpicon of adverse principles is falling to pieces, and its leaders live together in sleepless distrust." Whigs believed that the hodgepodge practice of always insisting the sky was falling was tiresome because it undermined social trust.[47]

Consequently, the public institutions that Jacksonians dreaded as corrupt and exploitative Whigs appreciated because they thought that they induced trust. In the Whig view, corporations were vehicles of broad public good, not state-sponsored efforts by the few to rob the many. Daniel Webster spoke for most Whigs in 1843 when he argued that acts of incorporation were "calculated to promote the happiness and prosperity of all classes of the people."[48] Far from oppressing the broad mass of people, they allowed collaboration for mutual gain. Boston Whigs agreed, noting that corporations allow "men of the smallest means to originate and carry on undertakings which, without the power, credit and facilities derived from such acts [of incorporation], would either not be undertaken at all, or only by individuals or great wealth and for their sole benefit."[49] Whig attitudes toward the future privileged collaboration, and most believed that corporations were an efficient way to overcome individual weakness and achieve success.

For Whigs, banks were another public institution promoting trust. Whigs like Webster rejected Jacksonian suspicion, arguing: "Banks, everywhere, and especially with us, are made for the borrowers. They are made for the good of the many, and not for the good of the few." Like corporations, banks, Whigs believed, extended prosperity's possibilities to more Americans by the efficient regulation of credit and paper money. Henry Clay agreed, stressing that banks were simply "organized agencies for the loan of money and the transaction of business."[50] Whigs clung to this principle even in the worst of times. In 1838, for example, during the nadir of the national economic depression that followed the 1837 Panic and Crash, Whigs like Horace Greeley urged Americans to *still* put their trust, and their money, in banks. "Let no man, then, think to relieve himself from the common troubles by means detrimental to the welfare of his neighbors," he declared, "by encrusting himself in the armor of narrow selfishness." In this view, trusting banks meant restoring confidence in the future. Pooling their resources allowed ordinary Americans to ensure mutual benefit. The future promised dark moments along with the light. When they came, Greeley noted, speaking for Whigs who wanted people to remember to rely on one another: "Let him rather prosper by feeding rather than starving his neighbors."[51]

Whigs carried their broader reading of trust up from interpersonal relationships, corporations, and banks, applying to it government too. Here, their differences with Jacksonians were stark. Democrats fought to limit the size and scope of government because they distrusted collected power. The *United States Magazine, and Democratic Review* spoke for most in 1837: "A strong and active democratic government, in the common sense of the term, is an evil, differing only in degree and mode of operation, and not in nature, from a strong despotism."[52] Thus, Democrats often echoed Jefferson's adage, only wanting a government that "neither picks my pocket, nor breaks my leg."[53] Whigs again found this perspective too narrow, believing instead in government's possibilities for building a prosperous future.

Consequently, Whig attitudes toward the future held out a positive role for government. "It is the object of republican institutions to encourage and stimulate improvement of the physical condition of the country," William Henry Seward explained in 1839, "and to promote the moral and intellectual advancement of its citizens."[54] Where Democrats wanted a minimalist government to enforce general order and leave them alone, Whigs wanted a government that would actively promote the common good. They tended to have a broader understanding of what this idea entailed, agreeing with the *American Whig Review,* which noted: "Whatever is national in character, or is evidently conducive to the common good, should be done at the common expense by the federal government."[55] Whigs trusted government more readily because they were confident in their ability to select wise leaders. As ever, this point of view carried a catch. Republican governments were mirrors of men, and, if the people were virtuous, sober, and prudent, so too would be the elected officials they chose to lead them. On the other hand, if they elected men of ungovernable will, low intellect, and narrow perspectives, then their government would be reckless, stupid, and inept.

Yet Whigs rejected cynicism, and their perspectives on the future saw vast opportunities for mutual benefit. In a larger sense, trust was important for the future because it represented a sacred charge as well. Most antebellum Americans agreed that preserving their nation was a generational responsibility, given to them by the founders with the expectation that it would be handed down again in turn. Whigs wanted to hand down something better than the nation as they had found it. "Man, therefore, was not made for himself alone—No!" John Quincy Adams thundered. "He was made for his country by the obligations of the social compact, he was made for all ages past by the sentiment of reverence for his forefathers; and he was made for all future times by the impulse of affection for his progeny." Where Democrats often stressed preserving the country in republican simplicity, middle-class Whigs like Adams saw their duty as continuing American development into the future. "No man in America is doomed by the necessity of his circumstances," urged Calvin Colton in 1832, "to die in the same condition in which he was born." If Whig ideas won the day, they believed, all that limited individual potential was each person's commitment to industry, prudence, and temperance. Whether strengthening interpersonal relations or honoring generational obligations, Whig thinking about the future relied on trust as a sturdy pillar for prosperity.[56]

As a result, Whigs believed that trust was the bedrock social principle that made collaborative effort possible. They argued that future progress required cooperation, not confrontation. It was only by working together that American greatness might be achieved. Whigs were deeply optimistic on this point, which was why they worked so hard to broaden individuals' self-interest and encourage them to trust. In this way, collaboration held the key to future prosperity so long as it was infused with bourgeois virtues.

## Cooperation

Whig attitudes toward the future stressed cooperation as crucial to progress. To make this possible, Whigs urged individuals to construe their interests broadly and extend trust to others. Further, their faith in voluntary associations, corporations, and government was part of their efforts to get people to work together. Most argued that cooperation helped individuals overcome isolation's weakness. It was a question of power. Whigs believed that, by working together, Americans could be more creative, efficient, and effective than was possible working alone. In the broadest sense, finally, their policies asked people to cooperate across class, state, and regional lines, culminating with what they argued would be a benign nationalism. In this way, they hoped that their emphasis on compromise facilitated people working together for larger ends. If cooperation along these lines was the rule, future widespread mutual benefit was assured. If these efforts failed, Whigs worried that Americans would slip back into barbarism.

Cooperation was crucial to bourgeois Whiggery. Isolated people might enjoy more autonomy and self-determinism, but they were also feeble. "In democratic people," Tocqueville explained, "all citizens are independent and weak." The old ties of kith, kin, and village were snapping under individualism's advance, making collaboration necessary to achieve all but the most rudimentary of aims: "[Free citizens] fall into impotence if they do not learn to aid each other freely."[57] Contrary to Democrats' suspicions, in their arguments for mutual aid Whigs asked Americans not to discard the local and the familiar but merely to broaden their sense of who constituted their communities. "All the world admits that identity of local origin is a tie of connection and sympathy," Daniel Webster agreed in 1849, "especially if it be strengthened by early association, by meeting with one another in the school-house, and in the society of early life."[58] Like Webster, most Whigs believed in the efficacy of local action, so long as it was qualified by social institutions.

Thus, Whigs' support for public institutions flowed from their desire to encourage collaboration. Individualism's corrosive tendencies would only worsen with time. In light of this, Whigs argued that education was vital because it strengthened individuals and encouraged them to work together. "The masses of the people must be taught to think for themselves before they can help themselves," the *American Whig Review* explained in 1851. Schools lifted individual Americans out of ignorance while also broadening their understanding of the common good. Whiggery was about elevating all classes of American society, and Whigs were "zealous friends of popular education because they [felt] that enlightened people will, necessarily, elevate itself."[59]

Beyond schools, Whigs supported banks and corporations because they argued that both harnessed collective public power for the common good. Banks were essential in this regard because they pooled capital to facilitate enterprise. "Such an institution acts beneficially," Webster explained, "by creating a currency that is of general credit everywhere."[60] Whigs maintained that credit was simply the public extension of the social values they were working to build. "What is credit?" asked Ohio Whigs in 1842. "It is an honest promise based upon the ability to do. It is a bond of honor between honest parties."[61] In this way, banks were vital to Whig attitudes toward the future because they encouraged collaboration by promoting trust while facilitating enterprise. Henry Clay explained this position in 1837 while refuting Jacksonian antibanking ideology: "In making war upon the banks, you wage war upon the people of the United States." In the Whig view, the idea of diverse, conflicting interests was wrongheaded. "We are all—People—States—Union—Banks," Clay stressed, "bound up and interwoven together, united in fortune and destiny." This view was central to Whiggery.[62]

Whigs also advocated incorporation because they believed that such acts strengthened American society by helping individuals work together. "They enable men," William Henry Seward explained, "of the smallest means, by a concentration of their capital and the credit created by that operation, to originate and to carry on undertaking which, without the power, credit, and facilities derived from such acts, would either not be undertaken at all, or only by individuals of great wealth for their sole benefit."[63] In the most generous view, corporations completed broad public improvement works that were otherwise untenable while also offering access to opportunities for individual advancement. Without cooperation and support, individuals simply could not build canals, major roads, or railways. New York Whigs argued that these "are projects of too vast moment and too universal an interest, to be left to the unaided efforts of individuals."[64] Thus, cooperation was both good for individuals and good for society.

Accordingly, infrastructure improvements were a dynamic, if obvious, example of the creative potential of collaborative effort. For example, canals united public and private interests in a collaborative effort to win the future. Whigs celebrated their construction because each canal demonstrated the fruits of cooperation, trust, and enlightened self-interest. The Erie Canal was the era's most famous and offered Whigs a tangible picture of the future they were trying to build. The uncertainty surrounding its construction and the subsequent success that it enjoyed seemed to Whig eyes portents of prosperity.

Whigs often lauded the Erie Canal to show the effectiveness of their ideas over time. "The present generation, enjoying as it does the daily benefits of the Erie Canal," Samuel Ruggles reminded Whigs in 1849, "can hardly realize the difficulties which its projectors were obliged to encounter." All those who supported the idea of a canal linking New York City to the Great Lakes were ridiculed: "The idea was treated as purely chimerical."[65] And scoffers had good reason to doubt. To complete the project, planners had to cross over three hundred miles, go through limestone rock and mountains, combat malarial conditions that eventually killed over one thousand workers, and come up with the financing to cover the staggering $7 million price tag, over $170 billion in 2019 terms.[66] Thus, the Erie Canal was a high-stakes wager on the best way to win to the future.

Few bets ever paid off so well. Finished in 1825, the canal retired its debts by 1840 and by 1845 was transporting over a million tons of goods each year. Though its construction predated Whiggery, Whigs lauded it from the beginning of the era through the end as an example of their principles properly understood. The *Western Record* dismissed criticism of the canal in 1830, noting that, while expenditures in 1829 were nearly $400,000, receipts easily exceeded $800,000, nearly doubling the investment.[67] Whigs believed that over $400,000 in profit was an effective way to silence naysayers, and those profits only increased over time.

The Erie Canal also encapsulated the Whigs' America writ small. Through a combination of public and private funding, an infrastructure development transformed Rochester, New York, from a sleepy village into a thriving city in a short two decades. In 1830, a hiccup over nine thousand people lived in Rochester. By 1850, the population had swelled by over 400 percent to north of thirty-six thousand, driven by the city's canal-fueled commercial success. Along with businesses, banks, and merchant houses, by 1857 Rochester also boasted a university and a hospital along with hundreds of churches and scores of schools.

Democrats saw a different picture when they looked at Rochester at midcentury. The canal brought factories and industry to towns and cities along its route, but the benefits of these developments were not, they believed, universally enjoyed or equally shared. The old colonial guild system that privileged almost familial relationships between master craftsmen and the apprentices and journeymen under their tutelage declined as skilled "mechanics" found themselves replaced by cheaper laborers with little to no connection to the finished product. Democrats blamed the Whigs' American System for this change. True, the guild system left a legacy of self-help and professional organizations that would become the first real labor groups, and workers attempted to organize for better wages and safer working conditions, yet those efforts usually failed. In the wake of public indifference and sometimes outright hostility to organized labor, many groups sought shelter within their churches and the Democratic Party. In Democratic eyes, the canal route offered a fertile ground for the Second Great Awakening because workers living there had little other recourse when seeking sympathy or aid.[68]

Whigs countered that the growing impersonal nature of work and working was not their fault, even if they were generally more comfortable with these changes. They also believed that they were building a middle-class social, cultural, and political network that would mitigate individualism's worst effects. In fact, most Whigs probably thought that Democratic efforts to thwart their plans only made workers' lives worse. That the two groups often talked past each other and doubted each other's motives is not shocking.[69]

Whigs across America looked to repeat the Erie Canal's success, supporting canal efforts throughout the antebellum era. In Virginia, the Chesapeake and Ohio Canal was a point of pride for most Whigs. "Our canals," Richmond Whigs boasted in 1834, "have turned out very handsomely."[70] This was not idle bragging. Though the Chesapeake and Ohio was never as lucrative an investment as the Erie, it was nonetheless profitable long after the Civil War. Whigs were quick to defend their record on these sorts of expenditures. "In the whole history of our Canals we find Whigs acting in concert," the *New York Daily Times* stressed, "and uniformly in favor of extending the benefits of the system, as far as was practicable."[71] Conversely, Whigs harangued Democrats for their opposition to these measures in the stark terms of sloth. They dismissed the instances in which public infrastructure projects failed to yield the promised results, focusing instead on the successes. "The most useless and disagreeable men in the world are those who do the least and complain the most," Albert Barnes explained in 1846. "The laziest are always the most captious on the enterprising, and they who are the least profit to the world themselves are sure to be most ambitious in deprecating the capacities they are too imbecile to emulate." Yet, beyond their profitability, canals also represented promise personified. They offered tangible evidence of the power of cooperative effort.[72]

Tariffs were another way in which Whigs looked to government to promote cooperation. Government protection of American industry benefited all because it strengthened social and commercial bonds and increased mutual reliance. "The question then," Calvin Colton argued, "the great, practical question—is shall European capital and labor, be permitted to bring American capital and labor, that is, American society down?" Whigs like Colton believed that it was a mistake to see tariffs through narrow local eyes. "No part of this nation can prosper without a protective tariff," he argued, "for the simple reason that the nation, as a whole cannot prosper without it."[73] Narrow sectional thinking missed the larger benefits that protection conferred. Tariffs wove disparate interests together, requiring trust, and broadening individual understandings of the common good. "What is this," John Pendleton Kennedy wondered, "but an ingenious method of stretching the blanket of a political faith to cover many bedfellows?"[74] Whigs argued that tariffs were good policies because ultimately they benefited everyone by linking the country together and aiding general prosperity.

For their part, Democrats tended to view tariffs suspiciously because they saw in them undue privilege for one section over another. Consequently, Jacksonians like William Leggett maintained the tariff was in truth "a device to tax the many for the benefit of the few."[75] Although the American economy as a whole enjoyed solid growth owing to increased production by protected northern manufacturers, the anger of southerners simmered because they were forced to purchase finished products at higher prices and sell their cotton domestically at lower rates than they could command overseas. And, when Andrew Jackson did not move quickly enough to mollify their concerns, South Carolinians, under the intellectual and political leadership of John C. Calhoun, argued for each state's right to nullify federal laws within its own borders. As many Whigs saw it, South Carolina recklessly transformed a debate over duties and imports into a conversation about federal power and the possibility of secession.[76]

But what does nullification have to do with cooperation? The South Carolina legislature's incendiary 1828 "Exposition and Protest," written secretly by Calhoun himself, marked a moment when the scales began falling from middle-class Whig eyes. In the Whig view, the document's language raised the bar for exaggeration and distortion. "The history of all has been the same, injustice, violence and anarchy," noted Calhoun, invoking an apocalyptic vision of the past to justify the rhetorical gymnastics of interposition, "succeeded by the government of one, or a few, under which the people seek refuge, from the more oppressive despotism of the majority."[77] This idea cut at the very bonds of unity that Whigs worked to promote.

Thus, most Whigs argued that the theory of state interposition was preposterous and disunion a perilous absurdity. Indeed, Virginia Whigs dismissed secession outright, arguing: "There is no middle ground between obedience and revolution. . . . [T]he doctrine of nullification is a dangerous political heresy."[78] The Whiggish Cincinnati *Philanthropist,* no fiery political broadsheet by any stretch, agreed, confirming a rock-ribbed resolve to preserve the Union: "We firmly believe that the North would PUT DOWN THE FANATICS."[79] So far so good. Whigs' response was a predictable conservative one to outrageous innovation, full of condemnation and resolve. Yet exactly zero nullification fanatics were put down in 1832, in South Carolina or elsewhere. The Union was not dissolved. And Whigs' belief in collaborative compromise is a major reason why.

Certainly, Henry Clay, Daniel Webster, and many other Whigs worked with Calhoun and a cadre of moderate Democrats to pass the Tariff of 1833, soothing South Carolina, and avoiding civil war. Yet cooperation is built on hope as well as enlightened self-interest and trust. Most Whigs, like most Americans in 1832, believed that the Union was something good that ought to be preserved. They had hope for the future and, thus, a reason to practice thrift through compromise, even if they believed the protective tariff to be sound policy for the whole country. "I agree with you, gentlemen," Henry Clay noted in a public letter to Virginia Whigs in 1834, "in regard to the present condition of our public affairs. In contemplating [the tariff] there is much to depress." Nullification, partisan acrimony, the reelection of Jackson followed by the election of Van Buren, the bank war—there was much about American public life that gave Whigs pause. But, as Clay noted: "Sentiments of despair are never to be indulged as to the fortune or fate of the Republic."[80] Whigs were usually willing to compromise because they believed unity to be more important over the long term.

Indeed, throughout the antebellum era, secessionists often leveraged the Whig proclivity for conciliation into short-term political triumphs. Most judged those setbacks an acceptable temporary price to ensure unity.

In a bigger sense, then, Whigs' emphasis on cooperation led to their particular brand of nationalism. Preserving the Union, Clay argued, was "the paramount desire which has influenced me throughout my whole public career."[81] Yet, for most Whigs, their bourgeois devotion to unity went deeper still. "The Union is not a temporary partnership of States," Daniel Webster insisted. "It is the association of the people, under a constitution of Government, uniting their power, joining together their higher interest, cementing their present enjoyments, and blending, in one indivisible mass, all their hopes for the future."[82] Thus, Whigs stressed compromise because they wanted a future full of self-controlled, middle-class people working together for larger ends. If Americans cultivated enlightened self-interest, extended trust, and practiced cooperation, the future would, Whigs believed, be bright. Whigs rejected the idea that their variety of nationalism meant that individuals or states must be someday subsumed into a faceless federal monolith. "The Union exists in absolute integrity," William Henry Seward explained, "without [the states] having relinquished any part of their individuality."[83] This view of political unity flowed from Whigs' understanding of the ideal society as one in which middle-class families were connected through churches and voluntary associations. The Union was "a family of states," Calvin Colton maintained, "where the harmony of familial relations must reign." Families members did not always agree, but they found room for compromise to pursue common goals. This was the ultimate aim of Whiggish cooperation, the promise Whigs wanted fulfilled in America.[84]

In the end, Whiggery was an optimistic reading of American potential. Whigs' middle-class striving, their faith in self-control, and their trust in collaborative effort were means to achieve a glorious future. Whigs wanted America to become a bustling capitalist world where manufacturing, trade, and agriculture all worked together for mutual benefit. Merchants, craftsmen, and farmers would all enjoy the fruits of progress and all realize that they shared a common interest. Whigs embraced modern transportation and communication advances because they believed that they all helped bind people together. Government power would be trustworthy because it would be primarily extended by legislatures of the people's representatives and because virtuous, enlightened statesmen filled its ranks. In a Whig future, the United States would offer opportunities for all to rise according to their merit and remain a place where the worthy got wealthy and the wealthy were worthy. America would be a vast country of many millions, all free, all united, and all committed to principles of temperance, prudence, and self-control.

Whigs imagined a country where moral reform would eventually become unnecessary. If all men and women controlled their baser instincts and practiced ordered liberty, then America would be a free country where law was almost superfluous. The United States that the Whigs sought to build would boast a society of educated and self-controlled people whose social life was undergirded by principles of association and cooperation. Middle-class families would instill bourgeois virtues and participate in Protestant church life, building a happy, moral country one individual at a time. Human nature might never be perfect, but Whigs believed that steady habits could perfect it. Ultimately, the Whigs' America was an optimistic conservative worldview that tempered hope with effort and achievement with merit. To do well, finally, Americans must first do good.

# Conclusion

So what happened to the Whigs? The antebellum political party died a slow death from 1845 to 1854. First, President James K. Polk provoked a morally bankrupt war with Mexico in 1845, annexing Texas, and extending the nation's borders to California's Pacific coastline along the way. The addition of so much new territory so quickly drove questions about slavery that moderate Whigs and Democrats alike had dodged for thirty years from the abstract into the public square. On the one hand, many Americans (mostly northern and middle western, mostly Whiggish) argued that slavery should not spread to any new states formed from the territories stolen from Mexico. To the contrary, many other Americans (mostly southern, mostly Democratic) argued that slaves were a legitimate form of constitutionally protected property that could not legally be excluded from territory won using the common treasury and national armies. The discovery of gold in California in 1849 only added fuel to the partisan fire because it inspired so many people to head west in search of fortune, hastening that state's ability to meet the demographic requirements for admission to the Union, and forcing the country at large to grapple with questions for which it was unprepared. Thus, the contest was joined over the central issue that was to dominate all American political life for the next dozen years, namely, the disposition of the territories. For the moment, moderates who desperately longed for a compromise that might stifle the underlying issue of slavery held the majority. However, it is a truism that happens to be true that, in crises of this sort, extremists grow in power, swallowing up all political space in the conciliatory center.

Such a prognosis seemed unlikely in 1850 because, in most respects, Americans had ample cause for optimism. Across the Northeast and parts of the Midwest, thick networks of canals, toll roads, and railroads spurred the growth of small, increasingly industrial cities such as Pittsburgh, Cincinnati, Louisville, and St. Louis, all linked to commercial centers in

Philadelphia, New York, and Boston. Across the South, cotton production was soaring to meet a seemingly endless global demand. A shade over twenty-three million people lived in the United States in 1850, representing an astounding jump of nearly 36 percent from 1840. In the places where Whiggery was strongest (i.e., the Border South, Upper Middle West, and Northeast), villages were growing into towns, which in turn were growing into cities. Colleges and universities were edging alongside older seminaries, and most new towns springing up as the country's borders raced west demanded a schoolmaster for their children, made room for lyceums and public lectures for their citizenry, and practiced a robust, observant Protestant Christianity. And, as map 6.1 illustrates, the American people were enjoying enormous demographic growth. Whiggery was enjoying a morning in the sun. If asked, most Americans probably would have agreed with Herman Melville's assessment of their country's prospects. "We Americans are the peculiar, chosen people—the Israel of our time; we bear the ark of the liberties of the world," Melville wrote in 1850. "God has predestinated, mankind expects, great things from our race; and great things we feel in our souls."[1] And it seemed that a crude greatness was within America's grasp. Polk's controversial war with Mexico stretched the country's borders to the Pacific Ocean, making manifest the two-ocean "destiny" that most white Americans considered a divine part of their nation's mission. In 1850, finally, more Americans were living longer, were eating better, and had more money than at any time in the nation's history. Yet this prosperity masked deep currents of restlessness and papered over the burning contradiction of black chattel slavery in a land loudly dedicated to liberty.[2]

Since 1820, the stability of American political power rested, in part, on the delicate balancing of slave states with free states, especially in the US Senate. As the antebellum years wore to a close, any tipping of the balance caused angry public consternation, and partisans of both sides saw in the territories won from Mexico a kind of looking glass hinting at the country's future. Would America be a slave nation or free soil? Democrats and Whigs alike groped desperately for an arrangement that would stem the sectional tide. It is fair to ask why. Why were Americans increasingly unable to reconcile American growth and the expansion of slavery given that they had done so since Dutch traders first sold Africans to Jamestown colonists in 1619?

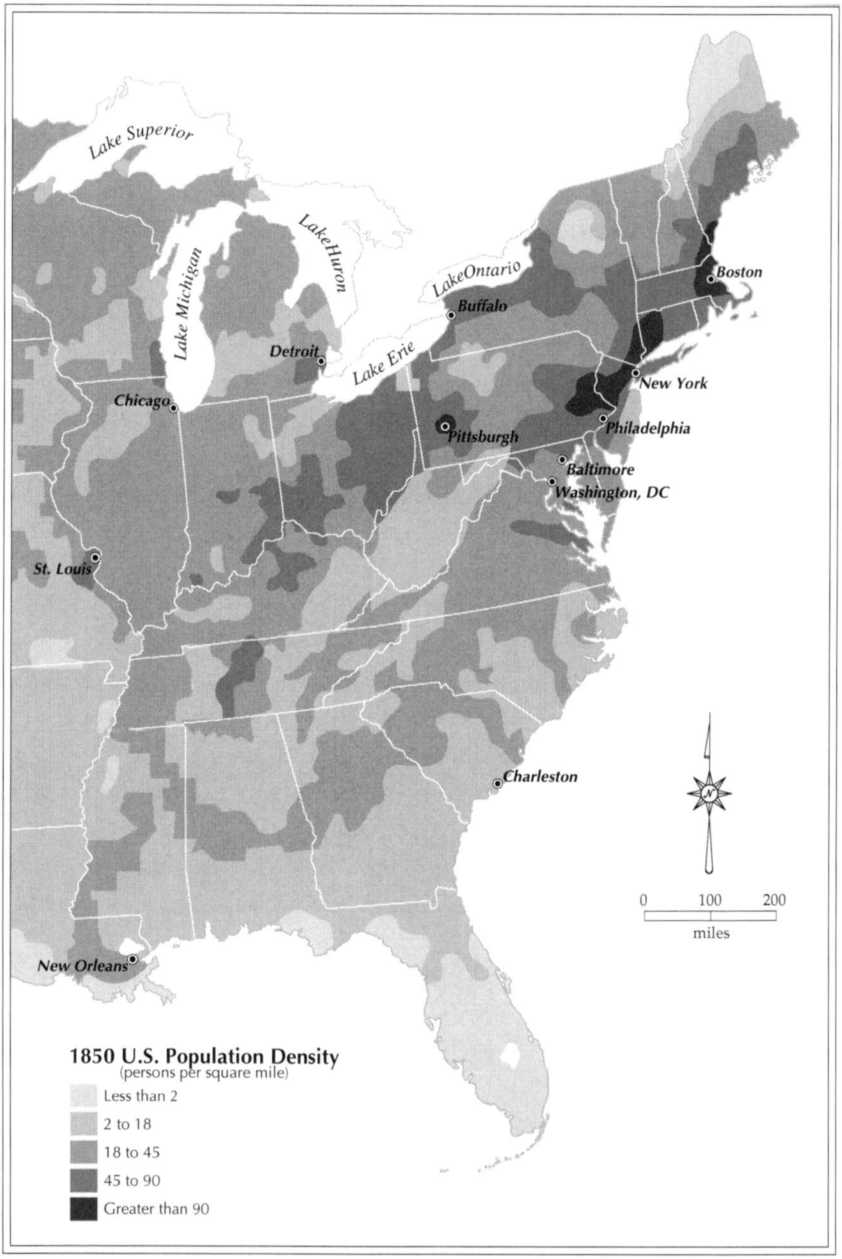


Map 6.1. 1850 US population density (persons per square mile).

One answer might look back to that deeply flawed, inconsistent founder Thomas Jefferson and the Declaration of Independence. "We hold these truths to be self-evident," Jefferson told the world in 1776, "that all men are created equal, that they are endowed by their Creator with certain unalienable Rights, that among these are Life, Liberty and the pursuit of Happiness."[3] It was an explosive idea at the time, with consequences bounding down to the present day. First, even though wealthy white men tried from the outset to limit its reach by class, then race, and finally gender, none of those boundaries held over the long term. Americans of varying means, creeds, colors, and genders forced the broader country to live up to the implications of its founding creed. Next, antebellum people, Whig and Democrat alike, probably agreed with Lincoln's argument at Gettysburg that theirs was or should be "a government of the people, by the people, for the people," though they might differ on how that end was best achieved.[4] In a deep way, the second party system formed around political debates about the partisan means that the people might use to control their government and reflect their values. One function that these parties performed was engineering compromises over slavery. Indeed, that compromises were required to save the Union in 1820 over Missouri and the extension of slavery, in 1832 over a slave state's proposed power to nullify federal laws (an argument that helped strengthen the intellectual bulwarks for secession), and again in 1850 over the expansion of slavery to the territories shows how uneasy that the peculiar institution rested in the minds of most Americans.

For some, Jefferson's creed did *not* apply to people of color, full stop. Blacks' inferiority was sanctioned by God, and their status as slaves was nothing more than natural law. For others, the mere fact of slavery in a country that was "conceived in Liberty, and dedicated to the proposition that all men are created equal," was a galling hypocrisy that grew harder to swallow over time.[5] The protection or limitation of slavery's expansion was set against the preservation of the Union. The Whiggish belief in conciliation, cooperation, and compromise often yielded on slavery to keep the country together, but each concession grew harder for middle-class Americans to stomach than the last. And, every time, the union that they preserved protected slavery too. America remained a slaveholding republic throughout the age of Jackson and Clay.

One way to look at that reality is to see a legacy of moral cowardice and political failure. Abolitionist voices grew louder and louder as the country expanded and there was no time when the condemnation of black chattel bondage was not heard somewhere in the growing United States. On the other hand, it is easy to celebrate the righteous work of the radical few and dismiss the fears of the conservative many. Part of the reason for this is probably that, when looking back upon past wrongs, too often too many find it seductive to assume that, because history has revealed the answer to be so glaring and obvious, past peoples must be benighted, moral pygmies to have missed it. Modern people fail to appreciate the sheer terror that the prospect of civil war generated in the minds and hearts of most antebellum Americans. Of course, everyday life was a terror-filled, arbitrary mess of depravity, cruelty, and barbarism for black men, women, and children living in bondage. Yet convincing a country where the vast majority took biting, nasty racism for granted to shoulder the butcher's bill to end black slavery was difficult. However, to middle-class Americans in the 1850s, it was becoming impossible to accommodate slavery's increasing demands and reconcile their own sense of the world as it ought to be.

Consequently, the Compromise of 1850 irritated everybody. Settlers in Utah and New Mexico, freed from Texas's dubious claims on their territory, could decide whether to allow slavery on the basis of popular sovereignty. Texas would take its current borders, while the federal government assumed the state's public debt. The South insisted on a more severe fugitive slave law and tried sweetening the bitter pill for outraged antislavery northerners by proposing to ban the slave trade (though not slavery itself) in the District of Columbia.[6] There was something for everyone, the moderates held the day, and no one was thrilled. The word *compromise* implies that both sides agreed to each other's terms, conceding some of what they wanted, to achieve a settlement with which all could live.

That is not what happened in 1850. Instead, the moderate middle accepted the various pieces of a patchwork, legislative quilt, quieting sectional strife for a time, but also allowing space for the unrepentant extremists to grind their axes for the next decade. A growing number of southerners began to see secession as the only concrete means to protect slavery, especially as "fire-eaters"—radical, prosecession southern polemicists—swelled to a shrill cacophony across Dixie calling for slavery's expansion or the death of the Union.[7] Middle-class northerners despised the Fugitive Slave Act most of all because it brought the horrors of slavery to their doorsteps with the disturbing pall of federal protection, forcing them at last to *participate* in the capture and return of runaway slaves. The layered federalism of the American legal system and the difficulties of travel meant that, until the 1850s, slavery was a distant, theoretical problem. Northerners who were uncomfortable with black chattel slavery could suppress their moral doubts because it was a southern problem hundreds of miles away. The Fugitive Slave Law ripped away this shoddy bandage, compelling all to get their hands dirty. Consequently, this law pushed many northern moderates toward the abolitionists, many northern states responded with personal liberty laws guaranteeing blacks' freedoms and angry mobs that answered slave-catching posses with violence.

Less than four years after Congress adopted the Compromise of 1850, the Whig Party dissolved. After the compromise failed to stem the tide of violence prompted by the proposed introduction of slavery in Kansas and Nebraska, many Whigs began questioning their party's leadership and direction. Whigs' ideological perspective, which informed their political agenda, was based on middle-class development over time, not space. The United States, most Whigs believed, should be improved by investment in transportation and communication and the prayerful attention to education, charity, and care for the infirm and insane. Yet their vision was slipping away, and many felt powerless. Crippled by sectional discord over slavery, in the eyes of most middle-class Americans Whiggery simply no longer offered the best avenue to pursue bourgeois goals. Territorial expansion was an accomplished fact by 1854, slavery seemed to overshadow everything, the sort of growth that mattered most to Whiggish Americans stalled, and Whigs were left to grapple with the consequences without a political party. The Whigs' America was going to smash as they watched in helpless horror.

Some disaffected Whigs found nativism a ready balm for their political discontent. Banning immigration and railing against the alleged failures in sobriety, cultivation, and intelligence of working-class Catholics was for many former Whigs much easier than reconciling slavery's expansion and national ideals celebrating individual liberty. Others saw through the thin crust of sectarian bigotry and found comfort in the new Republican Party that formed in Wisconsin in 1854. Republicans embraced nearly every aspect of the old Whig platform, including support for banks, a strong currency, the expansion of infrastructure through roads and railroads, and protective tariffs. What was missing? The Republicans reflected a growing middle-class consensus that refused to compromise on the extension of slavery, which was the political price that the South demanded for continued sectional harmony. Republican candidates made no concessions on the peculiar institution's expansion to the territories and, thus, drew little support in the South. Radicalism met radicalism as southerners came to see any Republican president as a direct threat to slavery. When the former Whig, now a Republican, Abraham Lincoln won the White House in 1860, the Lower South left the Union in the winter of 1860–1861, pushing the United States to the brink of civil war. On April 12, 1861, the armies of the newly constituted Confederate States of America began bombarding the Union troops stationed at Fort Sumter in the bay of the Charleston, South Carolina. Lincoln called for seventy-five thousand volunteers to suppress the southern rebellion, and the Upper South seceded. One side, Lincoln explained four years later, was "devoted altogether to saving the Union without war," while the other was "seeking to dissolve the Union, and divide effects, by negotiation": "Both parties deprecated war; but one of them would make war rather than let the nation survive; and the other would accept war rather than let it perish. And the war came."[8]

By 1864, along with several hundred thousand men already in the ground, slavery was dying. The short-war myth that supposedly everyone believed—that any war would be quick, cheap, and bloodless—is a durable fancy that privileges the views of professional soldiers and politicians over the darker fears of the women, blacks, and civilians who rightly expected a tidal wave of gore. It was largely an army of middle- and working-class white and black men whose war killed slavery, and, with over military 640,000 dead across the country and likely triple that number maimed or wounded, the price that they paid was high. For every three soldiers who died in battle, moreover, probably another five more died of disease, enduring horrific medical treatment in at best crude conditions. Surviving soldiers also suffered posttraumatic stress disorder and myriad other crushing psychological traumas mostly alone, usually uncataloged and uncared for by none save their families, friends, or churches.[9] But slavery was dead. A country full of deeply flawed men and women, most of whom probably still did not welcome the full extension of the Declaration's principles of equality and self-determinism to blacks, could no longer allow their bondage.[10]

Abraham Lincoln drew on the bigger picture to explain the war's deeper meaning. "If we shall suppose that American Slavery is one of those offences which, in the providence of God, must needs come, but which, having continued through His appointed time," he wondered, "He now wills to remove, and that He gives to both North and South, this terrible war, as the woe due to those by whom the offence came, shall we discern therein any departure from those divine attributes which the believers in a Living God always ascribe to Him?" Perhaps Whiggish people like Lincoln groped for an answer to the suffering in their midst and tried to convince themselves that civil war was a just penance for a middle-class people who tolerated slavery for so long: "Fondly do we hope, fervently do we pray, that this mighty scourge of war may speedily pass away." Bourgeois Whigs looked for moral purpose in public service, and many hoped that meaning could be drawn from shared sacrifice. "Yet, if God wills that it continue, until all the wealth piled by the bond-man's two hundred and fifty years of unrequited toil shall be sunk, and until every drop of blood drawn with the lash, shall be paid by another drawn with the sword," Lincoln laid out the gory moral bill in stark, clear language that was as lofty as it was harsh, "as was said three thousand years ago, so still it must be said 'the judgments of the Lord, are true and righteous altogether.'"[11] Thus, perhaps a fairer way to see the numerous compromises that preserved the Union throughout the antebellum era—and sadly slavery with it—is that they helped ensure that the country that they kept together was strong enough to survive the cataclysm of civil war and finally rid itself of slavery. It is also a fact that it was a former Illinois Whig who guided the nation through its darkest hours.

The middle-class political perspective survived the Civil War, outliving the Whigs, Abraham Lincoln, and sectional strife over slavery. Men and women of a certain publicly minded bent who valued education, self-restraint, and thrift found new political means to build a Whiggish world. Through the Gilded Age, and into the twentieth century, many Americans clung to the idea that cooperation, trust, and the tempering of self-interest with the common good could still build a better country, one broad-minded, civically engaged person at a time. In the end, they clung to the fragile hope that there was nothing wrong with America that could not be fixed by what was right with America.

It is an old-fashioned idea, true, but it has a certain staying power.

# Acknowledgments

As a much younger man, I was naive enough to wonder why authors wrote such ponderous acknowledgments. After working on this book for over a decade, the answer is obvious: nobody finishes such a project alone, and debts pile up. My wife, Erica, takes pride of place in my happy task of thanking those people who helped make this book possible. She is the love of my life, my raison d'être, and I am thankful each day that she chose to spend her life with me. Of course, I must next celebrate our dear children: Kieran, Isaac, Cora June, and Adeleine. They have enriched our lives immeasurably, and I am deeply proud of the young gentlemen and ladies that they are growing into. God bless our parents! Without their love, support, and encouragement, I truly doubt that we would enjoy even half of the modest success that we do.

Bruce Holle and Gretchen Starr-Lebeau are great teachers and good friends. Jim Klotter is a fantastic historian, a dear friend, and a Kentucky state treasure. He has steered me right more times than I can count. George Rable, Lawrence Kohl, and Kari Frederickson are fantastic scholars all and better people. I am proud to count them as friends. And thank you, thank you, *thank you* to all the generous archivists and librarians all across the Midwest and South who helped me track down materials and always answered questions. You ladies and gentlemen are the quiet stalwarts who keep scholarly efforts possible.

The University Press of Kentucky's (past and present) Leila Salisbury, Anne Dean Dotson, and David Cobb proved wonderful editors and stout champions of this book throughout the process. I appreciate that very much. Thanks also to the most diligent copyeditor in America, Joseph Brown. He saved me from numerous silly errors and mistakes; any that remain are my fault.

Finally, thank you also to the Union College Bulldog family. To the staff, students, and my colleagues in the faculty, I appreciate your conviviality, collegiality, and good-natured encouragement. I hope that this book makes you proud. Put one on the board for "Cannery Row."

# Notes

## Introduction

1. T. S. Eliot, "The Literature of Politics" (1955), in *To Criticize the Critic and Other Writings: Eight Essays on Literature and Education* (Lincoln: University of Nebraska Press, 1965; reprint, Lincoln: University of Nebraska Press, 1991), 144.

2. Deidre McCloskey, *The Bourgeois Virtues: Ethics for an Age of Commerce* (Chicago: University of Chicago Press, 2006), 66. The historiography of the bourgeoisie is varied and extensive. Peter Gay's magisterial five-volume *The Bourgeois Experience: Victoria to Freud* (New York: Norton, 1984–1998) remains the standard work on the topic. Other solid recent studies include Joseph F. Kett, *Merit: The History of a Founding Ideal from the American Revolution to the Twenty-First Century* (Ithaca, NY: Cornell University Press, 2013); Lawrence R. Samuel, *The American Dream: A Cultural History* (Syracuse, NY: Syracuse University Press, 2012); Deidre McCloskey, *Bourgeois Dignity: Why Economics Can't Explain the Modern World* (Chicago: University of Chicago Press, 2006); and Peter Gay, *Schnitzler's Century: The Making of Middle-Class Culture, 1815–1914* (New York: Norton, 2002).

3. McCloskey, *Bourgeois Dignity*, 6–7. On Jackson's fears, see Lawrence Frederick Kohl, *The Politics of Individualism: Parties and the American Character in the Jacksonian Era* (New York: Oxford University Press, 1989), 19–21.

4. Henry Clay, "On Mr. Foote's Motion for a Compromise Bill" (April 8, 1850), in *The Papers of Henry Clay*, ed. James F. Hopkins et al., 10 vols. (Lexington: University Press of Kentucky, 1959–1991), 10:698–99.

5. Henry Adams, *The Life of Albert Gallatin* (Philadelphia: J. B. Lippincott, 1880), 635.

To hear most antebellum political historians tell it, the Jacksonian Democrats were the party of ideas. Beginning with Arthur Schlesinger in 1945 and continuing through the first decade of the twenty-first century, waves of scholars portrayed Jacksonian Democrats as the party fighting for poor artisans, farmers, and mechanics against the Whiggish artifices of an entrenched "money power." This general analysis proved remarkably durable from Arthur M. Schlesinger Jr.'s *The Age of Jackson* (New York: Little, Brown, 1945; reprint, Old Saybrook, CT: Konecky & Konecky, 1971), Alan Dawley's *Class and Community* (Cambridge, MA: Harvard University Press, 1976; reprint; Cambridge, MA: Harvard University Press,

2000), and Harry L. Watson's *Liberty and Power: The Politics of Jacksonian America* (New York: Hill & Wang, 1990) to Charles Sellers's *The Market Revolution: Jacksonian America, 1815–1846* (New York: Oxford University Press, 1994) and Sean Wilentz's *The Rise of American Democracy: Jefferson to Lincoln* (New York: Norton, 2005), to name just a few. In this reading of the era, Democrats believed in ideas such as autonomy, liberty, and republicanism. And the Whigs? They were supposedly the party of wealthy bankers, southern planters, and eastern merchants. They were allegedly little more than a fractured coalition of evangelicals, modernizers, and moralizers, distantly linked by their baseless fears.

On the other hand, Michael F. Holt saw Whigs in a more favorable light than did other scholars. In the tightly argued *The Political Crisis of the 1850s* (New York: Wiley, 1978; reprint, New York: Norton, 1983) and the significantly longer, though less cogent, *The Rise and Fall of the American Whig Party: Jacksonian Politics and the Onset of the Civil War* (New York: Oxford University Press, 1999), he argued that Whiggery was a coalition of disparate social and sectional groups held together by a variety of centripetal outside factors (i.e., suspicion of mob politics, desire for banks, drive for internal improvements, etc.). As the parties grew closer on those issues, slavery and territorial expansion shattered Whig unity. For Holt, politics equaled politicians, and election results and ideas were largely dismissed.

Lawrence Frederick Kohl and Daniel Walker Howe offered the most innovative analyses in terms of ideology and cultural outlook. They were more receptive to the role of ideas and outlooks in shaping political thought and social activity. In *The Politics of Individualism,* Kohl argued that politics and political rhetoric mattered in Jacksonian America and that both reflected sharp differences in the minds and outlooks of people. As he understood things, Whigs believed so much in the destiny of America that they ceaselessly strove to release its creative energies for what they argued was the betterment of all. They did not push for moral reform or internal improvement, he urged, to secure wealth for the few at the expense of the many. Instead, they believed that the young American republic stood at a social, cultural, and political crossroads. Only by actively, even aggressively pushing people and institutions to improve their lives could they be assured that the country would achievement greatness.

First in *The Political Culture of the American Whigs* (Chicago: University of Chicago Press, 1979), and then much more forcefully in *What Hath God Wrought: The Transformation of America, 1815–1848* (New York: Oxford University Press, 2007), Daniel Walker Howe argued that innovations in transportation and communication such as railroads, steamboats, and telegraphs transformed antebellum America from loosely connected agricultural communities into a burgeoning economic powerhouse. The new technologies changed American politics and political culture, literature, and religion and sped up the exchange of and debate over contentious ideas.

6. Agreeing with Kohl, Howe maintained that Whigs were improvers, comfortable with modernity. They deeply believed in their own ability to advance the

minds and morals of their countrymen through temperance and education reforms. For Whigs, then, duties and obligations were as important as inchoate notions of rights. Individuals bore a responsibility to themselves and the country to restrain their passions, develop their minds, and achieve their potential. For Howe, those distinctions mattered. In his view, Whigs held a more subtle view of progress and a more optimistic vision of the future. This book builds on insights of Howe and Kohl.

7. Howe, *The Political Culture of the American Whigs,* 238–45. See also Scott A. Sandage, *Born Losers: A History of Failure in America* (Cambridge, MA: Harvard University Press, 2005), 75–77; and Howe, *What Hath God Wrought,* 577–88.

8. Thomas Jefferson quoted in Luigi Marco Bassani, *Liberty, State and Union: The Political Theory of Thomas Jefferson* (Macon, GA: Mercer University Press, 2010), 51. On Democratic criticisms of the Whigs, see Schlesinger, *The Age of Jackson,* 19–27; Kohl, *The Politics of Individualism,* 25–33; Wilentz, *The Rise of American Democracy,* 312–21; and Howe, *What Hath God Wrought,* 329–37.

Schlesinger, *The Age of Jackson,* 3. In a strict sense, the term *Whig* or *Whiggish* was not applied in party contexts until 1834. However, it remains one of the central arguments of this work that the people who later called themselves *Whigs* shared common beliefs, leanings, and fears before the formal structure was established and, indeed, after the party itself fell apart. John William Ward's *Andrew Jackson: Symbol for an Age* (New York: Oxford University Press, 1953) is probably still the best book on the various cultural and intellectual meanings Americans ascribed to Jackson's election. Other solid accounts include Schlesinger, *The Age of Jackson;* Watson, *Liberty and Power;* and Andrew Burstein, *The Passions of Andrew Jackson* (New York: Vintage, 2003).

9. This general overview was drawn from a mix of books such as, among others, Howe's *What Hath God Wrought;* Jill Lepore's *These Truths: A History of the United States* (New York: Norton, 2018); Wilentz's *The Rise of American Democracy;* and Daniel J. Boorstin's *The Americans: The Democratic Experience* (New York: Vintage, 1973).

10. Howe's *The Political Culture of the American Whigs* is the most durable study that divides the Whigs into subgroups such as modernizers, conservatives, and reformers. For more on this general overview, see Howe, *What Hath God Wrought,* 285–327. On time, see Martin Heidegger, *Being and Time,* trans. John Macquarrie and Edward Robinson (New York: Harper & Row, 1962); Eugene Minkowski, *Lived Time: Phenomenological and Psychopathological Studies,* trans. Nancy Metsel (Evanston, IL: Northwestern University Press, 1970); and David Carr, *Time, Narrative, and History* (Bloomington: Indiana University Press, 1986; reprint, Bloomington: Indiana University Press, 1991). These ideas on time (and others) are explored in intriguing detail, though in relation to how antebellum people imagined the coming Civil War in the decades before the conflict, in Jason Phillips, *Looming Civil War: How Nineteenth-Century Americans Imagined the Future* (New York: Oxford University Press, 2018).

## 1. The Individual

Epigraph: Philip Schaff quoted in Andrew Delbanco, *The Real American Dream: A Meditation on Hope* (Cambridge, MA: Harvard University Press, 1999), 62.

1. McCloskey, *Bourgeois Dignity,* 6–7.

2. Daniel Webster, "Address Delivered to the Citizens of Pittsburg [*sic*]" (July 8, 1833), in *The Works of Daniel Webster,* 14th ed., 6 vols. (Boston: Little, Brown, 1851–1866), 1:300.

3. Obviously, the concept of human nature has occupied historians, philosophers, and various other thinking men and women for nearly three thousand years. No list could do the subject justice, but, beyond religious texts or ancient accounts such as Plato's *The Republic* and St. Augustine's *City of God,* the most crucial works might include Niccolò Machiavelli's *The Prince* (1532), Thomas Hobbes's *Leviathan* (1651), John Locke's *Two Treatises of Government* (1689), Bernard Mandeville's *The Fable of the Bees; or, Private Vices, Publick Benefits* (1732), David Hume's *A Treatise on Human Nature* (1739), Adam Smith's *The Theory of Moral Sentiments* (1759), Samuel Johnson's *The History of Rasselas, Prince of Abissinia* (1759), Edmund Burke's *A Philosophical Enquiry into the Origin of Our Ideas of the Sublime and Beautiful* (1757), and Alexis de Tocqueville's *Democracy in America* (1835). See also McCloskey, *The Bourgeois Virtues,* 320–35; and McCloskey, *Bourgeois Dignity,* 10–16.

4. Henry Clay, "On Abolition Petitions: Speech in the Senate of the United States" (February 7, 1839), in Hopkins et al., eds., *The Papers of Henry Clay,* 9:278–79. For examples, see Abraham Lincoln, "The Perpetuation of Our Political Institutions: Address Before the Young Men's Lyceum of Springfield, Illinois" (1838), in *Abraham Lincoln: His Speeches and Writings,* ed. Roy P. Basler (Cleveland: World, 1946; reprint, Cambridge, MA: Da Capo, 2001), 77; Daniel Webster, "Reply to Hayne: A Speech in the United States Senate" (January 26, 1830), in *Pulpit and Rostrum: Sermons, Orations, Popular Lectures* (New York: H. H. Lloyd, 1861), 125; Horace A. Ackley, *Introductory Address of the Progress of the Science of Medicine* (Cleveland: Younglove, 1849); "Public Meeting," *National Banner and Nashville Whig,* August 5, 1835, 3; and M. M. Henkle, *The Moral Dignity and General Claims of Agricultural Science: An Address Delivered in the Chapel of Transylvania University* (Frankfort, KY: Hodges, Todd, & Pruett, 1843), 15.

5. "Introduction," *United States Magazine, and Democratic Review,* October 1837, 2.

"Domestic: Burning of the Charlestown Convent," *Pittsfield Sun,* August 21, 1834, 2. See also "Ursuline Report of the Burning of the Convent, August 11, 1834," Ursuline Convent, Charlestown, MA, Papers, box 1, folder 5, American Catholic History Research Center and University Archives, Washington, DC. The best scholarly accounts of the convent burning are Ray Allen Billington, *The Protestant Crusade, 1800–1860: A Study of the Origins of American Nativism* (New York: Rinehart, 1938); Nancy Lusignan Schultz, *Burning Down the House: The*

*Ursuline Convent Riot, Charlestown, Massachusetts, 1834* (Salem, MA: Salem State College Press, 1993); and Nancy Lusignan, *Fire and Roses: The Burning of the Charlestown Convent, 1834* (New York: Free Press, 2000). See also "Five Gamblers Hung without Trial," *New York Evangelist,* August 1, 1835, 213; and "Abuses of the Press Again!," *Catholic Telegraph,* February 27, 1835, 109.

6. David Grimstead's *American Mobbing, 1828–1861: Toward Civil War* (New York: Oxford University Press, 1998) is the best book on the rising violence of the antebellum era. For more on the Ursuline Convent burning and antebellum challenges to American Catholicism, see John T. McGreevy, *Catholicism and American Freedom* (New York: Norton, 2003). The violent possibilities beneath the Jacksonian culture of "go-ahead" that drove people in Vicksburg to hang recalcitrant gamblers are explored and explained in Joshua Rothman's *Flush Times and Fever Dreams: A Story of Capitalism and Slavery in the Age of Jackson* (Athens: University of Georgia Press, 2012). For more on the Anti-Rent Movement, see Henry Christman, *Tin Horns and Calico: A Decisive Episode in the Emergence of Democracy* (New York: Henry Holt, 1945); and Reeve Huston, *Land and Freedom: Rural Society, Popular Protest, and Party Politics in Antebellum New York* (New York: Oxford University Press, 2000). For grim details of the violent character of public life during the antebellum era, see Grimstead, *American Mobbing,* esp. 199–217 (chap. 7, "The Mobs of the Second Party System").

7. A growing body of interdisciplinary evidence suggests that Whigs had at least some reason to worry about the inherent savagery of individuals because the physiological and biochemical makeup of the human mind has not changed markedly since the late Paleolithic era, nearly forty to seventy-five thousand years in the past. Thus, no matter how sophisticated the civilization or how modern the society, a savage or righteous imagination was always present. The implications of these insights are explored in the chapters that follow. But, regarding individuals, as studies continue to show, human beings are hardwired by evolution to see their world in moral terms, and Western individualism is also psychologically welded onto a broader human need for the group. Consequently, parties and partisanship reflect both the moral interpretations that individuals invest in all they encounter and the desire to be surrounded by like-minded people who think and feel along similar lines. The anthropological and scientific evidence for this argument is both deep and, ironically enough, evolving. Jonathan Haidt's *The Righteous Mind: Why Good People Are Divided by Politics and Religion* (New York; Pantheon, 2012) is the single best book on the subject. Seminal works other than Charles Darwin's *On the Origin of Species* (1859) include Theodosius G. Dobzhansky, *Genetics and the Origin of Species* (New York: Columbia University Press, 1937); Claude Lévi-Strauss, *The Savage Mind* (Chicago: University of Chicago Press, 1966); John C. Eccles, *Evolution of the Brain: Creation of the Self* (New York: Routledge, 1989); Ian Tattersall, *The World from Beginnings to 4000 BCE* (New York: Oxford University Press, 2008); David Berreby, *Us and Them: The Science of Identity* (2005), 2nd ed. (Chicago: University of Chicago Press, 2008); Brian Fagan, *Cro-Magnon: How the*

*Ice Age Gave Birth to the First Modern Humans* (New York: Bloomsbury, 2010); *Evolution: The First Four Billion Years,* ed. Michael Ruse and Joseph Travis (Cambridge, MA: Belknap Press of Harvard University Press, 2011); Joshua Greene, *Moral Tribes: Emotion, Reason, and the Gap between Us and Them* (New York: Penguin, 2013); Robert M. Sapolsky, *Behave: The Biology of Humans at Our Best and Worst* (New York: Penguin, 2017); and Lisa Barrett, *How Emotions Are Made: The Secret Life of the Brain* (New York: Houghton Mifflin Harcourt, 2017).

8. "Lynching—*Vicksburg Sentinel and Expositor,*" *New-Yorker,* October 21, 1837, 494.

9. "The Progress of Democracy," *Subterranean,* April 24, 1847, 2.

10. "Jacobins," *Louisville Daily Journal,* June 28, 1845, 2; Horace Bushnell, "Barbarism the First Danger," *American National Preacher,* September 1847, 197. For a fair look at Democratic thinking on this point, see also "Abolition and Sectarian Mobs," *United States Magazine, and Democratic Review,* August 1854, 97; and "The Parricides of the Republic," *United States Magazine, and Democratic Review,* June 1851, 500. For more on Whig fears of barbarism and a glimpse of their view of its underlying causes, see "A Public Execution," *Spirit of the Age and Journal of Humanity,* October 17, 1833, 3; "July 12, 1834," *Albany Evening Journal,* July 15, 1834, 2; "Attempt at Assassination," *Louisville Journal,* July 8, 1835, 1; "Intelligence and Miscellany," *Law Reporter,* June 1844, 106–9; "Duelling in America," *Littell's Living Age,* December 4, 1847, 467–70; "Boyhood and Barbarism," *American Whig Review,* October 1851, 278; and "Modern Civilization," *Universalist Quarterly and General Review,* January 1858, 5–15. On Bushnell's Whiggish views, see Robert Bruce Mullin, *The Puritan as Yankee: A Life of Horace Bushnell* (Grand Rapids, MI: Eerdmans, 2002), 208–15.

11. M. Genung, "Lazy People," *Ladies' Repository: A Monthly Periodical, Devoted to Literature, Art and Religion,* October 1, 1857, 603. See also "Fanny Gossip and Susan Lazy," *Robert Merry's Museum,* February–July 1841, 145; "Laziness," *Maine Farmer and Mechanic's Advocate,* September 17, 1842, 1; "Morality: Lazy Boy," *Youth's Companion,* February 3, 1853, 163; and "Drones," *New World,* October 24, 1840, 334.

12. Abraham Lincoln, "Fragments of a Tariff Discussion" (December 1, 1847), in *The Collected Works of Abraham Lincoln,* ed. Roy P. Basler, 9 vols. (New Brunswick, NJ: Rutgers University Press, 1953), 1:412. Lincoln's bourgeois thinking on labor and what constitutes *work,* properly understood, reflects broader trends among the rising middle class across the Western world in the nineteenth century. See, e.g., Michael J. Novak, *Business as a Calling: Work and the Examined Life* (New York: Free Press, 1996), 125–31; Gay, *Schnitzler's Century,* 191–200; and McCloskey, *The Bourgeois Virtues,* 136–38.

13. "What Is Original Sin?," Religions, BBC, September 17, 2009, http://www.bbc.co.uk/religion/religions/christianity/beliefs/originalsin_1.shtml. See also McCloskey, *The Bourgeois Virtues,* 443–46; Haidt, *The Righteous Mind,* 35–36; and Greene, *Moral Tribes,* 55–56.

14. "Human Rights according to Modern Philosophy," *American Whig Review*, October 1845, 327–40, 332.

15. Henry Clay, "Speech in Lexington" (June 9, 1842), in Hopkins et al., eds., *The Papers of Henry Clay*, 9:712.

16. Daniel Webster, "Whig Principles and Purposes," in *The Works of Daniel Webster*, 2:42.

17. G. K. Chesterton, *Orthodoxy* (New York: John Lane, 1909), 212. For regional evidence of Whigs urging constant moral upkeep and improvement, see "Habits of Exercise," *Raleigh Register*, June 24, 1834, 1; "Public Baths," *National Banner and Nashville Whig*, July 3, 1835, 3; "Mechanics," *Vicksburg Register*, May 16, 1838, 3; and "A Word with Our Friends," *New York Tribune*, May 3, 1841, 2. A few national examples include "Public Education," *Godey's Lady's Book and Ladies' American Magazine*, February 1840, 51; "The True Aim of Life," *Ladies' Repository: A Monthly Periodical, Devoted to Literature, Art and Religion*, April 1854, 175; and Webster, "Whig Principles and Purposes."

18. From George Washington to a Continental Congress Camp Committee, January 29, 1778, Founders Online, National Archives, https://founders.archives.gov/documents/Washington/03-13-02-0335. For more on Washington and emerging American nationalism, see Paul C. Nagel, *This Sacred Trust: American Nationality, 1798–1898* (New York: Oxford University Press, 1971); Clinton Rossiter, *The American Quest, 1790–1860: An Emerging Nation in Search of Identity, Unity, and Modernity* (New York: Harcourt Brace Jovanovich, 1971); Henry Steele Commager, *Jefferson, Nationalism, and the Enlightenment* (New York: George Braziller, 1975); David Waldstreicher, *In the Midst of Perpetual Fetes: The Making of American Nationalism, 1776–1820* (Chapel Hill: University of North Carolina Press, 1997), esp. 117–26; and Reginald C. McGrane, "George Washington: An Anglo-American Hero," *Virginia Magazine of History and Biography* 63 (January 1955): 3–14.

19. James Madison, "The Federalist No. 51: The Structure of the Government Must Furnish the Proper Checks and Balances between the Different Departments," *Independent Journal*, February 6, 1788, Constitution.org, http://www.constitution.org/fed/federa51.htm. Similar founding examples include Alexander Hamilton, "The Federalist No. 78: The Judiciary Department," *Independent Journal*, June 14, 1788, Constitution.org, http://www.constitution.org/fed/federa78.htm; and James Wilson, "Speech of James Wilson" (October 6, 1787), in *The Anti-Federalist Papers*, ed. Ralph Ketchum (New York: Penguin, 1986; reprint, New York: Signet, 2003), 183–88. Madison, Wilson, and Hamilton, among many other founders, were quoted extensively in the partisan press. See, e.g., "Is the Law of God Eternal?," *Methodist Magazine and Quarterly Review*, January 1, 1833, 477; "The President's Message: The War," *American Whig Review*, January 1847, 1; and "Slavery," *National Era*, July 10, 1851, 110.

20. "Woman," *Musical Visitor*, April 30, 1841, 48; "Thoughts on Women," *Ladies' Garland and Family Wreath*, May 22, 1837, 45. See also "Men and

Gentlemen, Women and Ladies," *Michigan Farmer and Western Agriculturist,* October 16, 1843, 136; "The Women, God Bless Them," *New York Illustrated Magazine of Literature and Art,* January 1846, 393; "Woman's True Greatness," *American Penny Magazine and Family Magazine,* August 15, 1846, 448; and "Woman," *Godey's Lady's Book and Ladies' American Magazine,* February 1840, 76. Catherine E. Beecher's *A Treatise on Domestic Economy* (Boston: T. H. Webb, 1842) is among the more famous contemporary defenses of middle-class domesticity. See also Gay, *The Bourgeois Experience,* 2:46–58; and McCloskey, *The Bourgeois Virtues,* 132–38. The best scholarship on antebellum feminine virtue and domesticity include Nancy F. Cott, *The Bonds of Womanhood: "Woman's Sphere" in New England, 1780–1835* (New Haven, CT: Yale University Press, 1977); Christine Stansell, *City of Women: Sex and Class in New York, 1789–1860* (Champaign: University of Illinois Press, 1987); Gillian Brown, *Domestic Individualism: Imagining Self in Nineteenth-Century America* (Berkeley and Los Angeles: University of California Press, 1992); and Ann Douglas, *The Feminization of American Culture* (New York: Farrar, Straus & Giroux, 1998).

21. Daniel Webster, "Reception at Buffalo, New York" (May 22, 1851), in *The Works of Daniel Webster,* 2:522.

22. Henry Clay, "On Abolition" (February 7, 1839), quoted in Howe, *What Hath God Wrought,* 587. On the economic and political inconsistencies of the southern Whigs' position on slavery, see Howe, *What Hath God Wrought,* 585–88; Sven Beckert, *Empire of Cotton: A Global History* (New York: Vintage, 2014), 136–44; Calvin Schermerhorn, *The Business of Slavery and the Rise of American Capitalism, 1815–1860* (New Haven, CT: Yale University Press, 2015), 96–101; and Edward E. Baptist, *The Half Has Never Been Told: Slavery and the Making of American Capitalism* (New York: Basic, 2016), 261–67.

23. "The Whig Party, Its Position, and Duties," *American Whig Review,* December 1845, 547–60, 552; "The Rich against the Poor: The Laboring Classes," *Methodist Quarterly Review,* January 1841, 116. A few other examples include "Equality of Happiness," *New-Yorker,* November 14, 1840, 136; "Robert Owen—Universal Reform," *Liberator,* October 18, 1844, 168; "Whig Principle and Its Development," *American Whig Review,* February 1852, 124–34, 124; and William Henry Seward, "Annual Message to the Legislature" (January 7, 1840), in *The Works of William Henry Seward,* ed. George E. Baker, 5 vols. (Boston: Houghton, Mifflin, 1853–1884), 2:252. The bourgeoisie, American Whigs included, have long championed effort, striving, and discipline in their understanding of material disparities among a given set of people. For a deeper look at this point of view, see, e.g., Walter E. Houghton, *The Victorian Frame of Mind, 1830–1870* (New Haven, CT: Yale University Press, 1957), 191–95; Kohl, *The Politics of Individualism,* 188–90; Gay, *Schnitzler's Century,* 191–97; and McCloskey, *Bourgeois Dignity,* 143–45.

24. "Politics of the Day," *Niles' Weekly Register,* August 4, 1832, 408.

25. Daniel Webster, "The Character of Washington" (February 22, 1832), in *The Works of Daniel Webster,* 1:221.

26. William Henry Seward, "Annual Message to the Legislature" (January 1, 1839), in Baker, ed., *The Works of William Henry Seward,* 2:197. The best scholarship on the promise and possibility of America as an idea probably remains Henry Nash Smith's *Virgin Land: The American West as Symbol and Myth* (Cambridge, MA: Harvard University Press, 1950), R. W. B. Lewis's *The American Adam: Innocence, Tragedy, and Tradition in the Nineteenth Century* (Chicago: University of Chicago Press, 1959), Leo Marx's *The Machine in the Garden: Technology and the Pastoral Ideal in America* (New York: Oxford University Press, 1964; reprint, New York: Oxford University Press, 2000), Boorstin's *The Americans,* David E. Nye's *American Technological Sublime* (Cambridge, MA: MIT Press, 1994), and John F. Kasson's *Civilizing the Machine: Technology and Republican Values in America, 1776–1900* (New York: Hill & Wang, 1999).

27. "Human Nature," *New England Galaxy and United States Literary Advertiser,* August 20, 1836, 2. See also Orestes Brownson, "Tendency of Modern Civilization," *Boston Quarterly Review,* April 1838, 205.

28. "The Prospect Before Us," *Louisville Journal,* July 8, 1835, 1; "Social Intercourse," *Southern Whig,* April 9, 1841, 2; Joseph S. Tomlinson, "Our Country," *Ladies' Repository, and Gatherings of the West,* January 1842, 7; "Opinion of the World," *New York Tribune,* September 3, 1842, 1; "The Whig Cause," *Albany Evening Journal,* August 25, 1840, 3.

29. Abraham Lincoln, "Address at a Sanitary Fair in Baltimore" (April 18, 1864), in Basler, ed., *Abraham Lincoln: His Speeches and Writings,* 748; Noah Webster, *American Dictionary of the English Language* (New York: S. Converse, 1830), 498 (s.v. *liberty*). The definitions of *liberty* offered in the next two paragraphs are taken from Webster's *Dictionary.*

30. For evidence that the Western bourgeoisie valued liberty as long as it was checked by order and self-control, see McCloskey, *The Bourgeois Virtues,* 53; and Niall Ferguson, *Civilization: The West and the Rest* (New York: Penguin, 2011), 154–55.

31. "Our Liberty Its Own Danger," *New York Evangelist,* August 11, 1842, 128. See also "July 12, 1834," 2; "To the Public," *Louisville Journal,* July 8, 1835, 1; "Mr. Van Buren and the South," *Alabama Intelligencer,* September 19, 1835, 3; "The Polls," *Richmond Whig,* September 11, 1840, 1; "Democracy in France," *Augusta Chronicle,* February 16, 1849, 2; and "Speech of Ex-Gov. Neill S. Brown: The Public Lands and Alien Suffrage," *Republican Banner,* June 17, 1857, 2. Throughout most of his public career, Neill Brown was one of Tennessee's staunchest and most prolific Whigs. For more, see Joseph O. Baylen, "A Tennessee Politician in Imperial Russia, 1850–1853," *Tennessee Historical Quarterly* 14 (1955): 227–52.

32. "To the People of Virginia," *Niles' National Register,* March 2, 1844, 10; "The Result of the Election," *American Whig Review,* February 1845, 116. The charge of faction went up during each electoral cycle. For evidence, see "The Work Goes Bravely On," *The Rough and Ready,* January 30, 1847, 4–10; "Truth Is Mighty," *Raleigh Register,* July 7, 1840, 3; "Hartford Whig Convention," *New York*

*Herald,* February 21, 1842, 1; "A Word to Southern Democrats: By a Northern Conservative," *American Whig Review,* August 1849, 190–98; "Position of the Whig Party," *National Era,* February 12, 1852, 26; and "A Search After Democratic 'Principles,'" *American Whig Review,* July 1852, 79–85.

33. "The Crisis," *Tennessee Whig* (Elizabethon), May 23, 1839, 3. See also "Things in General," *Boston Courier,* March 29, 1832, 3; "New Riots—Law—Liberty—Order," *National Era,* May 24, 1849, 82; "An Apology for the Newest Whig Policy," *Albion: A Journal of News, Politics and Literature,* September 6, 1851, 425; Kohl, *The Politics of Individualism,* 146–48; McCloskey, *The Bourgeois Virtues,* 346–49; John A. Hall, *The Importance of Being Civil: The Struggle for Political Decency* (Princeton, NJ: University of Princeton Press, 2013), 19–25; and Mary Babson Fuhrer, *A Crisis of Community: The Trials and Transformation of a New England Town* (Chapel Hill: University of North Carolina Press, 2014), 108.

34. Edmund Burke, *Reflections on the Revolution in France* (1790), ed. Conor Cruise O'Brien (New York: Penguin, 1968; reprint, New York: Penguin, 1986), 89–90; "Christian Liberty," *Monthly Religious Magazine,* January 1844, 14. See also "Our Palladium of Liberty," *Knickerbocker,* September 1841, 247; "Progress of Civil Liberty," *Southern Literary Messenger,* December 1841, 848; "Ladies' Department: Influence of Women in the Present Time," *Boston Cultivator,* March 16, 1844, 83; Kohl, *The Politics of Individualism,* 157–60; Gregory Clark, *A Farewell to Alms: A Brief Economic History of the World* (Princeton, NJ: Princeton University Press, 2007), 259–62; and McCloskey, *Bourgeois Dignity,* 366–67. On Burke's resonance for Whigs, see "Edmund Burke," *Albion: A Journal of News, Politics and Literature,* November 29, 1834, 379; "Edmund Burke," *American Monthly Magazine,* May 1853, 625–30; and "Edmund Burke," *American Whig Review,* October 1852, 312.

35. Daniel Webster, "Reception at Buffalo" (1833), in *The Works of Daniel Webster,* 1:284. See also "Domestic," *Boston Recorder,* October 31, 1834, 175; "The Whig Party, Its Position, and Duties," 547–55; "Whig Principles," *Cincinnati Herald,* December 10, 1845, 1; and Ackley, *Introductory Address of the Progress of the Science of Medicine,* 15–16.

36. "The Spirit of Liberty," *American Whig Review,* December 1845, 614–22, 614.

37. McCloskey, *The Bourgeois Virtues,* 212–20; Haidt, *The Righteous Mind,* 142–46.

38. William Leggett, "The Monopoly Banking System," in *A Collection of the Political Writings of William Leggett,* ed. Theodore Sedgwick, 2 vols. (New York: Taylor & Dodd, 1840), 1:103–4. See also Kohl, *The Politics of Individualism,* 34–35; and Richard N. Current, *Daniel Webster and the Rise of National Conservatism* (Boston: Little, Brown, 1955), 75–79.

39. Sellers, *The Market Revolution,* 128; Wilentz, *The Rise of American Democracy,* 441; Watson, *Liberty and Power,* 43–44; Haidt, *The Righteous Mind,* 144–45. For an explanation of the Conservative/Liberal divide on authority, see Haidt, *The*

*Righteous Mind,* esp. 142–46 (chap. 7, "The Moral Foundations of Politics"). A few contemporary examples include "The Rationale of Political Representation," *American Quarterly Review,* September 1, 1836, 174–99; "Society in America," *North American Review,* October 1837, 418–25; "The Americans, in Their Moral, Social, and Political Relations," *North American Review,* January 1838, 106–7; "Authority against Reason," *United States Magazine, and Democratic Review,* September 1844, 272–80; and "American Civilization," *United States Magazine, and Democratic Review,* July 1858, 50–55.

40. "Letter from John W. Gildart to the President of the Democratic Convention at Jackson," *Mississippian,* November 21, 1834, 1; Leggett quoted in Kohl, *The Politics of Individualism,* 28. See also "Men and Manners in America," *Museum of Foreign Literature, Science, and Art,* October 1833, 468–74; "Epitome of the Times," *Atkinson's Saturday Evening Post,* December 7, 1833, 3; "Common Council," *Workingman's Advocate,* January 24, 1835, 2; "Money," *Huntress,* April 15, 1837, 3; "The Political Crisis," *United States Magazine, and Democratic Review,* June 1838, 312–19; Schlesinger, *The Age of Jackson,* 74–82; Sean Wilentz, *Chants Democratic: New York City and the Rise of the American Working Class, 1788–1850* (New York: Oxford University Press, 1984), 212–16; Sellers, *The Market Revolution,* 19–25; David S. Reynolds, *Waking Giant: America in the Age of Jackson* (New York: HarperCollins, 2008), 81–85; and William Leggett, "The Corporation Question," *Plaindealer,* December 24, 1836, 50. For Democrats, these fears were wide and deep. A few examples include "Notes," *Hampshire Republican,* August 3, 1836, 2; "Account of a Federal Whig Tippecanoe Meeting," *Arkansas State Gazette,* February 5, 1840, 1; and "Farming," *Weekly Argus and Rough-Hewer,* March 5, 1840, 3.

41. "Virginia Whig State Convention," *Niles' National Register,* October 19, 1839, 125.

42. John Pendleton Kennedy, "Explorations and Survey," in *Political and Official Papers* (New York: G. P. Putnam & Sons, 1872), 533.

43. See Howe, *The Political Culture of the American Whigs,* 216–20; Kohl, *The Politics of Individualism,* 212–14; Fuhrer, *A Crisis of Community,* 189–91; Clark, *A Farewell to Alms,* 36–37; McCloskey, *Bourgeois Dignity,* 125–29; and Haidt, *The Righteous Mind,* 137–38.

44. "Equality," *Boston Courier,* September 9, 1839, 3. See also "Human Equality," *Godey's Lady's Book and Ladies' American Magazine,* May 1835, 239; "Equality of the Rich and Poor," *Boston Recorder,* January 7, 1842, 1; "Social Inequality," *Christian Register,* May 9, 1846, 74; and "Natural Equality," *American Quarterly Register and Magazine,* September 1848, 475–76.

45. William Leggett, "The Inequality of the Human Condition" (*Plaindealer,* December 31, 1836), excerpted in *Democratic Editorials: Essays in Jacksonian Political Economy,* ed. Lawrence H. White (Indianapolis: Liberty Fund, 1984), 254–58, 257. A few examples of this thinking include "Liberty and Equality," *Banner of the Constitution,* May 30, 1832, 205–6; "Introduction to the Literature of Europe,"

*Albion: A Journal of News, Politics and Literature,* April 29, 1837, 129; "The Proper Sphere of Woman," *Hesperian* 2, no. 3 (January 1839): 181–82; and "Woman," *Ladies' National Magazine,* September 1844, 103. See also William R. Brock, *Parties and Political Conscience: American Dilemmas, 1840–1850* (Millbrook, NY: KTO, 1979), 265; Kohl, *The Politics of Individualism,* 187–88; and Howe, *What Hath God Wrought,* 380.

46. Calvin Colton, *The Americans* (London: Frederic Wesley & A. H. Davis), 362.

47. "The Nineteenth Century," *Southern Literary Messenger,* August 1851, 457–65, 461. See also "On Col. Johnson's Letter," *Louisville Journal,* July 3, 1835, 3; "Equality of Happiness," 136; "Whigs—Democrats—Equality," *Cincinnati Weekly Herald,* October 25, 1843, 2; "The Party of Progress," *Cincinnati Weekly Herald,* August 16, 1844, 1; "Movements of the Enemy," *American Whig Review,* September 1852, 193–200; and "Notes," *Louisville Journal,* December 22, 1853, 3.

48. Horace Mann, *A Few Thoughts for a Young Man* (Boston: Fuller, 1850; reprint, Boston: Lothrop, Lee, & Shepherd, 1870), 28.

49. Also relevant is the engraving by J. W. Barber *The Drunkard's Progress; or, The Direct Road to Poverty, Wretchedness and Ruin* (New Haven, CT: John Barber, 1826), Library of Congress, Prints and Photographs Online Catalog, http://www.loc.gov/pictures/resource/ppmsca.32721.

50. Abraham Lincoln, "Temperance Address Delivered Before the Springfield Washington Temperance Society" (February 22, 1842), in Basler, ed., *Abraham Lincoln: His Speeches and Writings,* 139–40.

51. "Employment," *New York Observer,* January 25, 1855, 30.

52. Lincoln, "Temperance Address Delivered Before the Springfield Washington Temperance Society," 139–40. See also Robert H. Wiebe, *The Segmented Society: An Introduction to the Meaning of America* (New York: Oxford University Press, 1976); Ronald G. Waters, *American Reformers: 1815–1860* (New York: Hill & Wang, 1978; reprint, New York: Hill & Wang, 1997), 132; W. J. Rorabaugh, *The Alcoholic Republic: An American Tradition* (New York: Oxford University Press, 1979), 200–201; Howe, *The Political Culture of the American Whigs,* 216–20; Kohl, *The Politics of Individualism,* 212–14; Fuhrer, *A Crisis of Community,* 189–91; Robert Nisbet, *The Quest for Community* (New York: Oxford University Press, 1953), 25–28; and McCloskey, *The Bourgeois Virtues,* 69–70.

53. "Loafer v. Lawyer," *New World,* July 30, 1842, 79.

54. "The Whigs and Their Candidate," *American Whig Review,* September 1848, 221.

55. "Loafer v. Lawyer," 79; "The Whigs and Their Candidate," 221; W. P. Tilden, *Temperance: A Sermon, Delivered to the First Congregational Society of Fitchburg, on Sunday, April 13, 1856* (Fitchburg, MA: E & J. Garfield, 1856), 4. See also Waters, *American Reformers,* 132–35; Rorabaugh, *The Alcoholic Republic,* 200–205; Howe, *The Political Culture of the American Whigs,* 266–70; Kohl, *The Politics of Individualism,* 72–74; and Howe, *What Hath God Wrought,* 598–99.

56. Daniel D. Barnard, *The Social System: An Address Before the House of Convocation, of Trinity College, Hartford, August 2, 1848* (Hartford, CT: Samuel Hanmer Jr./Calendar Press, 1848), 29. See also Kohl, *The Politics of Individualism,* 72; Houghton, *The Victorian Frame of Mind,* 191–95; Gay, *Schnitzler's Century,* 191–97; and McCloskey, *Bourgeois Dignity,* 143–45.

57. Sarah Josepha Hale, "The Mother," *Godey's Lady's Book and Ladies' American Magazine,* December 1848, 389. See also "The Proper Sphere of Woman," 181–82; and "Woman" (*Ladies' National Magazine*), 103. On the rural character of most antebellum Americans' lives, it is useful to consider that, as late as 1850, the US Census listed only a shade over 15 percent of the total population as living in urban places, urban places being considered towns of merely twenty-five hundred or more.

58. Daniel Webster, "Address to the Ladies of Richmond" (October 5, 1840), in *The Great Speeches of Daniel Webster* (Boston: Little, Brown, 1879), 479.

59. Webster, "Address to the Ladies of Richmond," 479. Karen Halttunen's *Confidence Men and Painted Women: A Study of Middle-Class Culture in America, 1830–1870* (New Haven, CT: Yale University Press, 1982), esp. 57–60, offers a detailed look at these caricatures and the importance they played in American culture, though her use of them and mine differ slightly. Thus, my analysis is more concerned with recovering bourgeois sincerity than with comparing new modes of femininity with older ones (i.e., sentimental womanhood). A few examples of this aspiring bourgeois pride include "Who Shall Tell of a Mother's Value?," *Christian Register,* October 2, 1847, 160; "My Dear Mother," *The Ladies' Repository: A Monthly Periodical, Devoted to Literature, Art and Religion,* October 1849, 293–94; and "The Mother," *Episcopal Recorder,* December 1, 1849, 152. See also Jack Larkin, *The Reshaping of Everyday Life, 1790–1840* (New York: HarperCollins, 1989), 66–70; James M. Volo and Dorothy D. Volo, *Family Life in 19th-Century America* (Westport, CT: Greenwood, 2007), 194–95; and Randolph Hollingsworth, "'Mrs. Boone, I presume?' In Search of an Idea of Womanhood in Kentucky's Early Years," in *Bluegrass Renaissance: The History and Culture of Central Kentucky, 1792–1852,* ed. James C. Klotter and Daniel Rowland (Lexington: University Press of Kentucky, 2012), 93–131, 119.

60. "A Mother's Influence," *Christian Advocate and Journal,* August 16, 1849, 129; "I Did It to Please a Mother," *New York Observer,* February 1, 1840, 3. See also "The Mother in Affliction," *Ladies' Repository, and Gatherings of the West,* July 1848, 204–5; "My Mother," *Christian Register,* February 3, 1849, 20; and McCloskey, *The Bourgeois Virtues,* 126–30.

61. Mrs. A. J. Graves, *Woman in America: Being an Examination into the Moral and Intellectual Condition of American Female Society* (New York: Harper & Bros., 1843), quoted in *Antebellum American Culture: An Interpretative Anthology,* ed. David Brion Davis (New York: D. C. Heath, 1979; reprint, New York: Routledge, 1998), 19; "Female Education," *Godey's Lady's Book and American Magazine,* July 1831, 29. Other examples include "To Mothers," *Evangelical Magazine and Gospel Advocate,* December 8, 1837, 389; Josiah Holbrook, "Domestic Education,"

*Journal of Education,* August 1838, 46; "The Duty of Mothers," *Common School Journal,* March 1, 1839, 72; "Duty of Mothers," *Poughkeepsie Casket: A Semi-Monthly Literary Journal, Devoted Exclusively to the Different Branches of Polite Literature,* June 15, 1839, 15; and "A Letter to Mothers: On the Home Education and Training of Children," *Ohio Cultivator,* January 15, 1851, 31. See also Ellen C. DuBois and Lynn Dumenil, *Through Women's Eyes: An American History with Documents* (Boston: Bedford/St. Martin's, 2012), 191; McCloskey, *The Bourgeois Virtues,* 223–27; and Fuhrer, *A Crisis of Community,* 152.

62. "Human Rights according to Modern Philosophy," 330; Beecher, *A Treatise on Domestic Economy,* 26. See also Houghton, *The Victorian Frame of Mind,* 191–95; Gay, *Schnitzler's Century,* 191–97; McCloskey, *The Bourgeois Virtues,* 227–29; and Fuhrer, *A Crisis of Community,* 152.

63. "The Priest—the Wife—the Family," *United States Magazine, and Democratic Review,* August 1845, 134. Other examples include "The Family State," *New York Evangelist,* November 11, 1837, 184; "Our Mistakes," *Ladies' Repository, and Gatherings of the West,* May 1844, 153; "Love and Marriage," *Harbinger, Devoted to Social and Political Progress,* October 28, 1848, 202; and "'Woman's Rights,'" *American Whig Review,* October 1848, 367–72.

64. "The Priest—the Wife—the Family," 134.

65. Leggett, "The Monopoly Banking System," 103–4. The terms *heroic artisan* and *self-made man* were drawn from Michael Kimmel's provocative *Manhood in America: A Cultural History* (1998), 3rd ed. (New York: Oxford University Press, 2012), chap. 1 ("The Birth of the Self-Made Man"), esp. 25–31. See also Lewis, *The American Adam,* 90–94; Marx, *The Machine in the Garden,* 227–29; Nye, *American Technological Sublime,* 65–72; and E. Anthony Rotundo, *American Manhood: Transformation in Masculinity from the Revolution to the Modern Era* (New York: Basic, 1993), 165–71.

66. Alexis de Tocqueville, *Democracy in America* (1835–1840), trans. and ed. Harvey C. Mansfield and Debra Winthrop (Chicago: University of Chicago Press, 2000), 482. See also Kohl, *The Politics of Individualism,* 11; and Howe, *What God Wrought,* 187–88.

67. Theodore Russell to Charles Russell, May 30, 1838, quoted in Rotundo, *American Manhood,* 168.

68. Henry Clay, "On the American System" (February 2, 1832), in *The Papers of Henry Clay,* 8:455–56; Daniel Webster, "Adams and Jefferson," in *The Works of Daniel Webster,* 1:122. See also McCloskey, *The Bourgeois Virtues,* 224–29, 241–47; Halttunen, *Confidence Men and Painted Women,* 13; Rotundo, *American Manhood;* Gay, *Schnitzler's Century,* 191–97; and Fuhrer, *A Crisis of Community,* 152.

69. Calvin Colton, *The Junius Tracts: No. VII* (New York: Greeley & McElrath, 1844), 111.

70. Schlesinger, *The Age of Jackson,* 19–27; Kohl, *The Politics of Individualism,* 25–33; Wilentz, *The Rise of American Democracy,* 312–21; Howe, *What Hath God Wrought,* 329–37.

## 2. Society

Epigraph: Pierre-Joseph Proudhon quoted in Gregory D. Sumner, *Dwight Macdonald and the Politics Circle: The Challenge of Cosmopolitan Democracy* (Ithaca, NY: Cornell University Press, 1996), 120.

1. Daniel Webster, "Mass Meeting in Saratoga" (1840), in *The Works of Daniel Webster,* 2:20; John Pendleton Kennedy, "A Review of Mr. Cambreleng's Report from the Committee of Commerce," in *Political and Official Papers,* 24. McCloskey's *The Bourgeois Virtues* is the single best account of the role of the seven virtues (i.e., faith, hope, love, temperance, courage, justice, and prudence) in the culture and thinking of Western bourgeoisie, but other solid work on the middle class/bourgeoisie includes Gay, *The Bourgeois Experience;* Peter Gay, *Modernism: The Lure of Heresy* (New York: Norton, 2008); McCloskey, *Bourgeois Dignity;* Franco Moretti, *The Bourgeois: Between History and Literature* (London: Verso, 2014); and Amy E. Wendling, *The Ruling Ideas: Bourgeois Political Concepts* (Lanham, MD: Lexington, 2014). Some of the best scholarship on southern Whigs and their middle-class sympathies includes Charles Grier Sellers Jr., "Who Were the Southern Whigs?," *American Historical Review* 59, no. 2 (January 1954): 335–46; Jonathan D. Wells, *The Origins of the Southern Middle Class, 1800–1861* (Chapel Hill: University of North Carolina Press, 2004); Paul Quigley, *Shifting Grounds: Nationalism and the American South, 1848–1865* (New York: Oxford University Press, 2011); Andrew R. Black, *John Pendleton Kennedy: Early American Novelist, Whig Statesman, and Ardent Nationalist* (Baton Rouge: Louisiana State University Press, 2014); and William J. Cooper Jr., *Approaching Civil War and Southern History* (Baton Rouge: Louisiana State University Press, 2019).

2. Colton, *The Americans,* 21; "Whigs—Whig Principles," *Nashville Republican,* August 1, 1837, 3.

3. "The Whig Party," *Republican Banner,* March 19, 1851, 2; Webster, "Address to the Ladies of Richmond," 479. The best scholarship on the changing social order includes Smith, *Virgin Land;* Lewis, *The American Adam;* Marx, *The Machine in the Garden;* Daniel J. Boorstin, *The Americans: The National Experience* (New York: Random House, 1965; reprint, New York: Vintage, 2002); Roderick Nash, *Wilderness and the American Mind* (New Haven, CT: Yale University Press, 1967; reprint, New Haven, CT: Yale University Press, 2001); Herbert Gutman, *Work, Culture, and Society in Industrializing America* (New York: Vintage, 1977); Kohl, *The Politics of Individualism;* and Howe, *What Hath God Wrought.*

4. Donald Scott, "Evangelicalism, Revivalism, and the Second Great Awakening," National Humanities Center, October 2000, http://nationalhumanitiescenter.org/tserve/nineteen/nkeyinfo/nevanrev.htm; Nathan O. Hatch, *The Democratization of American Christianity* (New Haven, CT: Yale University Press, 1989), 39–44; Jon Butler, *Awash in a Sea of Faith: Christianizing the American People* (Cambridge, MA: Harvard University Press, 1990), 258–65; Robert Abzug, *Cosmos Crumbling:*

*American Reform and the Religious Imagination* (New York: Oxford University Press, 1994), 32–39.

5. *A Memoir of S. S. Prentiss,* ed. George L. Prentiss, 2 vols. (New York: Charles Scribner, 1853; reprint, New York: Charles Scribner, 1899), 2:102. For further evidence of Whigs sharing Prentiss's view, see Albert Barnes, "Professional Industry," *Knickerbocker,* September 1846, 189. See also Daniel Dana, "Conversion the Work of God" (sermon delivered December 31, 1831), *American Baptist Magazine,* April 1832, 114–15; "Leisure Hours: The Maniac," *Evangelical Magazine and Gospel Advocate,* April 9, 1841, 118–19; McCloskey, *The Bourgeois Virtues,* 63–65; Moretti, *The Bourgeois,* 11–12; and Wendling, *The Ruling Ideas,* 87–92.

6. Lyman Beecher, "Sermon VI: The Design, Rights and Duties, of Local Churches," in *Beecher's Works,* vol. 2, *Sermons Delivered on Various Occasions* (Boston: John P. Jewett, 1852), 223.

7. "A Short Sermon," *Tennessee Farmer,* May 1835, 95; "The Importance of Sustaining a Good Moral Character," *Bellow Falls Gazette,* July 19, 1845, 3. For further evidence of Whigs sharing Prentiss's view, see Barnes, "Professional Industry," 189. See also Dana, "Conversion the Work of God," 114–15; "Leisure Hours: The Maniac," 118–19; McCloskey, *The Bourgeois Virtues,* 63–65; Moretti, *The Bourgeois,* 11–12; and Wendling, *The Ruling Ideas,* 87–92. Other examples include "Original Sermon," *Evangelical Magazine and Gospel Advocate,* February 21, 1840, 57–59; "The Goat and the Lamb," *Evangelical Magazine and Gospel Advocate,* October 29, 1841, 352; "The Influence of Early Piety," *Episcopal Recorder,* October 7, 1848, 118; "The Value of Man," *American Baptist Magazine,* September 1832, 277–81; "Thirsting for God," *Christian Reflector,* November 16, 1842, 1; and "Moral and Religious," *Trumpet and Universalist Magazine,* June 22, 1844, 1.

8. "Cox's Sermon—Means & Ends," *New York Evangelist,* November 26, 1831, 1.

9. Robert Page, "The Character and Blessedness of the Humble," *American National Preacher,* October 1838, 159–61; "Continued Extracts," *Episcopal Recorder,* September 12, 1840, 99. See also Gabor S. Boritt, *Lincoln and the Economics of the American Dream* (Memphis: Memphis State University Press, 1978); Shirley Samuels, *The Culture of Sentiment: Race, Gender, and Sentimentality in 19th-Century America* (New York: Oxford University Press, 1992), 150–57; Richard J. Carwardine, *Evangelicals and Politics in Antebellum America* (Knoxville: University of Tennessee Press, 1997); Abzug, *Cosmos Crumbling,* esp. 77–124 (pt. 2, "Evangelical Reform"); and Lori Merish, *Sentimental Materialism: Gender, Commodity Culture, and Nineteenth-Century American Literature* (Durham, NC: Duke University Press, 2000), 87–91.

10. 2 Thess. 3:10. Southern support for such ideas is shown in Wells, *The Origins of the Southern Middle Class,* 67–74; Quigley, *Shifting Grounds,* 33–41; Black, *John Pendleton Kennedy,* 111–18; and Cooper, *Approaching Civil War and Southern History,* esp. chap. 6 ("'The Only Door': The Territorial Issue, the Preston Bill, and the Southern Whigs").

11. Tocqueville, *Democracy in America,* 429. For more on Weber's thinking, see Max Weber, *The Protestant Ethic and the Spirit of Capitalism* (New York: Charles Scribner & Sons, 1905; reprint, New York: Routledge, 2013); and Joyce Appleby "Moderation in the First Era of Popular Consumption," in *Thrift and Thriving in America: Capitalism and Moral Order from the Puritans to the Present,* ed. Joshua J. Yates and James Davison Hunter (New York: Oxford University Press, 2011), 139–59, 152–54.

12. "An Essay on Industry," *Charleston Gospel Messenger,* April 1849, 8. See also "Young Men's Sermon," *Western Examiner,* January 11, 1835, 14; "Mr. Clayton's Address," *Niles' National Register,* September 14, 1844, 28–33; "Introductory to the Year 1849," *American Whig Review,* January 1849, 1–3; and "Religion and Health," *New York Observer,* July 22, 1852, 1.

13. "Young Men's Sermon," 14. See also "An Essay on Industry," 8; "Mr. Clayton's Address"; "Introductory to the Year 1849," 1–3; "Religion and Health," 1; and Kohl, *The Politics of Individualism,* 44–49. For evidence, see Brock, *Parties and Political Conscience,* 10–21. See also Howe, *What Hath God Wrought,* 288–96; Hatch, *The Democratization of American Christianity,* 194–98; Butler, *Awash in a Sea of Faith,* 265–72; and Abzug, *Cosmos Crumbling,* 39–43.

14. Dana, "Conversion the Work of God," 114–15. See also Clark, *A Farewell to Alms,* 166; McCloskey, *Bourgeois Dignity,* 125; and Appleby "Moderation in the First Era of Popular Consumption," 154. *Thrift* as a category of analysis is explored in depth in chapter 5 below.

15. Page, "The Character and Blessedness of the Humble," 160–61. See also "Heresies of Practice," *Episcopal Recorder,* April 25, 1835, 13; and "A Sunday Morning's Ramble," *Trumpet and Universalist Magazine,* May 28, 1842, 193.

16. "Young Men's Sermon," 14. See also "Thrift; or, Nothing Is Useless," *Zion's Herald,* October 8, 1845, 164; Wells, *The Origins of the Southern Middle-Class,* 73–74; "On the Duty of Servants," *Gospel Messenger and Southern Episcopal Register,* December 1830, 362–67; and "Striving for Perfection," *Trumpet and Universalist Magazine,* July 22, 1837, 17.

17. Ralph Waldo Emerson, "Society and Solitude" (1870), in *The Essential Writings of Ralph Waldo Emerson,* ed. Mary Oliver (New York: Modern Library, 2000), 663–72, 669; "The Spirit of Liberty," 622. Southern support is shown Wells, *The Origins of the Southern Middle Class,* 67–68; Quigley, *Shifting Grounds,* 22–27; and Black, *John Pendleton Kennedy,* 148–55.

18. "Charity Begins at Home," *New-Yorker,* July 16, 1836, 262.

19. "Good Humor," *Christian Register,* February 5, 1848, 22. Other examples include "The Life of William Wilberforce," *Christian Examiner,* May 1839, 191–204; "Whig Charity," *Philanthropist,* September 6, 1843, 4; "Speech of Hon. Daniel Webster: Delivered at Andover, Mass., Nov. 9, 1843," *Niles' National Register,* November 18, 1843, 186–90; "Summary," *New York Evangelist,* September 30, 1852, 159–60; Walters, *American Reformers,* 21–29; Kohl, *The Politics of Individualism,* 121–29; Steven Mintz, *Moralists and Modernizers: America's Pre–Civil War*

*Reformers* (Baltimore: Johns Hopkins University Press, 1995), 79–85; and Howe, *What Hath God Wrought,* 243–50.

20. Lyman Beecher to William Beecher, June 5, 1830, in *Autobiography, Correspondence, etc., of Lyman Beecher, D.D.,* ed. Charles Beecher, 2 vols. (New York: Harper & Bros., 1864–1866), 2:220.

21. "State Inebriate Asylum," *Christian Inquirer,* January 30, 1858, 3.

22. "Christianity in America," *Mercersburg Review,* October 1857, 493–501, 493–97. See also "Domestic," *Christian Reflector,* September 19, 1844, 151–52; "Democracy—True Democracy," *Cincinnati Weekly Herald,* April 16, 1845, 2; Carwardine, *Evangelicals and Politics in Antebellum America,* 33–41; McCloskey, *The Bourgeois Virtues,* 63–65; Moretti, *The Bourgeois,* 11–12; and Wendling, *The Ruling Ideas,* 87–92.

23. "Temperance and Politics—Church and State," *Wilmington (DE) Temperance Standard,* reprinted in *Liberator,* June 22, 1838, 100. On Clay's support for temperance reform, see James C. Klotter, *Henry Clay: The Man Who Would Be President* (New York: Oxford University Press, 2018), 63–69.

24. "State Inebriate Asylum," 3.

25. "The Spirit of Liberty," 614; "The American Democrat," *Boston Quarterly Review,* July 1838, 377. The idea of Jacksonians as traditionalists, uncomfortable with modernity, and Whigs as more comfortable modernists is explored in Kohl, *The Politics of Individualism,* 22–30, 108–14. See also Richard D. Brown, *Modernization: The Transformation of American Life, 1860–1865* (New York: Hill & Wang, 1976), 94–101; and Howe, *What Hath God Wrought,* 328–35.

26. Horace Mann, "[Letter to a Member of a Debating Society,] West Newton, June 16, 1851," in *A Few Thoughts for a Young Man,* 80.

27. John Pendleton Kennedy, "Letter to His Constituents," in *Political and Official Papers,* 274. See also Black, *John Pendleton Kennedy,* 137–45.

28. Kohl, *The Politics of Individualism,* 47–49; Howe, *What Hath God Wrought,* 330–31. See also Robert Rantoul, "Education the Duty of an American Citizen," *Common School Journal,* March 1, 1839, 77; and Marvin Meyers, *The Jacksonian Persuasion: Politics and Belief* (Stanford, CA: Stanford University Press, 1957; reprint, Stanford, CA: Stanford University Press, 1960), 206–12. The best scholarship on antebellum education includes Philip Greven, *The Protestant Temperament: Patterns of Child-Rearing, Religious Experience, and the Self in Early America* (Chicago: University of Chicago Press, 1977); Lawrence A. Cremin, *American Education: The National Experience, 1783–1876* (New York: Harper & Row, 1980); Carl F. Kaestle, *Pillars of the Republic: Common Schools and American Society, 1780–1860* (New York: Hill & Wang, 1983); and Stephen Mintz, *Huck's Raft: A History of American Childhood* (Cambridge, MA: Belknap Press of Harvard University Press, 2006), 75–84.

29. For evidence, see Cremin, *American Education,* 265–77; Kaestle, *Pillars of the Republic,* 14–20, 183–91; and Mintz, *Huck's Raft,* 77–81.

30. "The Christian Citizen's Duty," *Christian Reflector,* June 22, 1848, 98; Samuel R. Hall, *Lectures to School-Masters* (Boston: Carter, Hendee, 1835), 5.

31. "Address to the People of Renesselear County," *Common School Assistant,* July 1837, 49. See also Kaestle, *Pillars of the Republic,* 75–82; Kohl, *The Politics of Individualism,* 72; Clark, *A Farewell to Alms,* 223–25; and Wendling, *The Ruling Ideas,* 25.

32. "Address to the People of Renesselear County," 49. See also Hall, *Lectures to School-Masters,* 5–6; J. Orville Taylor, *The District School; or, National Education* (Philadelphia: Carey, Lea, & Blanchard, 1835), 285–95; and "American Legislation, Science, Art, and Literature," *De Bow's Commercial Review* 1–2 (1847): 114–16.

33. "Educational," *Weekly Messenger,* December 8, 1841, 1. See also "The Crisis," *Christian Advocate,* August 7, 1835, 198; "Common School Reader," *Massachusetts Ploughman,* November 2, 1844, 2; Wells, *The Origins of the Southern Middle Class,* 71–76; and Quigley, *Shifting Grounds,* 39–44.

34. "The Calling of the School Teacher," *Common School Journal,* August 1, 1846, 234. See also "School Discipline" (*American Annals of Education*), 224–29; "The Discipline of Life," *New York Evangelist,* May 26, 1853, 1; and Marx, *The Machine in the Garden,* 105–12.

35. "Lectures to Young People," *Quarterly Christian Spectator,* December 1, 1830, 651. See also Josef Pieper, *Leisure: The Basis of Culture* (New York: Pantheon, 1952; reprint, San Francisco: Ignatius, 2009), 36–38; Houghton, *The Victorian Frame of Mind,* 160; Kohl, *The Politics of Individualism,* 149; McCloskey, *The Bourgeois Virtues,* 349–50; Clark, *A Farewell to Alms,* 166; Howe, *What Hath God Wrought,* 288–92; McCloskey, *Bourgeois Dignity,* 125–32; and Wendling, *The Ruling Ideas,* 89–92.

36. William Henry Seward, "Schools—Catholics," in Baker, ed., *The Works of William Henry Seward,* 1:xliii; Daniel Webster, "Public Reception in Buffalo, on the 22d of May, 1851," in *The Works of Daniel Webster,* 2:46. See also "School Discipline," *Christian Watchman,* May 3, 1845, 1. On the changing emphases of parenting and schooling, see Greven, *The Protestant Temperament,* 32–40; Kaestle, *Pillars of the Republic,* 87; and Robin Fox, *The Tribal Imagination: Civilization and the Savage Mind* (Cambridge, MA: Harvard University Press, 2011), 287–90. Social notions of trust will continue to inform my analysis throughout the rest of this work. For a concise appraisal of these themes, see Francis Fukuyama, *Trust: The Social Virtues and the Creation of Prosperity* (New York: Free Press, 1995), esp. 33–41, 283–94.

37. "Address to the Pennsylvania Whig State Convention," *New York Daily Times,* July 24, 1854, 6; "Whig Meeting in Fayette," *Republican Banner,* September 16, 1842, 2. Whigs in Maine, Kentucky, and Ohio agreed. For evidence, see "Common School Reader," 2; "Common School Law," *Louisville Morning Courier,* January 8, 1845, 3; "Whig Ticket in Richland," *Ohio State Journal,* October 14, 1846, 2; and "David A. Bokee," *American Whig Review,* August 1851, 171.

38. "Regular Toasts," *Bangor (ME) Whig,* reprinted in *Niles' National Register,* October 23, 1841, 117.

39. "Franklin," *Literary Messenger* (Pittsburgh), June 1840, 4. See also "Views of Franklin," *New-Yorker,* October 28, 1837, 508; "Whig State Convention," *Ohio State Journal,* May 14, 1850, 1; and "Franklin's Advice to Young Tradesmen," *New-Yorker,* October 20, 1838, 68. For a solid scholarly exploration of Franklin's life and continuing resonance, see Edmund Morgan, *Benjamin Franklin* (New Haven, CT: Yale University Press, 2002).

40. See Edward Pessen, "Did Fortunes Rise and Fall Mercurially in Antebellum America? The Tale of Two Cities: Boston and New York," *Journal of Social History* 4, no. 4 (Summer 1971): 339–57; *American Economic Growth and Standards of Living Before the Civil War,* ed. Robert E. Gallman and John Joseph Wallis (Chicago: University of Chicago Press, 1993), 121–35; Sellers, *The Market Revolution,* 25–29; Margaret Coleman, "Labor Shortage, Wage and Labor Structures, and Poverty, 1810–1840, in the Northeastern United States" (PhD diss., New School for Social Research, 1996), 72–82; and Jonathan A. Glickstein, *American Exceptionalism, American Anxiety: Wages, Competition, and Degraded Labor in the Antebellum United States* (Charlottesville: University of Virginia Press, 2002).

41. "The New Female Academy," *American Magazine* (Boston: Bewick Co., 1836), 105. See also Kaestle, *Pillars of the Republic,* 84. I deal with white middle-class women in detail because that is how Whiggish women of varying social status and affluence tended to see themselves. The most enduring scholarship on antebellum women, as well as gender and sexuality, includes Stansell, *City of Women;* Cott, *The Bonds of Womanhood;* Carroll Smith-Rosenberg, *Disorderly Conduct: Visions of Gender in Victorian America* (New York: Oxford University Press, 1986); Halttunen, *Confidence Men and Painted Women;* Elizabeth R. Varon, *We Mean to Be Counted: White Women and Politics in Antebellum Virginia* (Chapel Hill: University of North Carolina Press, 1998); and Ronald G. Walters, *Primers for Prudery: Sexual Advice to Victorian America* (Baltimore: Johns Hopkins University Press, 2000). See also "What Every Teacher Can Do," *American Annals of Education,* December 1834, 541–45; "Influence of a Teacher," *Prairie Farmer,* February 1852, 65; "An Address on the Subject of Literary Associations to Promote Education," *Southern Literary Messenger,* February 1835, 282–91; "Primary Schools," *Godey's Lady's Book and Ladies' American Magazine,* May 1840, 219–21; "Leaves from the Diary of a New England School Teacher," *Home Magazine,* November 1854, 374–77; "The Cross-Bearing School Teacher," *Ladies' Repository: A Monthly Periodical, Devoted to Literature, Art and Religion,* December 1854, 548; and "A Good Teacher," *New York Evangelist,* November 27, 1856, 230.

42. "Methods of the First School," *American Annals of Education,* March 1834, 112–13; Emma Willard, *Last Leaves of American History* (New York: A. S. Barnes; Cincinnati: H. W. Derby, 1853), 234. See also William Grimshaw, *History of the United States* (1821), 3rd ed. (Philadelphia: John Grigg, 1830), 202–9; *The American's Guide* (Philadelphia: Hogan & Thompson, 1838), 2–14; Marcus Wilson, *American History: History of the United States* (Cincinnati: William H. Moore,

1847), 433–45; Cremin, *American Education;* Kaestle, *Pillars of the Republic,* 75–80; and Mintz, *Huck's Raft,* 75–84.

43. Grimshaw, *History of the United States,* 203; Tocqueville, *Democracy in America,* 503. The best work on American nationalism includes David M. Potter, "The Historian's Use of Nationalism and Vice Versa," *American Historical Review* 67, no. 4 (July 1962): 924–50; Paul C. Nagel, *One Nation Indivisible: The Union in American Thought, 1776–1861* (New York: Oxford University Press, 1964), 118–19; Nagel, *This Sacred Trust,* 140–56; Rossiter, *The American Quest;* and Waldstreicher, *In the Midst of Perpetual Fetes.*

44. Tocqueville, *Democracy in America,* 497.

45. Tocqueville, *Democracy in America,* 497; William Henry Seward, "California" (March 11, 1850), in Baker, ed., *The Works of William Henry Seward,* 1:57. See also "Condition of the Ministry," *Albion: A Journal of News, Politics and Literature,* April 1, 1837, 103; "Albany Convention," *Philanthropist,* April 28, 1840, 2; "Politics of the Day," *Niles' National Register,* October 31, 1840, 138–43; "Pleasure & Science," *Western Literary Journal,* April 1845, 367–72; "The Whig Party, Its Position, and Duties," 547–54; "Responsibility of the Ballot Box," *American Whig Review,* December 1845, 435–43; "General Intelligence," *Christian Observer,* August 20, 1847, 235–36; and "Liberty, Union, and No Compromise," *National Era,* April 11, 1850, 57–58.

46. "Address of Messrs. Webster, Leigh, Barbour, and Lyons, to the Ladies Assembled at the Log Cabin," *Niles' National Register,* October 17, 1840, 112. For similar arguments across the country, see also "Correspondence," *Cincinnati Weekly Herald,* February 25, 1846, 3; "Summary," *New York Evangelist,* May 29, 1851, 87; and "Domestic," *New York Observer,* June 10, 1851, 219–20.

47. "Questions on Lyceum No. 9," *Family Lyceum,* October 20, 1832, 40. See also Houghton, *The Victorian Frame of Mind,* 104; Kohl, *The Politics of Individualism,* 72–78; McCloskey, *The Bourgeois Virtues,* 315; Clark, *A Farewell to Alms,* 225–26; and Howe, *What Hath God Wrought,* 619–20.

48. "Drawing Card for Use in Schools and Lyceums," *Daily Courant,* April 17, 1838, 2; "The Statesman and the Mails," *Ohio State Journal,* May 10, 1853, 2.

49. "New York Lyceum Lectures," *New-Yorker,* November 14, 1840, 143. See also "Report of the Mass. Lyceum," *Family Lyceum,* April 16, 1833, 133; and "Huntingdon & Savage," *Literary World,* February 6, 1847, 1. Lyceums are an unfortunately understudied topic. After Josiah Holbrook's *American Lyceum* (Boston: Perkins & Marvin, 1829), which explains his idea for the lyceum movement, the best work includes Carl Bode, *The American Lyceum* (New York: Oxford University Press, 1956); Angela G. Ray, *The Lyceum and Public Culture in the Nineteenth-Century United States* (East Lansing: Michigan State University Press, 2005); and Carolyn Eastman, *A Nation of Speechifiers: Making an American Public* (Chicago: University of Chicago Press, 2009). Southern Whiggish interest is shown in Wells, *The Origins of the Southern Middle Class,* 42–55; and Quigley, *Shifting Grounds,* 17–25.

50. "Teacher's Lyceum," *Literary Messenger* (Pittsburgh), October 1841, 36. For evidence, see "Dr. Caldwell's Address," *Raleigh Register,* July 1, 1834, 2; "Public Debate: The Slavery Question in the U. States," *National Banner and Nashville Whig,* August 12, 1835, 3; "Meeting Today," *Alabama Times,* April 16, 1841, 3; "Dr. Hollick's Lecture," *Louisville Journal,* January 10, 1850, 3; Kohl, *The Politics of Individualism,* 72; McCloskey, *The Bourgeois Virtues,* 315–18; Clark, *A Farewell to Alms,* 226; and Howe, *What Hath God Wrought,* 621–25.

51. "Lyceums," *New-Yorker,* November 21, 1840, 157. See also "Winthrop Lyceum," *Maine Farmer and Mechanic's Advocate,* December 26, 1840, 407.

52. "Teacher's Lyceum," 36. For evidence, see "Dr. Caldwell's Address," 2; "Public Debate," 3; "Meeting Today," 3; "Dr. Hollick's Lecture," 3; Kohl, *The Politics of Individualism,* 72; McCloskey, *The Bourgeois Virtues,* 315–18; Clark, *A Farewell to Alms,* 226; Howe, *What Hath God Wrought,* 621–25; "Lyceums," 157; and "Winthrop Lyceum," 407.

53. "Fourteenth Annual Report of the American Bible Society," 223–24; Holdich, "American Bible Society," 45; Hackett, "Sketch of the Life and Character of John Jay," 59–69; "The Higher Law."

54. For more the society's history, Whiggish efforts to proselytize through voluntary associations, and the Bible's role in antebellum political thought and culture, see Peter J. Wosh, *Spreading the Word: The Bible Business in Nineteenth-Century America* (Ithaca, NY: Cornell University Press, 1994), 63–75; Carwardine, *Evangelicals and Politics in Antebellum America;* Varon, *We Mean to Be Counted,* 23; and Eran Shalev, *American Zion: The Old Testament as a Political Text from the Revolution to the Civil War* (New Haven, CT: Yale University Press, 2013), 147–50.

55. "Neglect of Bible Reading," *New York Evangelist,* August 28, 1856, 156. See also "The Advantages of Reading the Bible," *Evangelical Magazine and Gospel Advocate,* May 5, 1837, 141; "Daily Bible Reading," *Weekly Messenger,* March 9, 1842, 1; "What the Pulpit Wants," *New York Observer,* June 12, 1851, 186;Kohl, *The Politics of Individualism,* 151–52; Howe, *What Hath God Wrought,* 289; and McCloskey, *Bourgeois Dignity,* 63–67.

56. "Introductory to the Year 1849," 4; Ralph Waldo Emerson, "Thoughts on Modern Literature," *New-Yorker,* October 31, 1840, 102. See also "The Children of the Kingdom," *Apostolic Advocate,* December 1, 1835, 185–90; and "American Institute of Instruction," *Common School Journal,* September 15, 1843, 273–79.

57. "The United States," *Eclectic Magazine of Foreign Literature,* January 1851, 62. See also Wells, *The Origins of the Southern Middle-Class,* 56–62.

58. "Permit Me to Make a Donation," *Nashville Banner,* reprinted in *Reformer,* January 1830, 10.

59. Wosh, *Spreading the Word,* 63–64; Howe, *What Hath God Wrought,* 285–92.

60. "Domestic," *New York Observer and Chronicle,* September 11, 1851, 291.

61. "Receipts—A.B.S.," *Cincinnati Weekly Herald,* August 16, 1844, 1.

62. "Province of Texas, Mexico," *Religious Intelligencer,* July 25, 1835, 112. Other examples include "American Bible Society," *Workingman's Advocate,* January 30, 1830, 1; "Domestic Intelligence," *Weekly Messenger,* February 16, 1842, 1335–38; "Summary," *Boston Recorder,* June 29, 1843, 103–7; "To Our Subscribers," *Christian Observer,* November 29, 1844, 190; "Summary," *New York Evangelist,* February 20, 1845, 31–32; and "California Items," *Christian Secretary,* March 15, 1850, 3. See also Wosh, *Spreading the Word,* 228–35; Howe, *What Hath God Wrought,* 453–60; and McCloskey, *The Bourgeois Virtues,* 279–86.

63. Rorabaugh, *The Alcoholic Republic,* 8–12.

64. "Temperance and the Constitution," *United States Magazine, and Democratic Review,* August 1851, 105.

65. For Whig anxieties along these lines, see "The Prospect Before Us," 1; "Social Intercourse," 2; Tomlinson, "Our Country," 7; and Tilden, *Temperance,* 4.

66. "Washington Temperance Society," *Christian Secretary,* January 14, 1842, 3.

67. "National Temperance Society," *New York Observer and Chronicle,* September 11, 1851, 294. See also "Drunkenness in High Places," *Western Christian Advocate,* August 18, 1837, 66; and "A Letter from Mr. Wise," *Niles' National Register,* September 30, 1837, 66.

68. "A Letter from Mr. Wise." See also "Deception Unmasked," *Ohio State Journal,* August 21, 1844, 2; "Connecticut Blue Laws," *New York Herald,* September 4, 1844, 1; "National Temperance Society," *Independent,* May 20, 1852, 1; Howe, *What Hath God Wrought,* 189–97; and McCloskey, *The Bourgeois Virtues,* 241–45.

69. "Literature and Labor," *Ladies' Repository: A Monthly Periodical, Devoted to Literature, Art and Religion,* February 1855, 83. See also "Change of Customs," *New York Evangelist,* May 28, 1831, 244; "Albany Female Academy," *Albany Evening Journal,* July 2, 1834, 1; Pieper, *Leisure,* 43–46; and Fox, *The Tribal Imagination,* 325–30.

70. "A Temperance Appeal to the Women of Ohio," *Ohio Cultivator,* December 15, 1852, 378.

71. See also Houghton, *The Victorian Frame of Mind,* 273–80; Kohl, *The Politics of Individualism,* 150–57; McCloskey, *The Bourgeois Virtues,* 241–45; and Howe, *What Hath God Wrought,* 189.

72. Tocqueville, *Democracy in America,* 502; Nisbet, *The Quest for Community,* 25; "The Spirit of Liberty," 614.

## 3. The State

Epigraph: Ralph Waldo Emerson, "Journal V (1844–1845)," in *The Journals and Miscellaneous Notebooks of Ralph Waldo Emerson,* vol. 9, *1843–1847,* ed. Ralph H. Orth and Alfred R. Ferguson (Cambridge, MA: Belknap Press of Harvard University Press, 1971), 164.

1. Abraham Lincoln, "Fragment on Government," in Basler, ed., *The Collected Works of Abraham Lincoln,* 2:221.

2. Webster, "Whig Principles and Purposes," 42.

3. Daniel Webster, "Whig Convention at Richmond," in *The Works of Daniel Webster,* 2:91. On political bias see Haidt, *The Righteous Mind,* 219–25.

4. John Quincy Adams, "First Annual Message" (December 6, 1825), quoted in Lynn Hudson Parsons, *John Quincy Adams* (Indianapolis: Madison House, 1988; reprint, Lanham, MD: Rowman & Littlefield, 2001), 180.

5. Calvin Colton, *The Junius Tracts: No. V* (New York: Greeley & McElrath, 1844), 4.

6. George Caleb Bingham to James Sydney Rollins, December 12, 1853, quoted in Sarah Burns and John Davis, *American Art to 1900: A Documentary History* (Berkeley and Los Angeles: University of California Press, 2009), 456. Voting and electoral development descriptions are drawn from Watson, *Liberty and Power,* 172–86; Daniel Feller, *The Jacksonian Promise: America, 1815–1840* (Baltimore: Johns Hopkins University Press, 1995), 162–71; and Howe, *What Hath God Wrought,* 328–37.

7. George Washington, "First Inaugural Address" (April 30, 1789), American Presidency Project, https://www.presidency.ucsb.edu/documents/inaugural-address-16. See also Daniel Webster, "Speech of Daniel Webster, of Massachusetts" (January 26–27, 1830), in *The Webster-Hayne Debate on the Nature of the Constitution: Selected Documents,* ed. Herman Belz (Indianapolis: Liberty Fund, 2000), 81–154, http://oll.libertyfund.org/?option=com_staticxt&staticfile=show.php%3Ftitle=1557&chapter=166687&layout=html&Itemid=27.

8. Webster, "Second Reply to Hayne" (January 26–27, 1830), in *The Papers of Daniel Webster Digital Edition* (Charlottesville: University of Virginia Press, Rotunda, 2018), https://rotunda.upress.virginia.edu/founders/WBST-04-01-01-0003.

9. Lincoln, "The Perpetuation of Our Political Institutions," 81.

10. Seward, "Annual Message to the Legislature" (January 1, 1839), 197. A few other examples of this line of thinking include "July 12, 1834," 2; "Purging the Polls of Humbug," *Nashville Banner and Nashville Whig,* July 8, 1835, 3; "Office-Holding Villainy," *Wetumpka Whig,* November 12, 1844, 3; "The Position of Parties," *American Whig Review,* January 1845, 5–21, 20; and "History of a National Mistake," *Albion: A Journal of News, Politics and Literature,* October 24, 1846, 505.

11. For example, from 1840 to 1860, voter turnout averaged 76 percent of those eligible and was never lower than 69 percent. For evidence, see "Voter Turnout in Presidential Elections, 1828–2012," American Presidency Project, http://www.presidency.ucsb.edu/data/turnout.php.

12. Seward, "Annual Message to the Legislature" (January 7, 1840), 236.

13. "Whig Principle and Its Development," 124–25. See also "Domestic" (*Boston Recorder*), 183; "A Letter from Mr. Leigh," *Niles' National Register,* December 11, 1841, 232; Kohl, *The Politics of Individualism,* 130–31; and McCloskey, *Bourgeois Dignity,* 70–75.

14. George Bancroft, "An Oration, Delivered before the Democracy of Springfield, and Neighboring Towns, July 4th, 1836," *American Monthly Magazine,*

September 1836, 303–4. Bancroft was not alone. Other examples include James Buchanan, "The Right of Instruction," *Niles' Weekly Register,* February 7, 1835, 401–2; "The Right of Instruction," *Southern Literary Messenger,* October 1836, 684–93; "Instructions to Senators," *Maine Farmer and Mechanic's Advocate,* February 22, 1844, 3; and "Observation," *New York Evening Post,* September 9, 1836, 3. The best scholarship on the topic includes Meyers, *The Jacksonian Persuasion,* 20–23; Kohl, *The Politics of Individualism,* 123–25; and Howe, *What Hath God Wrought,* 498–501.

15. "Political Proscriptions," *American Whig Review,* May 1849, 445. See also "States of the Union," *Niles' National Register,* September 5, 1840, 2–6; "Domestic Intelligence," *Christian Observer,* May 26, 1843, 3; and "The English Middle Class," *Albion: A Journal of News, Politics and Literature,* October 7, 1854, 473.

16. "The Doctrine of Instruction," *Albany Evening Journal,* January 22, 1840, 2. See also McCloskey, *The Bourgeois Virtues,* 70–75; Kohl, *The Politics of Individualism,* 130–31; and McCloskey, *Bourgeois Dignity,* 70–75.

17. "The Policy to Be Pursued," *Boston Quarterly Review,* January 1841, 70. Whigs believed that their broad-mindedness was important. A few examples include "The Administration and the Country," *American Whig Review,* March 1846, 227–35; "Political Education," *American Whig Review,* April 1846, 354–63; "The Parties," *Cincinnati Weekly Herald,* October 14, 1846, 1; and "New Tenure of Statesmanship," *Littell's Living Age,* September 11, 1847, 524–25. See also McCloskey, *Bourgeois Virtues,* 70–73; Kohl, *The Politics of Individualism,* 130–31; and McCloskey, *Bourgeois Dignity,* 70–72.

18. "Theodore Frelinghuysen," *Niles' National Register,* May 18, 1844, 179. Similar appeals for Frelinghuysen include "Hon. Theodore Frelinghuysen," *New York Observer,* May 11, 1844, 76; "Theodore Frelinghuysen," *American Whig Review,* January 1845, 99–104; "Correspondence with Clay and Frelinghuysen," *Niles' National Register,* January 4, 1845, 283–84; and "Summary," *New York Evangelist,* January 23, 1845, 15.

19. *The Whig Party; Its Objects—Its Principles—Its Candidates—Its Duties—and Its Prospects* (Providence, RI: Knowles & Vose, 1844), 4 (emphasis added). See also "Improvements in Rail Roads—the Case Made Plain," *Louisville Journal,* July 8, 1835, 1; "Mob Law," *Western Messenger,* July 1838, 286–88; and "Human Rights according to Modern Philosophy," 327–37.

20. "The Murders by a Kentucky Mob," *New-Yorker,* September 11, 1841, 414. See also Haidt, *The Righteous Mind,* 320–29; and Greene, *Moral Tribes,* 213–20. On the clash of worldviews pulsing though politics and political culture, see also Meyers, *The Jacksonian Persuasion,* 234–37; Kohl, *The Politics of Individualism,* 39–41; Fox, *The Tribal Imagination,* 15; and Yuval Levin, *The Great Debate: Edmund Burke, Thomas Paine, and the Birth of Right and Left* (New York: Basic, 2014), 223–31.

21. "The Gatherer," *Godey's Lady's Book and Ladies' American Magazine,* July 1831, 53. See also "The Whigs," *Huntress,* February 6, 1841, 2; and "Ladies'

Department," *Boston Cultivator,* December 16, 1843, 394. Varon's *We Mean to Be Counted* is the best book on the topic, but other solid accounts include *The Abolitionist Sisterhood: Women's Political Culture in Antebellum America,* ed. Jean F. Yellin and John C. Van Horne (Ithaca, NY: Cornell University Press, 1994); Ronald J. Zboray and Mary Saracino Zboray, *Voices without Votes: Women and Politics in Antebellum New England* (Lebanon, NH: University Press of New England, 2010); and Carol Lasser and Stacey Robertson, *Antebellum Women: Private, Public, Partisan* (New York: Rowman & Littlefield, 2013).

22. "The Great Whig Convention," *Niles' National Register,* May 18, 1844, 183–84. See also "General Intelligence," *New York Evangelist,* October 17, 1844, 167; "General Intelligence," *Christian Observer,* October 24, 1845, 171; "The Future Policy of the Whigs," *American Whig Review,* April 1848, 329–36; Zboray and Zboray, *Voices without Votes,* 79–87; and Lasser and Robertson, *Antebellum Women,* 60–67.

23. "The Great Whig Convention." See also "General Intelligence" (*New York Evangelist,* October 17, 1844), 167; "General Intelligence" (*Christian Observer,* October 24, 1845), 171; "The Future Policy of the Whigs," 329–36; Zboray and Zboray, *Voices without Votes,* 64–70, 79–87; Lasser and Robertson, *Antebellum Women,* 60–67; and "Virginia Whig Convention at Richmond," *Niles' National Register,* October 17, 1840, 111.

24. "The Political Tendencies of America," *Littell's Living Age,* June 28, 1856, 6. Whigs were highly skeptical of the fitness of Catholics for citizenship. Ironically, they lumped all Catholics together, missing or overlooking the middle-class proclivities in German Catholics, and painting all Catholics with the broad brush of prejudice derived from caricatures of working-class Irish Catholics. A few examples include "The Irish in America," *Museum of Foreign Literature, Science, and Art,* April 1838, 519–23; "Nativism—Naturalized Citizens," *Cincinnati Weekly Herald,* October 30, 1844, 1; "Nativism," *Cincinnati Weekly Herald,* November 20, 1844, 1; "Foreign Immigration," *American Whig Review,* April 1848, 419–30; "William H. Seward," *American Whig Review,* June 1850, 622–30; "Domestic," *New York Observer,* February 6, 1851, 47; and "Christianity in America." See also Billington, *The Protestant Crusade,* 201–2; Holt, *The Political Crisis of the 1850s,* 121–25; and Kohl, *The Politics of Individualism,* 32–44.

25. Bernard Bailyn's *The Ideological Origins of the American Revolution* (Cambridge, MA: Harvard University Press, 1967) and *The Origins of American Politics* (New York: Vintage, 1970) remain the best two studies of the intellectual roots of America's political tradition. More recent solid scholarship includes Jeremy Black, *George III: America's Last King* (New Haven, CT: Yale University Press, 2009); and Andrew Jackson O'Shaughnessy, *The Men Who Lost America: British Leadership, the American Revolution, and the Fate of the Empire* (New Haven, CT: Yale University Press, 2013).

26. "Public Meeting," *Register of Pennsylvania,* April 19, 1834, 256. See also Schlesinger, *The Age of Jackson,* 3; Henry Clay, "Speech of Henry Clay [in the US

Senate]" (April 30, 1834), in *Register of Debates: Being a Report of the Speeches Delivered in the Two Houses of Congress* (Washington, DC: Duff Green, 1834), 606; "Dr. Caldwell's Address," 2; "Progress of the Harrison Nomination," *Investigator and Expositor,* January 1840, 91–93; "Summary," *New York Evangelist,* February 6, 1851, 23; "The Presidential Election of 1852," *American Whig Review,* November 1851, 434–40; McCloskey, *Bourgeois Virtues,* 33–35; Haidt, *The Righteous Mind,* 37–45; Greene, *Moral Tribes,* 207–11; and Levin, *The Great Debate,* 223–26. Whigs often charged Democrats with substituting passion for logic. Examples include "To the People of the United States," *Niles' Weekly Register,* July 30, 1831, 387–89; "Presidential Elections," *New-Yorker,* December 3, 1836, 171; "Interesting Correspondence," *Niles' National Register,* August 17, 1839, 397–98; "General Intelligence," *New York Evangelist,* April 27, 1843, 67; and "The True Issue between the Parties," *American Whig Review,* December 1850, 587–93.

27. "Edmund Burke" (*American Whig Review*), 312. See also "Burke," *American Monthly Magazine,* March 1830, 805–15; "General Intelligence," *New York Evangelist,* August 8, 1844, 127; "The Age of Pitt and Fox," *Eclectic Magazine of Foreign Literature,* September 1846, 124–32; Kohl, *The Politics of Individualism,* 42–50; McCloskey, *Bourgeois Virtues,* 105; Haidt, *The Righteous Mind,* 291; "Edmund Burke" (*American Whig Review*), 323–24; Greene, *Moral Tribes,* 199–202; and Levin, *The Great Debate,* 200–207.

28. Edmund Burke to Charles-Jean-François Depont, October 1789, in *The Portable Edmund Burke,* ed. Isaac Kramnick (New York: Penguin, 1999), 542.

29. "The Administration: The Party," *American Whig Review,* April 1852, 295. Harrison's 1841 inaugural address was the longest in American history. See William Henry Harrison, "Inaugural Address" (March 4, 1841), American Presidency Project, https://www.presidency.ucsb.edu/documents/inaugural-address-29. For Whig support for this sort of thinking, see "Edmund Burke," *Albion: A Journal of News, Politics and Literature,* September 28, 1833, 305–6; "The Science of Government," *American Monthly Magazine,* September 1838, 202; "The Crisis" (*Tennessee Whig*), 3; McCloskey, *Bourgeois Virtues,* 61–65; Levin, *The Great Debate,* 220–21; William Henry Seward, "Message of the Governor of New York" (1840), *Niles' National Register,* January 18, 1840, 331. See also "Balance of Party Power," *Niles' National Register,* February 20, 1841, 391.

30. "Conservative Policy," *Albion: A Journal of News, Politics and Literature,* September 11, 1841, 324; "Legislative Wisdom," *Philanthropist,* February 16, 1842, 2.

31. For evidence, see Kohl, *The Politics of Individualism,* 45–50; McCloskey, *Bourgeois Virtues,* 105–9; Haidt, *The Righteous Mind,* 289–95; Greene, *Moral Tribes,* 193–200; Levin, *The Great Debate,* 205–7; Mark Lilla, *The Once and Future Liberal: After Identity Politics* (New York: HarperCollins, 2017), 25–33; and Francis Fukuyama, *Identity: The Demand for Dignity and the Politics of Resentment* (New York: Farrar, Straus & Giroux, 2018), 8–12.

32. "Virginia Whig State Convention," 126; "Mr. Adams' Address," 112. See also "Architects of Ruin," *Albany Evening Journal,* June 25, 1838, 3; Kohl, *The*

*Politics of Individualism,* 93–95; McCloskey, *Bourgeois Virtues,* 40–45; Haidt, *The Righteous Mind,* 279–84; Levin, *The Great Debate,* 200–206; and Lilla, *The Once and Future Liberal,* 36–42.

33. "Presidential Veto," *American Whig Review,* August 1849, 112. Whigs across the country shared this fear. See, e.g., "The Veto," *New-Yorker,* August 28, 1841, 377; "The Veto Message," *Boston Recorder,* August 19, 1842, 131–32; "To the Whigs of Maryland," *Niles' National Register,* October 1, 1842, 77–79; "The Veto Power: Our Inland Trade," *American Whig Review,* October 1846, 325–30; and "Presidential Vetoes, Washington–Trump," American Presidency Project, http://www.presidency.ucsb.edu/data/vetoes.php.

34. "Political: President's Message," *Western Recorder,* December 14, 1830, 199; "Lexington and Maysville Road," *Louisville Daily Journal,* December 22, 1830, 2. See also "Speech of Henry Clay, Delivered at the Mechanics' Collation" (August 3, 1830), *Niles' Weekly Register,* September 4, 1830, 25–33. The best accounts of what the Maysville Road veto symbolized for Jackson and his supporters include Glyndon G. Van Deusen, *The Jacksonian Era, 1828–1848* (New York: Harper & Bros., 1959); Holt, *The Rise and Fall of the American Whig Party;* David P. Currie, *The Constitution in Congress: Democrats and Whigs, 1829–1861* (Chicago: University of Chicago Press, 2005); Craig Thompson Friend, *Along the Maysville Road: The Early American Republic in the Trans-Appalachian West* (Knoxville: University of Tennessee Press, 2005); and Howe, *What Hath God Wrought.*

35. "Speech of Henry Clay, Delivered at the Mechanics' Collation." For similar Whig sentiment on the subject, see "Pennsylvania and Internal Improvements," *Banner of the Constitution,* May 4, 1831, 178; and "Summary," *Western Luminary,* March 9, 1831, 351.

36. "The Whig Party, Its Position, and Duties," 547; "Whig Principles" (*Cincinnati Weekly Herald*), 1. See also Howe, *What Hath God Wrought,* 330–38; McCloskey, *Bourgeois Virtues,* 280–83; and Haidt, *The Righteous Mind,* 279–81.

37. Kohl, *The Politics of Individualism,* 129.

38. Webster, "Reply to Hayne," 135–37. Webster captures the sentiment of most Whigs, whether northern or southern. Other examples include "The Bridge," *National Banner and Nashville Whig,* November 28, 1829, 1; Abraham Lincoln, "To the People of Sangamo County: Political Announcement" (March 9, 1832), in Basler, ed., *Abraham Lincoln: His Speeches and Writings,* 53; Edward Everett, "Accumulation," *New-Yorker,* February 2, 1839, 312; and "The Position of Parties," 20.

39. Seward, "Annual Message to the Legislature" (January 1, 1839), 203.

40. Clay, "On the American System," 455–56. See also "The Whig Party, Its Position, and Duties," 552–55.

41. "American System," *North American Review,* January 1831, 128.

42. For more on the American System, see Clement Eaton, *Henry Clay and the Art of American Politics* (Chicago: Scott Foresman, 1957), 21–26; Maurice G. Baxter, *Henry Clay and the American System* (Lexington: University Press of Kentucky, 1995), 16–22; Howe, *What Hath God Wrought,* 583–87; W. H. Bartholomew,

"Henry Clay," *Register of Kentucky State Historical Society* 10, no. 28 (1912): 25–28; and Norman A. Graebner and George C. Herring, "Henry Clay, Realist," *Register of the Kentucky Historical Society* 107, no. 4 (2009): 551–76.

43. Kohl, *The Politics of Individualism,* 60; William Leggett, "True Functions of Government" (1834), in Sedgwick, ed., *A Collection of the Political Writings of William Leggett,* 1:163. The most durable and elegant explanation of this view is still found in Schlesinger's *Age of Jackson.*

44. Seward, "Annual Message to the Legislature" (January 1, 1839), 252.

45. "Whig Principle and Its Development," 124. See also John P. Kennedy, "Buckeye Celebration," *Niles' Weekly Register,* May 30, 1835, 225; "Internal Improvements," *American Farmer,* May 29, 1839, 7; and "The Whig Merchants' Meeting," *Niles' Weekly Register,* October 10, 1840, 92–93. That state governments and local municipalities pushed the American System forward is powerfully demonstrated in Herbert Ershkowitz and William G. Shade, "Consensus or Conflict? Political Behavior in the State Legislatures during the Jacksonian Era," *Journal of American History* 58, no. 3 (December 1971): 591–621.

46. John P. Kennedy, "An Address Delivered Before the American Institute, in the City of New-York, October 17, 1833," *Mechanics' Magazine,* October 1833, 230, 238, 239; "Town Meeting," *Nashville Banner and Nashville Whig,* May 29, 1832, 3; "Influence of the Trading Spirit upon the Social and Moral Life of America," *American Whig Review,* January 1845, 95. See also Howe, *What Hath God Wrought,* 243–50; and McCloskey, *Bourgeois Virtues,* 271–73.

47. "The Railroad Enterprise," *New Englander,* August 1851, 321. Other examples of similar Whig thinking include "Improvement in Social Condition," *Mechanics' Magazine,* June 1833, 300–301; "General Intelligence," *Michigan Farmer and Western Agriculturist,* January 15, 1848, 31–32; and "The History and Economy of Railroads," *Southern Quarterly Review,* April 1848, 372–80. See also Ershkowitz and Shade, "Consensus or Conflict?," 604; and Howe, *What Hath God Wrought,* 246–55.

48. "Whig State Convention," *Weekly Ohio State Journal,* October 20, 1847, 1. See also "Internal Improvements," *Western Journal of Agriculture, Manufactures, Mechanic Arts, . . . ,* May 1851, 71–76.

49. "Whig Principle and Its Development," 124–30; "A Community Virtue," *Circular,* September 28, 1853, 362.

50. Kennedy, "An Address Delivered before the American Institute," 239.

51. Edward Everett, "Oration" (1835), in *Orations and Speeches on Various Occasions,* 4 vols. (Boston: Little, Brown, 1850–1868), 1:518.

52. "Imprisonment for Debt," *New-Yorker,* October 20, 1838, 73; "The History and Economy of Railroads," 373; "The Railroad Enterprise," 345. See also "A Statistical View of Commerce," *American Quarterly Review,* June 1, 1835, 485–500; "Triumph of Humanity," *Christian Secretary,* December 26, 1851, 1; "Whig Principle and Its Development," 124–28; Kohl, *The Politics of Individualism,* 199–200; Holt, *The Rise and Fall of the American Whig Party,* 66–78; and Howe, *What Hath God Wrought,* 562–67.

53. "Louisville, Kentucky," *Gleason's Pictorial Drawing-Room Companion,* September 2, 1854, 140.

54. "Louisville, Kentucky," 140. During the initial construction, Congress paid 29 percent of the cost.

55. "Louisville and Portland Canal," *Niles' Weekly Register,* March 14, 1835, 28.

56. For evidence, see "Louisville and Portland Canal," *Louisville Daily Journal,* December 10, 1830, 2; Richard S. Coxe, "Chesapeake and Ohio Canal," *Niles' Weekly Register,* January 3, 1835, 308–11; "Interesting Account of the Illinois and Michigan Canal," *Ohio State Journal,* August 4, 1847, 2–3; "Chesapeake and Ohio Canal," *Ohio State Journal,* October 20, 1847, 3–4; "Commercial Relations," *Western Journal of Agriculture, Manufactures, Mechanic Arts, . . . ,* April 1848, 213–17; Ershkowitz and Shade, "Consensus or Conflict?," 604–5; Holt, *The Rise and Fall of the American Whig Party,* 53–62; and Howe, *What Hath God Wrought,* 560–69.

57. "The Whigs and Their Candidate," 221; "Internal Improvement," *New-Yorker,* February 29, 1840, 377.

58. "American Aristocracy," *United States Magazine, and Democratic Review,* August 1840, 132. See also "The Whig Leaders," *Aurora,* September 20, 1834, 120–21.

59. "The Permanency and Power of Whig Principles," *American Whig Review,* March 1852, 266. See also Ershkowitz and Shade, "Consensus or Conflict?," 607–8; Kohl, *The Politics of Individualism,* 115–20; and Howe, *What Hath God Wrought,* 241–55.

60. "Massachusetts Whig Convention," *Niles' National Register,* October 9, 1847, 84. See also Ershkowitz and Shade, "Consensus or Conflict?," 606–9; and Kohl, *The Politics of Individualism,* 123–28.

61. Seward, "Annual Message to the Legislature" (January 1, 1839), 203. See also "Virginia Whig State Convention," 125–27; "Internal Improvements," *New York State Mechanic,* May 20, 1843, 206–7; and "Movements of the Enemy," 193.

62. "Corporations," *Boston Courier,* February 26, 1836, 2; Daniel Webster et al., "Whig Mass Meeting: 100,000 Whigs in Council," *Niles' National Register,* September 24, 1844, 53. See also Ershkowitz and Shade, "Consensus or Conflict?," 616–17; Kohl, *The Politics of Individualism,* 213–14; and McCloskey, *Bourgeois Dignity,* 72–79.

63. Quoted in R. Kent Newmeyer, *Supreme Court Justice Joseph Story: Statesman of the Old Republic* (Chapel Hill: University of North Carolina Press, 1985), 158; On "royal levees," see "A Day in the Life of Louis XIV: The Daily Life of the King," n.d., Château de Versailles, http://en.chateauversailles.fr/discover/history/key-dates/day-life-louis-xiv#mornings.

64. Howard Bodenhorn, "Antebellum Banking in the United States," March 26, 2008, EH.Net Encyclopedia, https://eh.net/encyclopedia/antebellum-banking-in-the-united-states-2.

65. Andrew T. Hill, "The Second Bank of the United States, 1816–1841," Federal Reserve History, December 5, 2015, https://www.federalreservehistory

.org/essays/second_bank_of_the_us. See also Michael D., Bordo and Joseph G. Haubrich, "Credit Crises, Money, and Contractions: An Historical View," *Journal of Monetary Economics* 57, no. 1 (January 2010): 1–18; Ralph C. H. Catterall, *The Second Bank of the United States* (Chicago: University of Chicago Press, 1903); Bray Hammond, *Banks and Politics in America from the Revolution to the Civil War* (Princeton, NJ: Princeton University Press, 1957; reprint, Princeton, NJ: Princeton University Press, 1991); and Edward S. Kaplan, *The Bank of the United States and the American Economy* (Westport, CT: Greenwood, 1999).

66. Hill, "The Second Bank of the United States"; Catterall, *The Second Bank of the United States,* 93–104; Hammond, *Banks and Politics in America,* 251–65; and Kaplan, *The Bank of the United States and the American Economy,* 80–94.

67. Andrew Jackson, "State of the Union Address" (December 8, 1829), PresidentialRhetoric.com, http://www.presidentialrhetoric.com/historicspeeches/jackson/stateoftheunion1829.html; "The Bank," *Enquirer,* November 1, 1839, 2.

68. "President Jackson," *Argus of Western America,* June 30, 1830, 2; "Bank of the United States," *Workingman's Advocate,* July 16, 1831, 2. Hammond's *Banks and Politics in America* is still the best book on the Second Bank of the United States and the famous bank war. Other solid work includes Catterall, *The Second Bank of the United States;* Robert V. Remini, *Andrew Jackson and the Bank War: A Study in the Growth of Presidential Power* (New York: Norton, 1967); Kaplan, *The Bank of the United States and the American Economy;* Wilentz, *The Rise of American Democracy,* 358–65; and Howe, *What Hath God Wrought,* 373–86.

69. *The Correspondence of Nicholas Biddle,* ed. Reginald C. McGrane (New York: Houghton Mifflin, 1919), 222.

70. Andrew Jackson, "Bank Veto" (July 10, 1832), Miller Center, University of Virginia, http://millercenter.org/president/speeches/speech-3636; Andrew Jackson to Martin Van Buren, July 4, 1832, quoted in "The Autobiography of Martin Van Buren," ed. John Clement Fitzpatrick, *Annual Report of the American Historical Association for the Year 1918,* 130 vols. to date (Washington, DC: American Historical Society,1890–), 2:625. See also Catterall, *The Second Bank of the United States,* 95–102; Hammond, *Banks and Politics in America,* 251–59; and Kaplan, *The Bank of the United States and the American Economy,* 86–93.

71. Daniel Webster, "The Presidential Veto" (July 11, 1832), in *The Great Speeches of Daniel Webster,* 331.

72. Tocqueville, *Democracy in America,* 170.

73. See further Daniel Webster, "Reception at New York" (1837), in *The Works of Daniel Webster,* 1:80; "Bank of the United States," *New-Yorker,* April 10, 1841, 60; "United States Bank," *Ohio State Journal,* May 12, 1841, 1; and "Whig Candidates for the Assembly," *New York Herald,* October 26, 1841, 2.

74. Daniel Webster, "The Continuance of the Bank Charter" (March 18, 1834), in *The Works of Daniel Webster,* 4:94; "The Credit System," *Albany Evening Journal,* September 23, 1840, 1.

75. John P. Kennedy, “The Protective System,” in *Political and Official Papers,* 292; Calvin Colton, *The Junius Tracts: No. III* (New York: Greeley & McElrath, 1844), 15.

76. Nisbet, *The Quest for Community,* 25.

## 4. The Past

Portions of this chapter appeared in Joseph W. Pearson, “Dread Barbarism and the Pursuit of Power: American Whig Thought and the Purpose of the Past,” *Ohio Valley History* 19, no. 4 (Winter 2019): 3–18.

Epigraph: Thomas Hobbes, *Of Man, Being the First Part of Leviathan* (Cambridge, MA: Harvard Classic, 1909), 404–5 (chap. 13, “Of the Natural Condition of Mankind as concerning Their Felicity and Misery”).

1. No scholarly consensus exists as to exactly when the Middle Ages began and ended. See, e.g., Susan Wise Bauer, *The History of the Medieval World: From the Conversion of Constantine to the First Crusade* (New York: Oxford University Press, 2010); George Holmes, *The Oxford History of Medieval Europe* (New York: Oxford University Press, 2002); Maurice Keen, *The Penguin History of Medieval Europe* (New York: Penguin, 1991); and Morris Bishop, *The Middle Ages* (New York: American Heritage, 1968; reprint, New York: American Heritage, 2001). Most Whig authors were not precise when it came to chronology, though the vast majority point to the years after the founding of Norman rule in England in 1066 up until the beginning of the Protestant Reformation in 1517. As this chapter demonstrates, however, Whig nationalism and the importance Whigs placed on the future led many to look askance at peoples predating the American Revolution.

2. For a solid definition, see *Pocket Fowler's Modern English Usage,* 2nd ed. (New York: Oxford University Press, 2008), s.v. *barbarism, barbarity,* Oxford Reference, http://www.oxfordreference.com/view/10.1093/acref/9780199232581.001.0001/acref-9780199232581-e-336?rskey=0ge010&result=5.

3. McCloskey's *The Bourgeois Virtues* makes a powerful case for these seven virtues as the moral core of the modern middle class. Other crucial works on the middle class include Gay, *The Bourgeois Experience;* Houghton, *The Victorian Frame of Mind;* Mary P. Ryan, *Cradle of the Middle Class: The Family in Oneida County, New York, 1790–1865* (New York: Cambridge University Press, 1981); Smith-Rosenberg, *Disorderly Conduct;* Michael Mason, *The Making of Victorian Sexuality* (New York: Oxford University Press, 1995); and McCloskey, *Bourgeois Dignity.*

4. For more on these worldviews, see Kohl, *The Politics of Individualism.* A few other works supporting Kohl's position include Howe, *The Political Culture of the American Whigs;* Nisbet, *The Quest for Community;* Robert Putnam, *Bowling Alone* (New York: Simon & Schuster, 2000); Haidt, *The Righteous Mind;* and Greene, *Moral Tribes.* The argument that an urban/country or a rich/poor dichotomy

defined Whigs and Democrats, respectively, is best presented in Schlesinger, *The Age of Jackson;* Sellers, *The Market Revolution;* and Wilentz, *The Rise of American Democracy.*

5. *An Intermediate Greek-English Lexicon,* 7th ed. (New York: Oxford University Press, 1899; reprint, Oxford: Benediction Class, 1999), 872 (s.v. φρόνησις).

6. Ralph Waldo Emerson, "Prudence" (1841), in Oliver, ed., *The Essential Writings of Ralph Waldo Emerson,* 215–24, 215.

7. "Rev. Edward Irving," *New-Yorker,* October 24, 1840, 82; "Chronicle," *Niles' National Register,* September 9, 1843, 32. See also "The Message of the Governor," *New-Yorker,* January 6, 1838, 665–69; "Lynch Law and Vengeance," *American Whig Review,* February 1845, 121–24; "What Will They Do Now?," *National Era,* November 5, 1857; and McCloskey *The Bourgeois Virtues,* 253–57. The scholarship on virtues and ethics is vast. A few concise works include Josef Pieper, *The Four Cardinal Virtues* (South Bend, IN: University of Notre Dame Press, 1966); Linda Trinkaus Zagzebski, *Virtues of the Mind: An Inquiry into the Nature of Virtue and the Ethical Foundations of Knowledge* (New York: Cambridge University Press, 1996); and André Comte-Sponville, *A Small Treatise on the Great Virtues* (New York: Henry Holt, 2002).

8. "Taste," *Godey's Lady's Book and Ladies' American Magazine,* February 1840, 88; "The Materials of History," *Arcturus,* July 1841, 104. See also "How to Endure Poverty," *Journal of the Mechanics' Institute,* July 1833, 9; "The Nineteenth Century," 457–65; and "The Mouse and the Merchant," *National Magazine,* December 1853, 546–50.

9. "The Materials of History," 104.

10. "The Thirty Years' War," *New-Yorker,* October 20, 1838, 71. See also "The Voice of the Past," *New-Yorker,* September 4, 1841, 391; and J. F. Watson, "The Past and Present," *Home Journal,* August 28, 1847, 4.

11. "Slavery Forever!," *Louisville Courier,* June 26, 1849, 2. Time is another vast concept that has generated a prodigious amount of scholarship. A few important books include Heidegger, *Being and Time;* Minkowski, *Lived Time;* Carr, *Time, Narrative, and History;* Barbara Adam, *Timescapes of Modernity: The Environment and Invisible Hazards* (New York: Routledge, 1998); *Time and Memory: The Power of Repetitive Compulsion,* ed. Rosine Jozef Perelberg (London: Karnac, 2007); Mary Lynne Ellis, *Time in Practice: Analytical Perspectives on the Time of Our Lives* (London: Karnac, 2008); Eva Hoffman, *Time* (New York: Picador, 2009); and Phillips, *Looming Civil War.*

12. Henry Clay, "On the Public Lands" (December 20, 1835), in Hopkins et al., eds., *The Papers of Henry Clay,* 8:812; Colton, *Junius Tracts: No. III,* 10. A few examples of other Whigs who felt the same way include "The Past and the Present," *Scientific American,* July 15, 1848, 339; "The Martyr of Erromanga," *National Magazine,* February 1853, 145–47; "New England Generosity?," *Hartford Courant,* January 10, 1843, 2; and "The Age of Wonders," *Atkinson's Casket,* February 1833, 96. See also "A Touch of the Sentimental," *Bangor (ME) Whig-Courier,*

reprinted in *New-Yorker,* August 22, 1840, 360; "Hereditary Descent of Mental Talent," *New-York Mirror,* March 13, 1830, 283; Lewis, *The American Adam,* 191–93; Nash, *The Wilderness and the American Mind,* 78–80; Kohl, *The Politics of Individualism,* 47–48, 84; and Fuhrer, *A Crisis of Community,* 23–28.

13. "True Greatness," *New-Yorker,* August 1, 1840, 312; "The Drama at Paris," *National Magazine,* March 1839, 273.

14. "Macaulay's History of England," *American Whig Review,* April 1850, 349; "The Drama at Paris," 273. See also "Mr. Adams' Address: At the Meeting of the Boston Whig Young Men's Club, on Monday Evening, the 7th Instant," *Niles' National Register,* October 17, 1844, 105–12; "The Rival Brothers," *Philadelphia Album,* July 10, 1830, 217–19; "Traditions and Superstitions," *American Whig Review,* June 1846, 650–56; Kohl, *The Politics of Individualism,* 84; and Fuhrer, *A Crisis of Community,* 188–93.

15. "Romanism and Catholicism, or Romanism and Protestantism," *American Eclectic,* November 1841, 440. See also "Modern Improvements," *Southern Literary Journal,* July 1837, 421–23; and "The Life and Genius of Dante Alighieri," *American Whig Review,* August 1848, 125–30.

16. "The East and South," *Eclectic Museum of Foreign Literature, Science, and Art,* February 1843, 267–80.

17. "Romanism and Catholicism, or Romanism and Protestantism," 451. See also "The Afghanistan Expedition," *New-Yorker,* March 14, 1840, 405–6; "Reviews and Literary Notices," *Western Literary Journal,* March 1845, 287–92; "Whig Principle and Its Development," 124–35; and "Movements of the Enemy."

18. Calvin Colton, *A Lecture on the Railroad to the Pacific* (New York: A. S. Barnes, 1850), 15; "On the Use of Chloroform in Hangings," *American Whig Review,* September 1848, 283; Charles Sumner, "Freedom National, Slavery Sectional," *National Era,* September 2, 1852, 141–43. See also "Introduction to the Literature of Europe in the 15th, 16th, and 17th Centuries," *New-Yorker,* April 1, 1837, 22; "The Duty of the Citizen," *Philanthropist,* September 15, 1840, 2–3; "Alison's History of Europe: Introductory Note," *Eclectic Museum of Foreign Literature, Science, and Art,* January 1843, 34; and "Remarks on the Resolutions and Manifesto of the Southern Caucus," *American Whig Review,* May 1850, 443–50.

19. Abraham Lincoln, "Speech at Peoria, Illinois, in Reply to Senator Douglas, October 16, 1854," in *The Life and Writings of Abraham Lincoln,* ed. Phillips Van Doren Stern (New York: Random House, 1940; reprint, New York: Modern Library, 1990), 369.

20. Thomas E. Schott, *Alexander H. Stephens of Georgia: A Biography* (Baton Rouge: Louisiana State University Press, 1988), 62. See also Arthur C. Cole, *The Whig Party in the South* (Washington, DC: American Historical Association, 1913); Thomas B. Alexander, "Persistent Whiggery in the Confederate South, 1860–1877," *Journal of Southern History* 27, no. 3 (August 1961): 305–29; and Jonathan M. Atkins, "The Whig Party versus the 'Spoilsmen' of Tennessee," *The Historian* 57, no. 2 (1994): 329–40.

21. Abraham Lincoln, "Eulogy on Henry Clay" (July 6, 1852), in "Speeches and Writings," Abraham Lincoln Online, http://www.abrahamlincolnonline.org/lincoln/speeches/clay.htm.

22. Gay, *The Bourgeois Experience,* 1:56–60; Kohl, *The Politics of Individualism,* 82–86; McCloskey, *Bourgeois Dignity,* 10–14.

23. Thomas Cole to Luman Reed, September 18, 1833, in *The Life and Works of Thomas Cole* (1853), ed. Louis L. Noble, 3rd ed. (New York: Sheldon, Blakeman, 1856), 176–79, 176.

24. For more on this view among Jacksonians, see Schlesinger, *The Age of Jackson,* 8–16; Ward, *Andrew Jackson,* 30–35; Sellers, *The Market Revolution,* 21–33; and Reynolds, *Waking Giant,* 8–10.

25. Cole to Reed, September 18, 1833.

26. "The Tendency to Things of Monarchy," *Weekly Ohio State Journal,* April 6, 1842, 1; Henry Clay, "On the Commencement of Jackson's Administration" (May 16, 1829), in Hopkins et al., eds., *The Papers of Henry Clay,* 8:43; Daniel Webster, "Speech of Daniel Webster: Delivered at the Whig State Convention at Boston, Sept. 29, 1847," *Niles' National Register,* October 16, 1847, 104–6. For similar contemporary views, see Seward, "Annual Message to the Legislature" (January 1, 1839), 197; Sergeant S. Prentiss to George Prentiss, Vicksburg, MS, January 18, 1840, in Prentiss, ed., *A Memoir of S. S. Prentiss,* 2:150–51; Harrison, "Inaugural Address"; Calvin Colton, *Democracy* (New York: Horace Greeley, 1844), 2–3; and David Lowry Swain, "British Invasion of North Carolina, in 1776: A Lecture," in *Revolutionary History of North Carolina* (Raleigh: William D. Cooke, 1853), 101–5. See also Ralph A. Wooster, *Politicians, Planters, and Plain Folk: Courthouse and Statehouse in the Upper South, 1850–1860* (Knoxville: University of Tennessee Press, 1975), 71; Thomas Brown, *Politics and Statesmanship: Essays on the American Whig Party* (New York: Columbia University Press, 1985), 64–69; Kohl, *The Politics of Individualism,* 84–86; and Howe, *What Hath God Wrought,* 383.

27. "The Points of the Struggle," *Investigator and Expositor,* October 1838, 52. See also "The Tendency to Things of Monarchy," 1; "The Issues! The Issues!," *Carolina Watchman,* March 26, 1836, 2; "The Poor Man's Candidate," *Kentucky Gazette,* February 27, 1840, 3; Henkle, *The Moral Dignity and General Claims of Agricultural Science,* 1–3; and "The Points of the Struggle," 52. This sentiment was widely held. A few examples include "Friends of the Union," *Western Carolinian,* February 4, 1833, 3; "Tennessee," *Nashville Whig,* July 1, 1835, 2; John Thomas, "The Rest from Sin," *Apostolic Advocate,* November 1, 1835, 156; "To the Point," *Vermont State Journal,* March 22, 1836, 2; M. B. Hope, *A Discourse Delivered on the Occasion of the Death of David G. Aikin* (Princeton, NJ: J. T. Robinson, 1849), 8; "Kentucky Demonstrations," *Kentucky Whig,* December 31, 1852, 2; and "Observations," *Lexington Observer and Reporter,* November 8, 1854, 3.

28. "Some Thoughts on the History of American Government," *New-Yorker,* November 3, 1838, 98; "Political Regeneration," *American Monthly Magazine,* April 1838, 297; "A Lesson for Politicians," *American Whig Review,* September

1849, 252. See also "Letters from Mr. Brooks," *New-Yorker,* May 14, 1836, 117; "The Times," *American Monthly Magazine,* September 1837, 209–14; "Gems of Politics, Facts Stated," *New-Yorker,* February 24, 1838, 774–75; "Speech of C. M. [Cassius Marcellus] Clay," *Cincinnati Herald,* January 17, 1844, 2; "The Progress and Disorganization," *American Whig Review,* July 1845, 97–98; "Civilization: American and European," *American Whig Review,* June 1846, 611–20; "Summary," *New York Evangelist,* January 30, 1851, 19; "Imaginary Presidents: The Ideal of a National Administration," *American Whig Review,* April 1851, 2–7; and "The Nebraska Bill, and Its Results," *New Englander,* May 1854, 213–19.

29. Henry Clay, "Speech of Henry Clay at Hanover, VA" (July 10, 1840), *Niles' National Register,* July 25, 1840, 324; "The Whigs and Their Candidate," 223.

30. "Declaration of Independence," *American Quarterly Review,* January 1, 1834, 51. See also "Leaves and Notes," *Historical Family Library,* March 1, 1836, 145–50; "The Unpublished Chapters in the History of Tylerism," *New York Tribune,* July 6, 1843, 2; "The Age of Pitt and Fox," 124–32; "The Life of Oliver Cromwell," *Albion: A Journal of News, Politics and Literature,* July 1, 1848, 321; "The States," *Niles' National Register,* January 17, 1849, 41–43; *Elements of Intellectual Philosophy* (Portland, ME: Shirley & Hyde, 1827), 460; George Bancroft, *A History of the United States* (Boston: Charles Bowen, 1834), 306; William Martin, *The Moral and Intellectual School Book* (London: Darton & Clark, 1838), 169–70; and Wilson, *American History,* 358–59.

31. Quoted in Gamaliel Bradford, "Henry Clay," *Virginia Quarterly Review,* vol. 4, no. 1 (Winter 1928), https://www.vqronline.org/essay/henry-clay.

## 5. The Future

Epigraph: Loren Eiseley, *The Star Thrower* (New York: Times Books, 1978), 220.

1. "The Past and the Present," *Richmond (VA) Whig,* reprinted in *Southern Planter,* January 1855, 23.

2. Daniel Webster, "Lecture before the Society for the Diffusion of Useful Knowledge" (Boston, November 11, 1836), quoted in Kohl, *The Politics of Individualism,* 221; William H. Seward, "Extracts from Gov. Seward's Message," *American Railroad Journal and Mechanics' Magazine* 2 (1839): 11.

3. "Selfishness," *Ladies' Repository, and Gatherings of the West,* October 1848, 310. A few other examples of this thinking include "Society Based Not on Selfishness but Love," *Western Messenger,* June 1839, 129–31; "Religion Not Selfishness," *New York Observer,* March 6, 1847, 1; "The Spirit of Selfishness," *Christian Secretary,* January 28, 1848, 2; "How Indulgence Fosters Selfishness," *Weekly Intelligencer,* June 17, 1848, 95; "Benevolence and Selfishness," *Christian Register,* September 7, 1850, 1.

4. Tocqueville, *Democracy in America,* 482.

5. Colton, *The Americans,* 191; "Selfishness and Depravity," *Spirit of the Pilgrims,* November 1833, 623; "Human Selfishness," *Episcopal Recorder,* June 23, 1849, 58. A few other examples include "The Worth of Money," *Ladies' Magazine*

*and Literary Gazette,* February 1, 1830, 49–54; "Pursuit of Wealth," *Maine Farmer and Mechanic's Advocate,* May 4, 1839, 106–7; "The Importance of Money," *Cincinnati Weekly Herald,* November 22, 1843, 1; "The Money Diggers," *American Monthly Review,* August 1840, 81–87; and "The Pursuit," *Home Journal,* October 19, 1850, 1. See also "Whig Promises Fulfilled," *Ohio State Journal,* March 29, 1843, 2; "To the Whig Party of Tennessee," *Republican Banner,* October 3, 1851, 2; and Andrew Delbanco, *The Real American Dream: A Meditation on Hope* (Cambridge, MA: Harvard University Press, 1999), 88–89.

6. Tocqueville, *Democracy in America,* 502.

7. "Virtue and Happiness—Sin and Misery," *Evangelical Magazine and Gospel Advocate,* August 28, 1840, 278; "Temperance Cause at a Stand," *Boston Recorder,* April 22, 1836, 66–67.

8. "Temperance: Radical and Conservative," *New York Evangelist,* April 8, 1837, 59–60; "Temperance Town," *New-Yorker,* August 20, 1836, 339; *Western Christian Advocate,* August 18, 1837, 66–69. See also "General Intelligence," *Christian Observer,* August 8, 1845, 127; and "Letter Written in a Wheelbarrow," *The Rough and Ready,* January 2, 1847, 4.

9. "The Moral Principle of the Temperance Movement," *Christian Examiner,* November 1841, 252. See also "The Origin, Nature, Principles, and Prospects of Temperance Reform," *American Quarterly Observer,* July 1834, 46–52; "Temperance," *New York Evangelist,* February 23, 1839, 1; and "Temperance Celebration," *Boston Recorder,* July 12, 1839, 110–11.

10. "Temperance," *United States Magazine, and Democratic Review,* August 1851, 115. See also Schlesinger, *The Age of Jackson,* 266–67; Sellers, *The Market Revolution,* 210–17; and Wilentz, *The Rise of American Democracy,* 456–57.

11. Sergeant S. Prentiss, "Speech at Portland, Maine" (1840), in Prentiss, ed., *A Memoir of S. S. Prentiss,* 2:167.

12. "Political Motives for 1851–2: American National Ideas," *American Whig Review,* January 1851, 10. See also "Return of the Whig Flag," *Niles' Weekly Register,* November 21, 1835, 200; "Whig Victories and Prospects," *Huntress,* August 26, 1837, 3; "The Democratic and Whig Parties," *Philanthropist,* April 19, 1843, 2; "Whig Patriotism," *Liberator,* January 8, 1847, 7–8; and "On Wealth and Fortune," *Trumpet and Universalist Magazine,* October 9, 1847, 68.

13. Clay, "On the American System," 455–56.

14. "Editors' Table," *New York Monthly Magazine,* January 1847, 80.

15. See also "Youths' Department," *Christian Advocate,* June 24, 1831, 172–73; "A Self Made Man," *New York Observer and Chronicle,* April 10, 1841, 60; "Association—It's [*sic*] Aims," *Harbinger, Devoted to Social and Political Progress,* November 15, 1845, 361; "A Self-Made Man: The Late Judge Buel," *Farmer's Register,* April 30, 1840, 240; Daniel Walker Howe, *Making the American Self: Jonathan Edwards to Abraham Lincoln* (Cambridge, MA: Harvard University Press, 1997), 136–37; Delbanco, *The Real American Dream,* 64–71; and McCloskey, *The Bourgeois Virtues,* 258–62.

16. "Our Politics," *Western Argus,* August 6, 1828, 2. Kendall's view is the stock explanation of Whig political motivation in many of the most important works on the topic, including Schlesinger, *The Age of Jackson,* 267–75; Sellers, *The Market Revolution,* 202–12; and Wilentz, *The Rise of American Democracy,* 456–60.

17. "The Federal Party and the People," *The Crisis,* May 16, 1840, 86–87.

18. "The Maniac's Story," *Godey's Lady's Book and Ladies' American Magazine,* September 1833, 112–16.

19. "Retribution of Madness," *New York Evangelist,* January 18, 1855, 10. See also "What Creates Mobs?," *Zion's Herald,* September 2, 1835, 138; Houghton, *The Victorian Frame of Mind,* 329–31; Kohl, *The Politics of Individualism,* 147; and McCloskey, *The Bourgeois Virtues,* 253–59.

20. "Illustrations of Insanity," *American Journal of Insanity* 1 (July 1844): 46–50, 46. See also Houghton, *The Victorian Frame of Mind,* 77–82; Kohl, *The Politics of Individualism,* 74; McCloskey, *The Bourgeois Virtues,* 314–15; Howe, *What Hath God Wrought,* 193; McCloskey, *Bourgeois Dignity,* 391–92; and Wendling, *The Ruling Ideas,* 89.

21. "Madness," *American Whig Review,* August 1852, 126. See also "The Golden Madness," *Friend,* September 30, 1848, 12; and "Excessive Joy," *Christian Observer,* November 12, 1853, 184.

22. Abraham Lincoln, "My Childhood Home I See Again" (1846), in Basler, ed., *Abraham Lincoln: His Speeches and Writings,* 191. See also Howe, *The Political Culture of the American Whigs,* 282–83; Kohl, *The Politics of Individualism,* 74–78; McCloskey, *The Bourgeois Virtues,* 3–8; and Howe, *What Hath God Wrought,* 193–96.

23. G. Ferrus, "On the Insane," *American Journal of the Medical Sciences* (Boston) 19 (1836): 124. See also "Insanity in the United States," *New York Evangelist,* May 30, 1840, 88; "Starving Mad," *Spirit of the Times,* March 8, 1845, 10; "Progress of Home Medical Literature," *Boston Medical and Surgical Journal,* April 12, 1848, 224–25; "Insanity Increasing in Our Country," *Zion's Herald,* July 17, 1850, 116; Howe, *The Political Culture of the American Whigs,* 281–85; Kohl, *The Politics of Individualism,* 76–79; Delbanco, *The Real American Dream,* 83–90; McCloskey, *The Bourgeois Virtues,* 9–14; and Howe, *What Hath God Wrought,* 192–95.

24. *The American Heritage Medical Dictionary,* s.v. *melancholia attonita,* https://medical-dictionary.thefreedictionary.com/melancholia+attonita. Some of the better recent books on this topic include Edward Shorter, *A History of Psychiatry: From the Era of the Asylum to the Age of Prozac* (New York: Wiley, 1998); Carla Yanni, *The Architecture of Madness: Insane Asylums in the United States* (Minneapolis: University of Minnesota Press, 2007); and Benjamin Reiss, *Theaters of Madness: Insane Asylums and Nineteenth-Century American Culture* (Chicago: University of Chicago Press, 2008).

25. "A Letter about Hard Times," *Lowell Offering,* June 1843, 203; "The Issue at Stake," *United States Magazine, and Democratic Review,* November 1843, 545.

See also Kohl, *The Politics of Individualism,* 225; "Greenville," *Western Monthly Magazine,* June 1837, 293–99; "Items of News," *The Crisis,* June 6, 1840, 112; and "State Credit," *United States Magazine, and Democratic Review,* January 1842, 3–8.

26. Sandage, *Born Losers,* 46 (see generally 44–50).

27. William Henry Seward, "The Six Million Loan" (April 10, 1840), in Baker, ed., *The Works of William Henry Seward,* 1:49.

28. "General Bankrupt Law," *New-Yorker,* May 30, 1840, 169. A few other examples of this sort of thinking include "To the Whig Party in Kentucky," *Louisville Daily Journal,* July 24, 1840, 2; "Congressional Whig Meeting: Monday, September 13, 1841," *Niles' National Register,* September 18, 1841, 35–36; "Western Reserve," *Ohio State Journal,* August 4, 1842, 2; and "The Whig Convention: The Candidate and the Campaign," *American Whig Review,* August 1852, 97–102.

29. Henry Clay, "Beginning of Jackson's Administration" (May 16, 1829), in Mallory, ed., *Life and Speeches of the Hon. Henry Clay,* 1:572.

30. "The Pursuit of Wealth," *Flag of Our Union,* March 13, 1858, 85. See also Kohl, *The Politics of Individualism,* 201–5; Delbanco, *The Real American Dream,* 100–102; McCloskey, *The Bourgeois Virtues,* 242–47, 394–98; and Howe, *What Hath God Wrought,* 225–35.

31. "Inordinate Pursuit of Riches," *The Friend,* November 25, 1848, 78.

32. "Wealth and Poverty," *Lowell Offering,* May 1844, 151.

33. "On Wealth," *American Monthly Magazine,* March 1834, 21. See also Howe, *The Political Culture of the American Whigs,* 283; Kohl, *The Politics of Individualism,* 86–90; Howe, *What Hath God Wrought,* 200–212; "Improvement," *American Monthly Magazine,* November 1836, 516; "Temperance Reform," *New-Yorker,* April 3, 1841, 41; "Temperance," *Christian Secretary,* January 7, 1842, 2–4; and "General Intelligence," *New York Evangelist,* June 21, 1849, 155–56.

34. Abraham Lincoln, "Address Before the Wisconsin State Agricultural Society, Milwaukee, Wisconsin" (September 30, 1859), in Basler, ed., *The Collected Works of Abraham Lincoln,* 9:478–79.

35. "Political Responsibilities," *American Whig Review,* November 1851, 365.

36. Tocqueville, *Democracy in America,* 404; "Whig Mass Meeting at Boston," *Niles' National Register,* September 28, 1844, 53. Other examples include "Political Economy of Intemperance," *American Quarterly Observer,* July 1834, 1–4; "Political Items," *New-Yorker,* October 22, 1836, 75; "Wealth—Two Kinds," *Common School Assistant,* December 1838, 92–95; "A Plea for Usefulness," *Christian Register,* January 30, 1841, 1; "Indiana," *Niles' National Register,* September 16, 1843, 3; and "Hon. John P. Kennedy," *American Whig Review,* January 1851, 13–15. See also Howe, *The Political Culture of the American Whigs,* 282–83; Kohl, *The Politics of Individualism,* 115–23; McCloskey, *The Bourgeois Virtues,* 346–50; and Howe, *What Hath God Wrought,* 215–19.

37. *Oxford Pocket Dictionary of Current English,* s.v. *trust,* Oxford Dictionaries, http://www.oxforddictionaries.com/us/definition/american_english/trust.

38. Tocqueville, *Democracy in America,* 482. See also Howe, *The Political Culture of the American Whigs,* 278–79; McCloskey, *The Bourgeois Virtues,* 275–81; and Howe, *What Hath God Wrought,* 199–200.

39. "Trust the Proof of Faith," *Circular,* January 17, 1854, 76. See also "A Letter from Mr. Rush," *Niles' Weekly Register,* June 17, 1837, 245–47; "And Still Another," *Cincinnati Weekly Herald,* September 18, 1844, 1; and "The Whig Party, Its Position, and Duties," 547–53.

40. "Subterfuge," *Richmond (VA) Enquirer,* April 10, 1840, 3.

41. "Whig Intrigue," *Michigan Argus,* September 20, 1838, 3; "American Democracy," *United States Magazine, and Democratic Review,* March 1852, 278. Throughout the antebellum era, O'Sullivan spoke for most Democrats. A few examples of like-minded thinking on this issue include "An Old Democrat," *The Crisis,* September 2, 1840, 216; "The Farm and Farming of the Rev. J. H. Turner," *Farmers' Register,* April 30, 1842, 154–58; "Messr. Editors—," *Louisville Morning Courier and American Democrat,* November 25, 1845, 2; "The Mexican War—Its Origin, Its Justice and Consequences," *United States Magazine, and Democratic Review,* February 1848, 106–11; and "Arkansas News," *Memphis Daily Appeal,* May 13, 1856, 2.

42. "Thoughts on the Times," *United States Magazine, and Democratic Review,* December 1839, 458–59.

43. "Privilege," *Ohio Statesman,* October 13, 1840, 3.

44. "American Civilization," 50.

45. "Whig Meeting," *Alabama Journal,* January 15, 1840, 1.

46. "True Principles," *Boston Atlas,* January 19, 1837.

47. "The Locofoco Pot," *Nashville Tennessean,* January 16, 1843, 2. See also "Principle Events of 1837," *New-Yorker,* December 30, 1837, 649; "Great Whig Meeting in New York," *Cincinnati Weekly Herald,* May 15, 1844, 3; "Necessity of Party," *American Whig Review,* July 1848, 8–10; "The Whig Convention: The Candidate and the Campaign," 97–99; "Tennessee," *Niles' National Register,* October 14, 1843, 104; Howe, *The Political Culture of the American Whigs,* 272–74; and Howe, *What Hath God Wrought,* 300–312. The term *locofoco* was a pejorative used by Whigs to imply that Democrats were rash and reactionary. For evidence, see Hans Sperber and Travis Trittschuh, *American Political Terms: An Historical Dictionary* (Detroit: Wayne State University Press, 1962), 245.

48. "Speech of Hon. Daniel Webster," 186.

49. "Incorporation Principle," *Boston Courier,* February 22, 1836, 3. See also "General Intelligence," *American Monthly Review,* November 1833, 353–57; "Rights of Corporations," *New-Yorker,* March 16, 1839, 409; and "From Washington," *Boston Recorder,* September 3, 1841, 142.

50. Daniel Webster, "The Continuance of the Bank Charter" (March 18, 1834), in *The Writings and Speeches of Daniel Webster,* 18 vols. (Boston: Little, Brown, 1903), 7:94; Henry Clay, "Speech in the Senate" (February 19, 1838), in Hopkins et al., eds., *The Papers of Henry Clay,* 9:158.

51. Horace Greeley, "The Return of Prosperity," *New-Yorker,* March 31, 1838, 25. See also Kohl, *The Politics of Individualism,* 61–62; Howe, *What Hath God Wrought,* 525–32; and Hammond, *Banks and Politics in America,* 451–60.

52. "Introduction" (*United States Magazine, and Democratic Review*), 6.

53. Thomas Jefferson, *Notes on the State of Virginia* (1787), query 17, Avalon Project, http://avalon.law.yale.edu/18th_century/jeffvir.asp.

54. William Henry Seward, "Address, August 15, 1839," in Baker, ed., *The Works of William Henry Seward,* 2:213.

55. "The Position of Parties," 19.

56. John Quincy Adams, "An *Oration,* Delivered [December 22] at Plymouth . . ." (Boston, 1802), 6; Calvin Colton, *Manual for Immigrants to America* (London: F. Westley & A. H. Davis, 1832), 171. Adams's speech was cited by Adams himself and other Whigs throughout the era. Evidence of reverence for these ideas includes "Mr. Adams," *New York Review,* January 1842, 55–57; "Speech of Hon. John Quincy Adams," *Liberator,* April 29, 1842, 66–68; "Sermon on the Death of Hon. John Quincy Adams," *Boston Recorder,* March 3, 1848, 34–35; and William H. Seward, "The Life of John Quincy Adams," *Methodist Quarterly Review,* April 1850, 197–205. See also Brown, *Modernization,* 94–99; and Kohl, *The Politics of Individualism,* 63–69.

57. Tocqueville, *Democracy in America,* 490.

58. Daniel Webster, "Festival of the Sons of New Hampshire," in *The Works of Daniel Webster,* 2:498. See also "School Discipline: A Practical Lesson & Personal Duty," *American Annals of Education,* May 1833, 227–28; "The Discipline of Life," 4–5; Kaestle, *Pillars of the Republic,* 74–75, 82; Clark, *A Farewell to Alms,* 212–13; and Wendling, *The Ruling Ideas,* 22–25.

59. "Whig Principle and Its Development," 134.

60. "The Whig Merchants' Meeting," 93.

61. "Banks—Banking—Currency—Politics," *Weekly Ohio State Journal,* May 18, 1842, 2.

62. Henry Clay, "On the Sub-Treasury Bill" (September 25, 1837), in Hopkins et al., eds., *The Papers of Henry Clay,* 9:7.

63. William Henry Seward, "Annual Message to the Legislature" (January 4, 1842), in Baker, ed., *The Works of William Henry Seward,* 2:312.

64. "Public Works," *New York Enquirer,* November 16, 1839, 3. See also McCloskey, *The Bourgeois Virtues,* 344–49; Clark, *A Farewell to Alms,* 157–61; Howe, *What Hath God Wrought,* 278–82; and McCloskey, *Bourgeois Dignity,* 130–32.

65. "Canal Policy of New York," *American Whig Review,* December 1849, 1.

66. https://www.measuringworth.com/calculators/uscompare. Translating monetary values across historical eras is always a tricky business. The best economists can do is compare a bundle of certain goods at different moments for which we have evidence.

67. "Domestic," *Western Recorder,* January 26, 1830, 15. See also "Progress of Mr. Clay," *Niles' National Register,* August 31, 1839, 8; "Summary," *New York*

*Evangelist,* July 17, 1841, 115; and "A Search After Democratic Principles," 79–82.

68. For evidence, see Schlesinger, *The Age of Jackson,* 74–82; Whitney R. Cross, *The Burned-Over District: The Social and Intellectual History of Enthusiastic Religion in Western New York, 1800–1850* (Ithaca, NY: Cornell University Press, 1950; reprint, Ithaca, NY: Cornell University Press, 1981), 56–63; Paul E. Johnson, *A Shopkeeper's Millennium: Society and Revivals in Rochester, New York, 1815–1837* (New York: Hill & Wang, 1978; reprint, New York: Hill & Wang, 2004), 29–35; Wilentz, *Chants Democratic,* 202–16; Watson, *Liberty and Power,* 173–80; and Sellers, *The Market Revolution,* 19–25.

69. Kohl, *The Politics of Individualism,* 214–20; Howe, *What Hath God Wrought,* 568–75.

70. "Richmond Whigs," *Niles' National Register,* September 13, 1834, 26.

71. "Who Built the Canals?," *New York Daily Times,* October 6, 1852, 6.

72. Barnes, "Professional Industry," 189. See also Dana, "Conversion the Work of God," 114–15; and "Leisure Hours: The Maniac," 118–19. Solid works on the Chesapeake and Ohio Canal include Mike High, *The C&O Canal Companion* (Baltimore: Johns Hopkins University Press, 2001); Joel Achenbach, *The Grand Idea: George Washington's Potomac and the Race to the West* (New York: Simon & Schuster, 2004); and Robert Kapsch, *The Potomac Canal, George Washington and the Waterway West* (Morgantown: West Virginia University Press, 2007).

73. Colton, *Junius Tracts: No. III,* 15, 7.

74. John P. Kennedy, "On the Protective Tariff," in *Political and Official Papers,* 280.

75. William Leggett, "Despotism of Andrew Jackson" (May 22, 1834), in Sedgwick, ed., *A Collection of the Political Writings of William Leggett,* 1:282.

76. William Freehling's magisterial *Prelude to Civil War: The Nullification Controversy in South Carolina, 1816–1836* (New York: Oxford University Press, 1965) is still the standard work on the subject. Other credible treatments include Lacy K. Ford, *Origins of Southern Radicalism: The South Carolina Upcountry, 1800–1860* (New York: Oxford University Press, 1991); and Elizabeth R. Varon, *Disunion! The Coming of the American Civil War, 1789–1859* (Chapel Hill: University of North Carolina Press, 2008).

77. John C. Calhoun, "[South Carolina] Exposition and Protest, Dec. 19, 1828," in *The Papers of John C. Calhoun,* vol. 10, *1825–1829,* ed. Clyde N. Wilson and W. Edwin Hemphill (Columbia: University of South Carolina Press, 1977), 531.

78. "Anti-Nullification," *Niles' Weekly Register,* August 4, 1832, 406. See also "Mr. Calhoun's Address," *Atkinson's Saturday Evening Post,* August 27, 1831; "Progress of Nullification," *Banner of the Constitution,* April 18, 1832, 158, "Epitome of the Times," *Atkinson's Saturday Evening Post,* February 16, 1833, 3; and "Parties in This Country," *Knickerbocker,* August 1835, 85–89.

79. "Dissolution of the Union," *Philanthropist,* April 21, 1837, 5.

80. Henry Clay, "To the Whigs of Nansemond County [VA]" (May 25, 1839), in Hopkins et al., eds., *The Papers of Henry Clay,* 9:319. See also Kohl, *The Politics of Individualism,* 130–35; and Howe, *What Hath God Wrought,* 570–85.

81. Henry Clay, "A Speech at Buffalo, New York" (July 17, 1839), in Hopkins et al., eds., *The Papers of Henry Clay,* 9:331.

82. Daniel Webster, "The Constitution Is Not a Compact between Sovereign States" (February 16, 1833), in *The Writings and Speeches of Daniel Webster,* 6:211.

83. William Henry Seward, "Henry Clay" (June 30, 1852), in Baker, ed., *The Works of William Henry Seward,* 3:107.

84. Calvin Colton, *The Junius Tracts: No. I* (New York: Greeley & McElrath, 1844), 69. See also Kohl, *The Politics of Individualism,* 133–35; Delbanco, *The Real American Dream,* 50–52; and Howe, *What Hath God Wrought,* 243–50.

## Conclusion

1. Herman Melville, *White-Jacket; or, The World in a Man-of-War* (London: Richard Bentley, 1850; reprint, Boston: St. Botolph Society, 1892), 144.

2. For evidence, see Howe, *What Hath God Wrought,* 787–91; Amy S. Greenberg, *A Wicked War: Polk, Clay, Lincoln, and the 1846 U. S. Invasion of Mexico* (New York: Knopf, 2012), 243–47; and Steven Hahn, *A Nation without Borders: The United States and Its World in an Age of Civil Wars, 1830–1910* (New York: Penguin, 2016), 132–39.

3. "Declaration of Independence," National Archives, https://www.archives.gov/founding-docs/declaration-transcript.

4. Abraham Lincoln, "The Gettysburg Address" (November 19, 1863), Abraham Lincoln Online, http://www.abrahamlincolnonline.org/lincoln/speeches/gettysburg.htm.

5. Lincoln, "The Gettysburg Address."

6. David M. Potter, *The Impending Crisis: America Before the Civil War, 1848–1861* (New York: Harper & Row, 1976), 99–101; Robert V. Remini, *Henry Clay* (New York: Norton, 1991), 733–39; Harlow Giles Unger, *Henry Clay: America's Greatest Statesman* (Philadelphia: Da Capo, 2015), 253–57.

7. Potter, *The Impending Crisis,* 109–11.

8. Abraham Lincoln, "Second Inaugural Address" (March 4, 1865), Teaching American History, https://teachingamericanhistory.org/library/document/second-inaugural-address.

9. "The Cost of War: Killed, Wounded, Captured, and Missing," American Battlefield Trust, Civil War History, https://www.battlefields.org/learn/articles/civil-war-casualties.

10. Phillips, *Looming Civil War,* 6–8. See also Harry S. Stout, *Upon the Altar of the Nation: A Moral History of the Civil War* (New York: Viking, 2006), 61; Drew

Gilpin Faust, *This Republic of Suffering: Death and American Civil War* (New York: Knopf, 2008), 3; George C. Rable, *God's Almost Chosen Peoples: A Religious History of the American Civil War* (Chapel Hill: University of North Carolina Press, 2010), 168–74; and Mark W. Summers, *The Ordeal of the Reunion: A New History of Reconstruction* (Chapel Hill: University of North Carolina Press, 2014), 10–12.

11. Lincoln, "Second Inaugural Address."

# Bibliography


Abzug, Robert H. *Cosmos Crumbling: American Reform and the Religious Imagination.* New York: Oxford University Press, 1994.

Achenbach, Joel. *The Grand Idea: George Washington's Potomac and the Race to the West.* New York: Simon & Schuster, 2004.

Ackley, Horace A. *Introductory Address of the Progress of the Science of Medicine.* Cleveland: Younglove, 1849.

Adam, Barbara. *Timescapes of Modernity: The Environment and Invisible Hazards.* New York: Routledge, 1998.

Adams, Henry. *The. Life of Albert Gallatin.* Philadelphia: J. B. Lippincott, 1880.

Ahlstrom, Sydney E. *A Religious History of the American People.* 1972. 2nd ed. New Haven, CT: Yale University Press, 2004.

Alexander, Thomas B. "Persistent Whiggery in the Confederate South, 1860–1877." *Journal of Southern History* 27, no. 3 (August 1961): 305–29.

*The American's Guide.* Philadelphia: Hogan & Thompson, 1838.

Anderson, Benedict. *Imagined Communities: Reflections on the Origin and Spread of Nationalism.* New York: Verso, 1983.

*Antebellum American Culture: An Interpretative Anthology.* Edited by David Brion Davis. New York: D. C. Health, 1979. Reprint, New York: Routledge, 1998.

*The Anti-Federalist Papers.* Edited by Ralph Ketchum. New York: Penguin, 1986. Reprint Signet, 2003.

Applebaum, Diana Karter. *The Glorious Fourth: An American Holiday, an American History.* New York: Facts on File, 1989.

Atkins, Jonathan M. "The Whig Party versus the 'Spoilsmen' of Tennessee." *The Historian* 57, no. 2(1994): 329–40.

Bailyn, Bernard. *The Ideological Origins of the American Revolution.* Cambridge, MA: Harvard University Press, 1967.

———. *The Origins of American Politics.* New York: Vintage, 1970.

Balleisen, Edward J. *Navigating Failure: Bankruptcy and Commercial Society in Antebellum America.* Chapel Hill: University of North Carolina Press, 2001.

Bancroft, George. *A History of the United States.* Boston: Charles Bowen, 1834.

Barnard, Daniel D. *The Social System: An Address Before the House of Convocation, of Trinity College, Hartford, August 2, 1848.* Hartford, CT: Samuel Hanmer Jr./Calendar Press, 1848.

Bauer, Susan Wise. *The History of the Medieval World: From the Conversion of Constantine to the First Crusade.* New York: Oxford University Press, 2010.

Baylen, Joseph O. "A Tennessee Politician in Imperial Russia, 1850–1853." *Tennessee Historical Quarterly* 14 (1955): 227–52.

Beecher, Catherine E. *A Treatise on Domestic Economy.* Boston: T. H. Webb, 1842.

Beecher, Lyman. *Autobiography, Correspondence, etc., of Lyman Beecher, D.D.* Edited by Charles Beecher. 2 vols. New York: Harper & Bros., 1864–1866.

Benson, Lee. *The Concept of Jacksonian Democracy: New York as a Test Case.* New York: Atheneum, 1961.

Biddle, Nicholas. *The Correspondence of Nicholas Biddle.* Edited by Reginald C. McGrane. New York: Houghton Mifflin, 1919.

Billington, Ray Allen. *The Protestant Crusade, 1800–1860: A Study of the Origins of American Nativism.* New York: Rinehart, 1938.

Bishop, Morris. *The Middle Ages.* New York: American Heritage, 1968. Reprint, New York: American Heritage, 2001.

Black, Andrew R. *John Pendleton Kennedy: Early American Novelist, Whig Statesman, and Ardent Nationalist.* Baton Rouge: Louisiana State University Press, 2014.

Black, Jeremy. *George III: America's Last King.* New Haven, CT: Yale University Press, 2009.

*Bluegrass Renaissance: The History and Culture of Central Kentucky, 1792–1852.* Edited by James C. Klotter and Daniel Rowland. Lexington: University Press of Kentucky, 2012.

Bode, Carl. *The American Lyceum.* New York: Oxford University Press, 1956.

Boorstin, Daniel J. *The Americans: The National Experience.* New York: Random House, 1965. Reprint, New York: Vintage, 2002.

———. *The Americans: The Democratic Experience.* New York: Vintage, 1973.

Bordo, Michael D., and Joseph G. Haubrich. "Credit Crises, Money, and Contractions: An Historical View." *Journal of Monetary Economics* 57, no. 1 (January 2010): 1–18.

Boritt, Gabor S. *Lincoln and the Economics of the American Dream.* Memphis: Memphis State University Press, 1978.

Brock, William R. *Parties and Political Conscience: American Dilemmas, 1840–1850.* Millbrook, NY: KTO, 1979.

Brooke, John L. *Columbia Rising: Civil Life on the Upper Hudson from the Revolution to the Age of Jackson.* Chapel Hill: University of North Carolina Press, 2010.

Brown, Gillian. *Domestic Individualism: Imagining Self in Nineteenth-Century America.* Berkeley and Los Angeles: University of California Press, 1992.

Brown, Richard D. *Modernization: The Transformation of American Life, 1860–1865.* New York: Hill & Wang, 1976.

Brown, Thomas. *Politics and Statesmanship: Essays on the American Whig Party.* New York: Columbia University Press, 1985.

Burke, Edmund. *Reflections on the Revolution in France.* 1790. Edited by Conor Cruise O'Brien. New York: Penguin, 1968. Reprint, New York: Penguin, 1986.

Burns, Sarah, and John Davis. *American Art to 1900: A Documentary History.* Berkeley and Los Angeles: University of California Press, 2009.

Burstein, Andrew. *The Passions of Andrew Jackson.* New York: Vintage, 2003.

Butler, Judith. *Gender Trouble: Feminism and the Subversion of Identity.* New York: Routledge, 1990.

Calhoun, John C. *The Papers of John C. Calhoun.* Vol. 10, *1825–1829.* Edited by Clyde N. Wilson and W. Edwin Hemphill. Columbia: University of South Carolina Press, 1977.

Carr, David. *Time, Narrative, and History.* Bloomington: Indiana University Press, 1986. Reprint, Bloomington: Indiana University Press, 1991.

Carwardine, Richard. *Evangelicals and Politics in Antebellum America.* Knoxville: University of Tennessee Press, 1997.

Catterall, Ralph C. H. *The Second Bank of the United States.* Chicago: University of Chicago Press, 1903.

Christman, Henry. *Tin Horns and Calico: A Decisive Episode in the Emergence of Democracy.* New York: Henry Holt, 1945.

Clark, Gregory. *A Farewell to Alms: A Brief Economic History of the World.* Princeton, NJ: Princeton University Press, 2007.

Clay, Henry. *The Papers of Henry Clay.* Edited by James F. Hopkins et al. 10 vols. Lexington: University of Press of Kentucky, 1959–1991.

Coleman, Margaret. "Labor Shortage, Wage and Labor Structures, and Poverty, 1810–1840, in the Northeastern United States." PhD diss., New School for Social Research, 1996.

Colton, Calvin. *Manual for Immigrants to America.* London: F. Westley & A. H. Davis, 1832.

———. *The Americans.* London: F. Westley & A. H. Davis, 1833.

———. *Democracy.* New York: Horace Greeley, 1844.

———. *The Junius Tracts: Nos. 1–7.* New York: McElrath & Greeley, 1844.

———. *Public Economy for the United States.* New York: A. S. Barnes, 1848.

———. *A Lecture on the Railroad to the Pacific.* New York: A. S. Barnes, 1850.

Commager, Henry Steele. *Jefferson, Nationalism, and the Enlightenment.* New York: George Braziller, 1975.

Comte-Sponville, André. *A Small Treatise on the Great Virtues.* New York: Henry Holt, 2002.

Cooper, William J., Jr. *Approaching Civil War and Southern History.* Baton Rouge: Louisiana State University Press, 2019.

Cott, Nancy F. *The Bonds of Womanhood: "Woman's Sphere" in New England, 1780–1835.* New Haven, CT: Yale University Press, 1977.

Crawford, T. Hugh. "Images of Authority, Strategies of Control: Cooper, Weems, and George Washington." *South Central Review* 11, no. 1 (Spring 1994): 61–74.

Cremin, Lawrence A. *American Education: The National Experience, 1783–1876.* New York: Harper & Row, 1980.

Cross, Whitney R. *The Burned-over District: The Social and Intellectual History of Enthusiastic Religion in Western New York, 1800–1850.* Ithaca, NY: Cornell University Press, 1981.

Currie, David P. *The Constitution in Congress: Democrats and Whigs, 1829–1861.* Chicago: University of Chicago Press, 2005.

Curti, Merle. *The Growth of American Thought.* New York: Harper & Bros., 1943.

Dearinger, Ryan L. "Violence, Masculinity, Image, and Reality on the Antebellum Frontier." *Indiana Magazine of History* 100, no. 1 (March 2004): 26–55.

Delbanco, Andrew. *The Real American Dream: A Meditation on Hope.* Cambridge, MA: Harvard University Press, 1999.

———. *Melville: His World and Work.* New York: Vintage, 2007.

*Democratic Editorials: Essays in Jacksonian Political Economy.* Edited by Lawrence H. White. Indianapolis: Liberty Fund, 1984.

Dierks, Konstantin. *In My Power: Letter Writing and Communications in Early America.* Philadelphia: University of Pennsylvania Press, 2011.

Dobzhansky, Theodosius G. *Genetics and the Origin of Species.* New York: Columbia University Press, 1937.

Douglass, Ann. *The Feminization of American Culture.* New York: Farrar, Straus & Giroux, 1998.

DuBois, Ellen C., and Lynn Dumenil. *Through Women's Eyes: An American History with Documents.* Boston: Bedford/St. Martin's, 2012.

Eastman, Carolyn. *A Nation of Speechifiers: Making an American Public.* Chicago: University of Chicago Press, 2009.

Eccles, John C. *Evolution of the Brain: Creation of the Self.* New York: Routledge, 1989.

*Elements of Intellectual Philosophy.* Portland, ME, 1827.

Eliot, T. S. *The Literature of Politics.* London: Conservative Political Centre, 1955.

Emerson, Ralph Waldo. *The Essential Writings of Ralph Waldo Emerson.* Edited by Mary Oliver. New York: Modern Library, 2000.

Erikzsn, Thomas Hylland. *Time in Practice: Analytical Perspectives on the Time of Our Lives.* London: Karnac, 2008.

Ershkowitz, Herbert, and William G. Shade. "Consensus or Conflict? Political Behavior in the State Legislatures during the Jacksonian Era." *Journal of American History* 58, no. 3 (December 1971): 591–621.

Everett, Edward. *Orations and Speeches on Various Occasions.* 4 vols. Boston: Little, Brown, 1850–1868.

*Evolution: The First Four Billion Years.* Edited by Michael Ruse and Joseph Travis. Cambridge, MA: Belknap Press of Harvard University Press, 2011.

*An Extensive Republic: Print, Culture, and Society in the New Nation, 1790–1840.* Edited by Robert A. Gross and Mary Kelly. Vol. 2 of *A History of the Book in America.* Chapel Hill: University of North Carolina Press, 2011.

Fagan, Brian. *Cro-Magnon: How the Ice Age Gave Birth to the First Modern Humans.* New York: Bloomsbury, 2010.

Faust, Drew Gilpin. *This Republic of Suffering: Death and American Civil War.* New York: Knopf, 2008.

Ferguson, Niall. *Civilization: The West and the Rest.* New York: Penguin, 2011.

Ferrus, G. "On the Insane." *American Journal of the Medical Sciences* (Boston) 19 (1836): 103–25.

Ford, Lacy K. *Origins of Southern Radicalism: The South Carolina Upcountry, 1800–1860.* New York: Oxford University Press, 1991.

Fox, Robin. *The Tribal Imagination: Civilization and the Savage Mind.* Cambridge, MA: Harvard University Press, 2011.

Freehling, William. *Prelude to Civil War: The Nullification Controversy in South Carolina, 1816–1836.* New York: Oxford University Press, 1965.

Friend, Craig Thompson. *Along the Maysville Road: The Early Republic in the Trans-Appalachian West.* Knoxville: University of Tennessee Press, 2005.

Fuhrer, Mary Babson. *A Crisis of Community: The Trials and Transformation of a New England Town, 1815–1848.* Chapel Hill: University of North Carolina Press, 2014.

Fukuyama, Francis. *Trust: The Social Virtues and the Creation of Prosperity.* New York: Free Press, 1995.

———. *Identity: The Demand for Dignity and the Politics of Resentment.* New York: Farrar, Straus & Giroux, 2018.

Gallman, Robert E., and John Joseph Wallis, eds. *American Economic Growth and Standards of Living Before the Civil War.* Chicago: University of Chicago Press, 1993.

Gay, Peter. *The Bourgeois Experience from Victoria to Freud.* 5 vols. New York: Oxford University Press, 1984–1998.

———. *Schnitzler's Century: The Making of Middle-Class Culture, 1815–1914.* New York: Norton, 2002.

Glickstein, Jonathan A. *American Exceptionalism, American Anxiety: Wages, Competition, and Degraded Labor in the Antebellum United States.* Charlottesville: University of Virginia Press, 2002.

Graves, A. J. *Woman in America: Being an Examination into the Moral and Intellectual Condition of American Female Society.* New York: Harper & Bros., 1843.

Greenberg, Amy S. *A Wicked War: Polk, Clay, Lincoln, and the 1846 U.S. Invasion of Mexico.* New York: Knopf, 2012.

Greene, Joshua. *Moral Tribes: Emotion, Reason, and the Gap between Us and Them.* New York: Penguin, 2013.

Gregory, Brad S. *The Unintended Reformation: How a Religious Revolution Secularized Society.* Cambridge, MA: Harvard University Press, 2012.

Greven, Philip. *The Protestant Temperament: Patterns of Child-Rearing, Religious Experience, and the Self in Early America.* Chicago: University of Chicago Press, 1977.

Grimshaw, William. *History of the United States.* Philadelphia: John Grigg, 1830.

Grimstead, David. *American Mobbing, 1828–1861: Toward Civil War.* New York: Oxford University Press, 1998.

Gutman, Herbert. *Work, Culture, and Society in Industrializing America.* New York: Vintage, 1977.

Habermas, Jürgen. *The Structural Transformation of the Public Sphere: An Inquiry into a Category of Bourgeois Society.* 1962. Translated by Thomas Burger. Cambridge, MA: MIT Press, 1989.

Hahn, Steven. *A Nation without Borders: The United States and Its World in an Age of Civil Wars, 1830–1910.* New York: Penguin, 2016.

Haidt, Jonathan. *The Righteous Mind: Why Good People Are Divided by Politics and Religion.* New York: Pantheon, 2012.

Hall, David D. *Worlds of Wonder, Days of Judgment: Popular Religious Belief in Early New England.* Cambridge, MA: Harvard University Press, 1989.

Hall, John A. *The Importance of Being Civil: The Struggle for Political Decency.* Princeton, NJ: Princeton University Press, 2013.

Hall, Samuel R. *Lectures to School-Masters.* Boston: Carter, Hendee, 1835.

Halttunen, Karen. *Confidence Men and Painted Women: A Study of Middle-Class Culture in America, 1830–1870.* New Haven, CT: Yale University Press, 1982.

Hammond, Bray. *Banks and Politics in America.* Princeton, NJ: Princeton University Press, 1957. Reprint, Princeton, NJ: Princeton University Press, 1991.

Harris, Christopher. "Mason Locke Weems's Life of Washington: The Making of a Bestseller." *Southern Literary Journal* 19, no. 2 (Spring 1987): 92–101.

Hay, Robert Pettus. "Freedom's Jubilee: One Hundred Years of the Fourth of July, 1776 to 1876." PhD diss., University of Kentucky, 1967.

Heidegger, Martin. *Being and Time.* 1927. Translated by John Macquarrie and Edward Robinson. New York: Harper & Row, 1962.

Henkle, M. M. *The Moral Dignity and General Claims of Agricultural Science: An Address Delivered in the Chapel of Transylvania University.* Frankfort, KY: Hodges, Todd, & Pruett, 1843.

Hietala, Thomas R. *Manifest Design: American Exceptionalism and Empire.* Ithaca, NY: Cornell University Press, 1985.

High, Mike. *The C&O Canal Companion.* Baltimore: Johns Hopkins University Press, 2001.

Hoffman, Eva. *Time.* New York: Picador, 2009.

Holbrook, Josiah. *American Lyceum.* Boston: Perkins & Marvin, 1829.

Holmes, George. *The Oxford History of Medieval Europe.* New York: Oxford University Press, 2002.

Holt, Michael F. *The Political Crisis of the 1850s.* New York: Wiley, 1978. Reprint, New York: Norton, 1983.

———. *Political Parties and American Political Development from the Age of Jackson to the Age of Lincoln.* Baton Rouge: Louisiana State University Press, 1992.

Hope, M. B. *A Discourse Delivered on the Occasion of the Death of David G. Aikin.* Princeton, NJ: J. T. Robinson, 1849.

Horwitz, Morton J. *The Transformation of American Law, 1780–1860.* Cambridge, MA: Harvard University Press, 1979.

Houghton, Walter. *The Victorian Frame of Mind, 1830–1870.* New Haven, CT: Yale University Press, 1957.

Howe, Daniel Walker. *The Political Culture of the American Whigs.* Chicago: University of Chicago Press, 1984.

———. *Making the American Self: Jonathan Edwards to Abraham Lincoln.* Cambridge, MA: Harvard University Press, 1997.

———. *What Hath God Wrought: The Transformation of America, 1815–1848.* New York: Oxford University Press, 2007.

Huston, Reeve. *Land and Freedom: Rural Society, Popular Protest, and Party Politics in Antebellum New York.* New York: Oxford University Press, 2000.

"Illustrations of Insanity." *American Journal of Insanity* 1 (July 1844). 9–49.

Kaestle, Carl F. *Pillars of the Republic: Common Schools and American Society, 1780–1860.* New York: Hill & Wang, 1983.

Kammen, Michael. *Mystic Chords of Memory: The Transformation of Tradition in American Culture.* New York: Vintage, 1991.

Kaplan, Edward S. *The Bank of the United States and the American Economy.* Westport, CT: Greenwood, 1999.

Kapsch, Robert. *The Potomac Canal, George Washington and the Waterway West.* Morgantown: West Virginia University Press, 2007.

Kasson, John F. *Civilizing the Machine: Technology and Republican Values in America, 1776–1900.* New York: Hill & Wang, 1999.

Keen, Maurice. *The Penguin History of Medieval Europe.* New York: Penguin, 1991.

Kennedy, John Pendleton. *Political and Official Papers.* New York: G. P. Putnam & Sons, 1872.

Kimmel, Michael. *Manhood in America: A Cultural History.* 1998. 3rd ed. New York: Oxford University Press, 2012.

Klotter, James C. *Henry Clay: The Man Who Would Be President.* New York: Oxford University Press, 2018.

Kohl, Lawrence F. *The Politics of Individualism.* New York: Oxford University Press, 1989.

Larkin, Jack. *The Reshaping of Everyday Life, 1790–1840.* New York: HarperCollins, 1989.

Lasser, Carol, and Stacey Robertson. *Antebellum Women: Private, Public, Partisan.* New York: Rowman & Littlefield, 2013.

Leary, Lewis. *The Book-Peddling Parson: An Account of the Life and Works of Mason Locke Weems, Patriot, Pitchman, Author and Purveyor of Morality to the Citizenry.* Chapel Hill, NC: Algonquin, 1984.

Leggett, William. *A Collection of the Political Writings of William Leggett.* Edited by Theodore Sedgwick. 2 vols. New York: Taylor & Dodd, 1840.

Lepore, Jill. *These Truths: A History of the United States.* New York: Norton, 2018.

Lévi-Strauss, Claude. *The Savage Mind.* 1962. Translated by George Weidenfeld. Chicago: University of Chicago Press, 1966.

Levin, Yuval. *The Great Divide: Edmund Burke, Thomas Paine, and the Birth of the Right and Left.* New York: Basic, 2014.

Lewis, R. W. B. *The American Adam: Innocence, Tragedy, and Tradition in the Nineteenth Century.* Chicago: University of Chicago Press, 1959.

*The Life and Works of Thomas Cole.* 1853. 3rd ed. Edited by Louis L. Noble. New York: Sheldon, Blakeman, 1856.

*The Life and Writings of Abraham Lincoln.* Edited by Phillips Van Doren Stern. New York: Random House, 1940. Reprint, New York: Modern Library, 1990.

Lilla, Mark. *The Once and Future Liberal: After Identity Politics.* New York: HarperCollins, 2017.

Lincoln, Abraham. *Abraham Lincoln: His Speeches and Writings.* Edited by Roy P. Basler. Cleveland: World, 1946. Reprint, Cambridge, MA: Da Capo, 2001.

———. *The Collected Works of Abraham Lincoln.* Edited by Roy P. Basler. 9 vols. New Brunswick, NJ: Rutgers University Press, 1953.

Lockridge, Kenneth A. *A New England Town: The First Hundred Years, 1636–1736.* New York: Norton, 1970.

Lusignan, Nancy. *Fire and Roses: The Burning of the Charlestown Convent, 1834.* New York: Free Press, 2000.

Mann, Horace. *A Few Thoughts for a Young Man.* Boston: Fuller, 1850. Reprint, Boston: Lothrop, Lee, & Shepherd, 1870.

Martin, William. *The Moral and Intellectual School Book.* London: Darton & Clark, 1838.

Marx, Leo. *The Machine in the Garden: Technology and the Pastoral Ideal in America.* New York: Oxford University Press, 1964. Reprint, New York: Oxford University Press, 2000.

Mason, Michael. *The Making of Victorian Sexuality.* New York: Oxford University Press, 1995.

McCloskey, Deirdre. *The Bourgeois Virtues.* Chicago: University of Chicago Press, 2006.

———. *Bourgeois Dignity: Why Economics Can't Explain the Modern World.* Chicago: University of Chicago Press, 2010.

McCormick, Richard P. *The Second American Party System: Party Formation in the Jacksonian Era.* New York: Norton, 1973.

McCoy, Drew. *The Elusive Republic: Political Economy in Jeffersonian America.* Chapel Hill: University of North Carolina Press, 1980.

McGrane, Reginald C. "George Washington: An Anglo-American Hero." *Virginia Magazine of History and Biography* 63 (January 1955): 3–14.

McGreevy, John T. *Catholicism and American Freedom.* New York: Norton, 2003.

Melville, Herman. *White-Jacket; or, The World in a Man-of-War.* New York: Harper & Bros., 1850. Reprint, Evanston, IL: Northwestern University Press, 1963.

Merish, Lori. *Sentimental Materialism: Gender, Commodity Culture, and Nineteenth-Century American Literature.* Durham, NC: Duke University Press, 2000.

Merk, Frederick, and Lois Bannister Merk. *Manifest Destiny and Mission in American History: A Reinterpretation.* New York: Knopf, 1963.

"Methods of the First Schools." *American Annals of Education,* March 1834, 113–15.

Meyers, Marvin. *The Jacksonian Persuasion: Politics and Belief.* Stanford, CA: Stanford University Press, 1957. Reprint, Stanford, CA: Stanford University Press, 1960.

Miller, Perry. *The New England Mind: The Seventeenth Century.* Cambridge, MA: Harvard University Press, 1939. Reprint, Cambridge, MA: Harvard University Press, 1982.

———. *Errand into the Wilderness.* Cambridge, MA: Harvard University Press, 1956. Reprint, Cambridge, MA: Harvard University Press, 1984.

Minkowski, Eugene. *Lived Time: Phenomenological and Psychopathological Studies.* Translated by Nancy Metsel. Evanston, IL: Northwestern University Press, 1970.

Mintz, Steven. *Moralists and Modernizers: America's Pre–Civil War Reformers.* Baltimore: Johns Hopkins University Press, 1995.

———. *Huck's Raft: A History of American Childhood.* Cambridge, MA: Belknap Press of Harvard University Press, 2006.

Moretti, Franco. *The Bourgeois: Between History and Literature.* London: Verso, 2014.

Morgan, Edmund S. *The Puritan Dilemma: The Story of John Winthrop.* New York: HarperCollins, 1958.

———. *Benjamin Franklin.* New Haven, CT: Yale University Press, 2002.

Mullin, Robert Bruce. *The Puritan as Yankee: A Life of Horace Bushnell.* Grand Rapids, MI: Eerdmans, 2002.

Nagel, Paul C. *One Nation Indivisible: The Union in American Thought, 1776–1861.* New York: Oxford University Press, 1964.

———. *This Sacred Trust: American Nationality, 1798–1898.* New York: Oxford University Press, 1971.

Nash, Roderick. *Wilderness and the American Mind.* New Haven, CT: Yale University Press, 1967. Reprint, New Haven, CT: Yale University Press, 2001.

*New England Primer; or, An Easy and Pleasant Guide to the Art of Reading.* Boston: Massachusetts Sabbath School Society, 1843.

Newmeyer, R. Kent. *Supreme Court Justice Joseph Story: Statesman of the Old Republic.* Chapel Hill: University of North Carolina Press, 1985.

Nisbet, Robert. *The Quest for Community.* New York: Oxford University Press, 1953.

———. *Conservatism: Dream and Reality.* Minneapolis: University of Minnesota Press, 1986.

Novak Michael J., *Business as a Calling: Work and the Examined Life.* New York: Free Press, 1996.

Nye, David E. *American Technological Sublime.* Cambridge, MA: MIT Press, 1994.

O'Shaughnessy, Andrew Jackson. *The Men Who Lost America: British Leadership, the American Revolution, and the Fate of the Empire.* New Haven, CT: Yale University Press, 2013.

Parsons, Lynn Hudson. *John Quincy Adams.* Indianapolis: Madison House, 1988. Reprint, Lanham, MD: Rowman & Littlefield, 2001.

Pearson, Joseph W. "The Dilemma of Dissent: Kentucky's Whigs and the Mexican War." *Ohio Valley History* 12, no. 2 (Summer 2012): 24–47.

Perelberg, Rosine Jozef, ed. *Time and Memory: The Power of Repetitive Compulsion.* London: Karnac, 2007.

Pessen, Edward. "Did Fortunes Rise and Fall Mercurially in Antebellum America? The Tale of Two Cities: Boston and New York." *Journal of Social History* 4, no. 4 (Summer 1971): 339–57.

Phillips, Jason. *Looming Civil War: How Nineteenth Century Americans Imagined the Future.* New York: Oxford University Press, 2018.

Pickering, John. *The Working Man's Political Economy.* Cincinnati: Thomas Varney, 1847.

Pieper, Josef. *The Four Cardinal Virtues.* South Bend, IN: University of Notre Dame Press, 1966.

———. *Leisure: The Basis of Culture.* New York: Pantheon, 1952. Reprint, San Francisco: Ignatius, 2009.

*Pocket Fowler's Modern English Usage.* 2nd ed. New York: Oxford University Press, 2008.

*The Portable Edmund Burke.* Edited by Isaac Kramnick. New York: Penguin, 1999.

Potter, David M. "The Historian's Use of Nationalism and Vice Versa." *American Historical Review* 67, no. 4 (July 1962): 924–50.

———. *The Impending Crisis: America Before the Civil War, 1848–1861.* New York: Harper & Row, 1976.

Prentiss. Sergeant S. *A Memoir of S. S. Prentiss.* Edited by George L. Prentiss. 2 vols. New York: Charles Scribner, 1853. Reprint, New York: Charles Scribner, 1899.

*Pulpit and Rostrum: Sermons, Orations, Popular Lectures.* New York: H. H. Lloyd & Co., 1861.

Quigley, Paul. *Shifting Grounds: Nationalism and the American South, 1848–1865.* New York: Oxford University Press, 2011.

Rable, George C. *God's Almost Chosen Peoples: A Religious History of the American Civil War.* Chapel Hill: University of North Carolina Press, 2010.

Ray, Angela G. *The Lyceum and Public Culture in the Nineteenth-Century United States.* East Lansing: Michigan State University Press, 2005.

*Register of Debates: Being a Report of the Speeches Delivered in the Two Houses of Congress.* Washington, DC: Duff Green, 1834.

Reiss, Benjamin. *Theaters of Madness: Insane Asylums and Nineteenth-Century American Culture.* Chicago: University of Chicago Press, 2008.

Remini, Robert V. *Andrew Jackson and the Bank War: A Study in the Growth of Presidential Power.* New York: Norton, 1967.

*Revolutionary History of North Carolina.* Raleigh: William D. Cooke, 1853.

Reynolds, David S. *Waking Giant: America in the Age of Jackson.* New York: HarperCollins, 2008.

Rorabaugh, W. J. *The Alcoholic Republic: An American Tradition.* New York: Oxford University Press, 1979.

Rossiter, Clinton. *Conservatism in America: The Thankless Persuasion.* New York: Knopf, 1962.

———. *The American Quest, 1790–1860: An Emerging Nation in Search of Identity, Unity, and Modernity.* New York: Harcourt Brace Jovanovich, 1971.

Rothman, Joshua. *Flush Times and Fever Dreams: A Story of Capitalism and Slavery in the Age of Jackson.* Athens: University of Georgia Press, 2012.

Rotundo, E. Anthony. *American Manhood: Transformation in Masculinity from the Revolution to the Modern Era.* New York: Basic, 1993.

Ryan, Mary P. *Cradle of the Middle Class: The Family in Oneida County, New York, 1790–1865.* New York: Cambridge University Press, 1981.

Samuel, Lawrence R. *The American Dream: A Cultural History.* Syracuse, NY: Syracuse University Press, 2012.

Samuels, Shirley. *The Culture of Sentiment: Race, Gender, and Sentimentality in 19th-Century America.* New York: Oxford University Press, 1992.

Sandage, Scott. *Born Losers: A History of Failure in America.* Cambridge, MA: Harvard University Press, 2006.

Schlesinger, Arthur M., Jr. *The Age of Jackson.* New York: Little, Brown, 1945. Reprint, Old Saybrook, CT: Konecky & Konecky, 1971.

"School Discipline." *American Annals of Education,* May 1833, 224–31.

Schott, Thomas E. *Alexander H. Stephens of Georgia: A Biography.* Baton Rouge: Louisiana State University Press, 1988.

Scott, Donald. "The Popular Lecture and the Creation of a Public in Mid-Nineteenth-Century America." *Journal of American History* 66, no. 4 (March 1980): 791–809.

Schultz, Nancy Lusignan. *Burning Down the House: The Ursuline Convent Riot, Charlestown, Massachusetts, 1834.* Salem, MA: Salem State College Press, 1993.

Sellers, Charles. *The Market Revolution: Jacksonian America, 1815–1846.* New York: Oxford University Press, 1994.

Seward, William Henry. *The Works of William Henry Seward.* Edited by George E. Baker. 5 vols. Boston: Houghton, Mifflin, 1853–1884.

Shalev, Eran. *American Zion.* New Haven, CT: Yale University Press, 2013.

Shorter, Edward. *A History of Psychiatry: From the Era of the Asylum to the Age of Prozac.* New York: Wiley, 1998.

Smith, Henry Nash. *Virgin Land: The American West as Symbol and Myth.* Cambridge, MA: Harvard University Press, 1950.

Smith-Rosenberg, Carroll. *Disorderly Conduct: Visions of Gender in Victorian America.* New York: Oxford University Press, 1986.

Sperber, Hans, and Travis Trittschuh. *American Political Terms: An Historical Dictionary.* Detroit: Wayne State University Press, 1962.

Stansell, Christine. *City of Women: Sex and Class in New York, 1789–1860.* Champaign: University of Illinois Press, 1987.

Summers, Mark W. *The Ordeal of the Reunion: A New History of Reconstruction.* Chapel Hill: University of North Carolina Press, 2014.

Tattersall, Ian. *The World from Beginnings to 4000 BCE.* New York: Oxford University Press, 2008.

Taylor, J. Orville. *The District School; or, National Education.* Philadelphia: Carey, Lea, & Blanchard, 1835.

Thompson, E. P. "Time, Work-Discipline, and Industrial Capitalism." *Past and Present,* no. 38 (December 1967): 56–97.

Tocqueville, Alexis de. *Democracy in America.* 1835–1840. Translated and edited by Harvey C. Mansfield and Debra Winthrop. Chicago: University of Chicago Press, 2000.

Unger, Harlow G. *Henry Clay: America's Greatest Statesman.* Philadelphia: Da Capo, 2015.

Van Deusen, Glyndon G. *The Jacksonian Era, 1828–1848.* New York: Harper & Bros., 1959.

Varron, Elizabeth R. *We Mean to Be Counted: White Women and Politics in Antebellum Virginia.* Chapel Hill: University of North Carolina Press, 1998.

———. *Disunion! The Coming of the American Civil War, 1789–1859.* Chapel Hill: University of North Carolina Press, 2008.

Volo, James M., and Dorothy D. Volo. *Family Life in 19th-Century America.* Westport, CT: Greenwood, 2007.

Waldstreicher, David. *In the Midst of Perpetual Fetes: The Making of American Nationalism, 1776–1820.* Chapel Hill: University of North Carolina Press, 1997.

Walters, Ronald G. *Primers for Prudery: Sexual Advice to Victorian America.* Baltimore: Johns Hopkins University Press, 2000.

Ward, John William. *Andrew Jackson: Symbol for an Age.* New York: Oxford University Press, 1953.

Waters, Ronald G. *American Reformers, 1815–1860.* New York: Hill & Wang, 1978. Reprint, New York: Hill & Wang, 1997.

Watson, Harry L. *Liberty and Power: The Politics of Jacksonian America.* New York: Hill & Wang, 1990.

Weber, Max. *The Protestant Ethic and the Spirit of Capitalism.* New York: Charles Scribner & Sons, 1905. Reprint New York: Routledge, 2013.

Webster, Daniel. *The Works of Daniel Webster.* 14th ed. 6 vols. Boston: Little, Brown, 1851–1866.

———. *The Great Speeches of Daniel Webster.* Boston: Little, Brown, & Co., 1879.

———. *The Papers of Daniel Webster Digital Edition.* Charlottesville: University of Virginia Press, Rotunda, 2018.

Webster, Noah. *American Dictionary of the English Language.* New York: S. Converse, 1830.

*The Webster-Hayne Debate on the Nature of the Constitution: Selected Documents.* Edited by Herman Belz. Indianapolis: Liberty Fund, 2000.

Weems, Mason Locke. *The Life of Washington.* New York: Weems, 1800. Reprint, Cambridge, MA: Belknap Press of Harvard University Press, 1962.

Wells, Jonathan D. *The Origins of the Southern Middle Class, 1800–1861.* Chapel Hill: University of North Carolina Press, 2004.

Wendling, Amy E. *The Ruling Ideas: Bourgeois Political Concepts.* Lanham, MD: Lexington, 2014.

"What Every Teacher Can Do." *American Annals of Education,* December 1834, 5441–44.

*The Whig Party; Its Objects—Its Principles—Its Candidates—Its Duties—and Its Prospects.* Providence, RI: Knowles & Vose, 1844.

Wiebe, Robert. *Opening of American Society: From the Adoption of the Constitution to the Eve of Disunion.* New York: Knopf, 1984.

———. *Self-Rule: A Cultural History of American Democracy.* Chicago: University of Chicago Press, 1996.

Wilentz, Sean. *Chants Democratic: New York City and The Rise of the American Working Class, 1788–1850.* New York: Oxford University Press, 1984.

———. *The Rise of American Democracy: Jefferson to Lincoln.* New York: Norton, 2006.

Willard, Emma. *Last Leaves of American History.* Cincinnati: H. W. Derby & Co., 1853.

Wilson, Major. *Space, Time, and Freedom: The Quest for Nationality and the Irrepressible Conflict.* Westport, CT: Greenwood, 1974.

Wilson, Marcus. *American History: History of the United States.* Cincinnati: William H. Moore, 1847.

Wooster, Ralph A. *Politicians, Planters, and Plain Folk: Courthouse and Statehouse in the Upper South, 1850–1860.* Knoxville: University of Tennessee Press, 1975.

Wosh, Peter J. *Spreading the Word: The Bible Business in Nineteenth-Century America.* Ithaca, NY: Cornell University Press, 1994.

Yanni, Carla. *The Architecture of Madness: Insane Asylums in the United States.* Minneapolis: University of Minnesota Press, 2007.

Yates, Joshua J., and James Davison Hunter, eds. *Thrift and Thriving in America: Capitalism and Moral Order from the Puritans to the Present.* New York: Oxford University Press, 2011.

Yellin, Jean F., and John C. Van Horne, eds. *The Abolitionist Sisterhood: Women's Political Culture in Antebellum America.* Ithaca, NY: Cornell University Press, 1994.

Zagzebski, Linda Trinkaus. *Virtues of the Mind: An Inquiry into the Nature of Virtue and the Ethical Foundations of Knowledge.* New York: Cambridge University Press, 1996.

Zboray, Mary S., and Ronald J. Zboray. *Voices without Votes: Women and Politics in Antebellum New England.* Lebanon, NH: University Press of New England, 2010.

# Index